Volume II

Tell Me More

The Winds of Change

Trebbiano

CONTENTS

CHAPTER 1 1

CHAPTER 2 21

CHAPTER 3 31

CHAPTER 4 64

CHAPTER 5 82

CHAPTER 6 87

CHAPTER 7 109

CHAPTER 8 124

CHAPTER 9 148

CHAPTER 10 198

CHAPTER 11 205

CHAPTER 12 228

CHAPTER 13 239

CHAPTER 14 269

CHAPTER 15 303

VOLUME 2

THE WINDS OF CHANGE

CHAPTER 1

When the Vice President of Food & Beverage announced the addition of three junior Vice Presidents as his assistants, the news was received as a dirty bomb by the Hotels and likewise, all the Regional Directors.

It was the added position, but his choice of abrasive personalities which rubbed everybody the wrong way.

Developing new restaurant concepts for the new hotels was a smart addition and long overdue. New outside blood will bring fresh ideas. With his versatile experiences to his credit, he sounded prepared for the challenge.

The other two men were picked from the group of Regional Directors.

Their names and aggressive characters are well known for their abrasive style. The one picked from the Washington DC area had shown care and creativity managing in this region. Well educated and hungry for more management skills, he read every book and put it to practice. A man with considerable confidence, he also projected a good amount of arrogance.

The other appointee was a typical product of India. I had known the character traits of this country's privileged sons, who were afforded to study in a foreign country with the full support of foreign aid. With his nose held up high he displayed his autocratic style.

The dividing line will be from North to south, giving each the same number of projects. The list includes all future hotels in development or under construction.

I know the character; he is an Indian working in a foreign country. This Man received my region.

From the beginning, I knew this would be a fight, and he does not fight fair.

Because of his lack of knowledge and practical experience, he resulted with bully tactics.

I expressed concerns to Charles and my RVP, but the plan was set; nothing would be changed.

The hotels in the Florida region performed exceptionally well; the P&L statement showed great results and strong management.

His first tour to visit the hotels was a superficial walk-through. He looked for flaws but could not pin anything on me nor the properties.

After the third hotel, he started to get pushy, yet nothing was found. He showed his irritation.

I had scheduled the resort properties for the last two days of his visit.

When he noticed water spots on glassware or the gasket on one refrigerator showing wear, which required replacement he took pleasure to rub it in my face.

The two resorts catered to distinct markets.

Award ceremonies following a three day conference, or sports tournament, political conventions or themed parties required the food department to go the extra mile and source unusual food items. Of course, these customer demands had not been entered into the corporate recipe file. It demanded the skills of an experienced Chef to produce it.

"You are not allowed to do this." Arguments flared up, and we would not reason or listen to justification. He found his angle and kept digging and aggravating the property management and me.

At the Fort Lauderdale Beach Hotel, he started a new argument.

"This hotel is not even a company hotel in the way it is operated in F&B! How can you let them violate all the SOPs?"

A four-star hotel calls for an upgrade; none are yet on the department's books.

The Hotel owner's vision had directed us. For that, we obtained variances. From corporate.

He hammered away at every item he considered outside the company's guidelines. I was desperately looking for anything to gain the upper hand.

When we reached the Seafood restaurant, he stopped and looked at the menu.

He was momentarily lost for an answer and then harped on specifics about the seafood recipes. I pulled the menu out of his hand and said that all food items are company-specified, and recipes are documented and approved.

A separate SOP chapter will be set up for future four-star properties. It is the first hotel to offer this level of luxury. We are pioneering many procedures and are still in the testing mode. Full documentation will follow.

Let's have a look at the other specialty restaurant. What do you make of this menu?

"All in French!."

I thought you spoke French.

"No, only speak Hindi, English, and Dutch. My wife is from Holland."

Yes, I know that! "You do?"

Then he wanted to go to the ballroom. He met the Catering Director, who was setting up for dinner.

He was shown an afternoon refreshment buffet for a meeting group. The setup included props to stage a theme.

More props came out for the dinner setup.

He was lost, searching for a question, and said, "You have a sophisticated clientele."

Have a look at this coffee break. Have you ever seen something like this?

"Not really. All our hotels operate on a strict budget."

We are well within the financial guidelines. These props are used often and have been paid for times over.

Our coffee breaks cost as much as breakfast. Notice the salty and spicy dry snacks. We get them ready for the cocktail party following the meeting. We wet the whistle in advance.

Shaking his head, he was lost for words.

Midafternoon at a busy pool, vacationers had every lounge chair occupied.

The kiddie area is noisy, with children playing under the waterfall. The bar serves tropical cocktails in unbreakable glasses.

"Are you using glassware at the pool with a grin?" Now I have something to think about.

Take a look at this. These items had been featured at the conference in California just in time to get supplies into this hotel.

A five-year-old child approached the bar, called the bartender by his first name, and asked for another cocktail. "Please, and a little more of the red stuff." He added all the ingredients behind the counter, poured it into a shaker can, and gave it to the boy to give the final shake.

A bright smile from the boy. "Did I do good?"

"Yes, another star for you!"

That shook Kumar to his knee. "What is this all about?"

The bartender answered coolly, "It's marketing; you know we are catering to the future!"

He was shaking his head; it was too much for him, and he walked away.

"Will you have dinner with me?"

No, I have an appointment tonight with the hotel's owner. I can ask him if he wants to meet you. He will clarify all these out-of-the-ordinary things.

"I think I'll pass, make it an early night, and look around at the other hotel."

The dinner appointment was a bluff, but he took the bait.

The restaurant director met him and knew him from the home office. She spoke to him about the efforts and creative juices it took to get this hotel on its feet. "The effort is well worth it. We are exceeding budget, profit is over projection, and guest responses are out of this world."

"The owner is happy and will cash in when he sells 40 percent ownership to an insurance company".

He left with a blank face.

In my heart, I knew that the bastard would distort the truth, leave nothing to the fact, and twist it to make himself look good at my expense.

"Watch out. He is a snake. Only cutting the head off will get rid of a snake. I was getting the warnings from everyone who knew him.

Meanwhile, Charles has to support him to save his face.

The report did not surprise, but it is now recorded on paper.

It made us look like the renegade's region. My boss called the VP of Food and Beverage, defending the hotels and me. His defaming language is unacceptable; I will take it to the EVP.

Knowing I did the right thing, the team brushed it off and banked on the granted variances.

We had been given a mission, and we delivered. The hotel was initially awarded a four-diamond rating from AAA, and after their testing, a four-star rating from Michelin Guide was promised.

My defense was justified, and I gave it to my boss. He can use it or file it. I couldn't care less. I was angry.

✳✳✳✳✳✳

We had an office meeting in the boss's style, and the entire office participated.

He reflected on the past events while drinks came to the table, hard liquor for all and nonalcoholic stuff for the Mormon controller. The secretaries all had Chardonnay, even the tea toddler.

Raunchy jokes came from marketing. The secretaries wanted to hear more, but he pleaded the fifth. He could not go there with a smirk on his face!

A preview trip for me to Panama was not approved.

I met with the man who contracted to deliver all the hotel supplies out of Miami at his office, and his dark-haired secretary greeted me. She knew her attributes and began to flirt.

"First, the bad news. The furniture has been in the warehouse for the past two years and is turning rusty. Salty air that is close to the ocean is a detriment.

We don't have a good inventory since three different owners were involved and walked away from the project.

"The warehouse had neglected keeping good delivery records. I can give you a list of what I know and what we have now. You can compare it with your documents from other hotels of the same size. It should cover the basics."

I took the list from his secretary and compared the items to a standard city hotel procurement list.

"Remember, this is in Panama, and the hotel has a specialty restaurant. I do not see enough silverware or chinaware to cover the needs."

It gave me a headache when I learned that no funds were allocated to adjust shortcomings.

Any missing items must be funded out of operating money.

******

The monthly meeting at the corporate office addressed the usual management changes. The director of F&B was requesting a transfer from the Lake of Ozark to Panama.

A Cuban national came as a teenager, entered the hotel industry, and then worked up to his current job. His language skills would be essential, and the Chef had Spanish language skills to get started and build on them. All other managers must come from local sources per government directive.

The creation of a specialty menu and the regular restaurant menu had to be set up.

The menu department was at a loss. Here we go again!

"We do not even know what products are available, let alone the food quality."

Being behind schedule, time is of the essence! I pressed for a team to fly to Panama City and research the availability and products we could incorporate into what would resemble a company menu.

We have a General manager and the Food and Beverage director on site, yet the feedback has been next to nothing.

The GM was not a foodie by heart. He just told me, "You deal with it. I will let you know when you get off track!" Who needs this kind of help?

I finally proposed to the VP that I take people to the country, research the marketplace and vendor source, and then sit on-site to work on a frame for the menus. Fine-tuning and proofing can be done back home. Purchasing officials have been dispatched, but nobody told me.

The corporate Chef and my former carpool woman Ginny got the marching orders. Everything came into high gear.

I briefed my boss in Florida. "Okay, go ahead. You have a mission to accomplish." I took my missing item list and would have the local management follow up on it.

7

Going to the market first will give us an overview and flavor of life in Panama.

The German corporate Chef, Willy, had seen open-air food markets in tropical climates, but Ginny had never been to any Latin American country. She needed to obtain a passport for her first trip outside the USA.

Spanish-speaking people with a fast tongue were irritating to her. "How can anyone understand this? They speak so fast!"

Nestor, the F&B man, explained that the words get connected in the language, and often, the vowels do not get sounded aloud but get lost in the pronunciation. "This is the most difficult part of the language aside from assigning masculine and feminine definitions."

The explanation was lost on her.

Then Nestor pointed to the telephone pole. "What are these?"

"Buzzards, vultures, waiting for the cleanup crew to get their fill! "Disgusting!" she proclaimed. She was living a sheltered life in the USA!

Finally, the procurement guy made himself known. We did not even know of him. He will be able to save us time. He had an approved vendor list on his schedule. How can he aid us with a product list?

He produced such a list, which aided us in our task.

"The fish is great and fresh but comes as a whole fish and needs to be cleaned. Fillet and cot in portions."

No problem. I will teach the cooks, the Chef said.

"The meat from Argentina is leaner than what we are used to but relatively tender and better tasting. It is grass-fed, natural, not corn-fed, and fattened like in Colorado feed lots."

"Chicken comes as whole dressed birds. The pork was perfect, lean, and a little smaller, and butchering was needed. "You should not have any problems hiring trained help. Produce you have seen in the market, as well as dry goods from local sources and the US, are all excellent."

"Make sure to refrigerate all grain products to keep the weevils out."

"What is that?" Let me explain, Ginny!

It comes from flies laying eggs into the food source to feed the larva and reproduce. The flower received added protein and cannot be used. It will be disposed of.

Then birds get to eat the larva while the vultures live the good life at the market. Have you seen them?

"Yuck, yes. Don't like their looks."

The menu can now be written according to the corporate guidelines with minimal deviation, including local vegetables, fruit, and fish. Recipes from Barbados are on file, and the others will be sent from the hotel once the chef has tested them.

Now, the specialty restaurant! It must reflect the flavor of the region.

Colombian and Peruvian food. I suggest we go to a Peruvian restaurant, order everything on the menu, and graze through the choice. If we cannot bribe the host or hostess, Ginny must bring a big handbag to bury a menu.

She looked at me with big eyes. "You do stuff like this?"

While we worked through the menu and had ordered twice the food a standard table would buy, the owner came to see who these crazy people were.

At first, he questioned the waitress, then greeted us and inquired about the orders. "Are you that hungry?"

Nestor offered his business card and revealed the mission.

"This building is finally going to be a hotel. It had been sitting there for years. Nobody knew the reasons, only an occasional newspaper story when another investor failed to complete it."

Compliments on great food! Nestor, the wheeler dealer, worked to get more out of him by inviting him to a preview.

"I am honored to receive such a privileged invitation." We conduct extensive training and practice meals. We would like you to participate in this process and share your opinion.

The owner offered us an after-dinner drink, his finest Aqua diente. Straight down the hatch is the way to take it.

Firewater! It was appropriately named as it put our throats on fire.

"It helps to digest the food!"

Okay, while coughing, but it does nothing to put out the fire down my throat.

"You will be feeling better in minutes. It is medicine."

The Chef agreed, "Us culinary guys know a thing or two about health, don't we?"

******

The boss gave me a set of blueprints for the new mega hotel that will be built or has broken ground near the entrance to Disney World in Orlando.

"Look it over, it is in your region. Here are the rooms, a monster with huge ballrooms and meeting spaces. Get back to me if you see anything not irregular."

By now, I had reviewed the blueprints and seen the finished space, which gave me a natural feel for how it would turn out.

My past experience included serving banquets, thousands of guests in Switzerland and also in Montreal was now put to the test.

The central kitchen was well-planned, and there was a good flow of products from the stores to the cleaning and commissary. The cooking was excellent. The emphasis was on group business, which would be fed in banquet ballrooms.

On the opposite side of the building was the space for food production to service the banquet rooms. A 3,500-guest capacity demands a carefully planned kitchen. The traffic areas for the servers, space for dishing up the food, and the dishwashing flashed through my head.

Where is it? I did see spaces marked on the prints, but is this all they have set aside?

I looked and looked and could not see how this was going to work. I closed my eyes, envisioned the kitchen where I had worked and cooked five thousand meals, and compared it to this layout.

It looked as if the planner had left it out of the grand plan and then searched for space to make it work.

Attempting to squeeze it into an unused space became a makeshift kitchen.

I took another look at it the following day. Am I not seeing this correctly, or is the scale misguiding me?

A piece of supplemental equipment drawing with a list of ovens and dish-up belts gave me the decisive answers.

Counting the number of ovens, ranges, and worktables showed me that this space and equipment layout will never support the food we need to serve a large banquet.

I looked at this and put it aside for another viewing the next day. A fresh mind would see it differently.

Nothing satisfied me that this was not a workable space to produce such a quantity.

I told my boss straight out what I found. I hope it gets corrected, and he, as the RVP, will take it to the architect and present the issues.

My know-it-all junior VP, Kumar called me and told me I was wrong. Okay, then you work on this property. Whoever gets that job will become the sacrificial lamb.

A meeting was scheduled to review my findings. Somehow, the architect had indeed forgotten the kitchen. To cover his mistake, he squeezed as much as possible into an unsuitable space.

My attendance with Mr. Charles was demanded.

At once, I was put on the spot by the architect. His boss was in attendance, and now, I was unsure if I should say I am sorry or just shut up. Somehow I needed to hedge my bet.

I could be wrong; I am not in the building trade and do not see this correctly.

When I counted the equipment list and calculated the need for 31/2 thousand prime rib portions or any other cut meat, it must be cooked in this kitchen. There is no other way.

The central kitchen is on the opposite side of this large building. Do you agree with my analysis?

This man turned red and started to stutter, and in as much admitting the oversight. His VP looked at him with a stern face.

I had ruffled their feathers. Charles smiled at me for having the courage to ask how this error could be corrected.

"He is right. We had not seen this ourselves. Thank you for your keen eye and for disclosing it to us."

The focus returned to me. "Can you see a way out of this?"

Roasting ovens came to mind. If we can replace these ovens that are taking up space and replace them with electric roasting ovens on wheels, the same size as a warming cart, we can cancel the carts and have a dual purpose for cooking. It will give us space back. However, the logistical area to support people moving around is too small. Is there a way to extend the roof line and expand the space?

I thought that by raising questions, I was not making accusations and staying clear of controversy.

"Are you an architect?"

No, but luckily, I will have my son in the family as an architect.

Charles patted me on the back. "I just knew, just knew it."

"Let us not forget the equipment list, I handed him my wish list.

******

The menu for the specialty restaurant will be printed in Panama. You could not proofread it because Spanish terminology makes this impossible for you, Ginny.

The list of missing equipment I had left behind in Panama was being filled individually. The banquet chairs were cleaned and repainted. The boys were working hard to get ahead of the game.

Now, the state government has announced that it has requested the company to train twice the needy hotel employees and produce a pool of skilled labor.

"You are the best at doing that. We will give tax holidays in exchange."

The entire training period was now extended by another week.

It would be a traffic jam inside the hotel. The theoretical classroom training can be done simultaneously, but the hands-on, the most important task, becomes the challenge.

These people had to take colorful buses to the hotel. HR and the local agency had done an exemplary job selecting all personnel. Reporting time at 8:00 a.m. allows for travel time with the bus, but most employees were at the door by 6:30 and 7:00 a.m. They must have left the house by 5:00 a.m.

I was impressed with the attendance; paying attention to the interpreter, acknowledging what was clear, and asking intelligent questions convinced me we were on the right path.

The classroom training was taken slowly and deliberately and was well worth the extra time,

Applicants came with a notepad for personal notes and looked highly motivated.

Then, the hands-on activity was divided into two groups, and all the steps were repeated.

While waiting for their turn, cleaning duties were assigned on a rotation basis.

The kitchen hired a good team, and skilled cooks from restaurants in the city came with professional pride. I was visible in their faces.

The banquet department, staffed by all locals and headed up by Julio, was starting slowly. I would catch up with him if he fell behind.

He is an experienced man, and he knows the market. Nestor assured me of his attributes.

The office staff, secretaries, banquet salespeople, and food and beverage employees arrived at the work desk like fashion models. They were skilled and bilingual in a professional office environment.

I noticed a little flirt from a dark-haired sales associate. Every time I passed by her desk, she said a kind word and engaged me in conversation.

******

Then came the Boss's Day. It was celebrated as a special day recognizing the managers in charge of departments that warranted secretarial assistance.

It is not a customary celebration in the US, but Isabel recognized me with a big bouquet of tropical flowers. I was at ahh, could not get a word out, but I finally thanked her with a hug and kiss.

"Thank you; you are very nice. We usually get a handshake. I like the extra touch; it makes me feel appreciated."

"I know I do not work directly in your department, but I am not a designated secretary, so I will be overlooked."

" I thought you would appreciate this gesture since you are away from your office."

I told her this is not a custom in the USA, but I appreciate the attention.

The aroma from the hair smelled of flowers. I know which one. It's the same as from the bouquet. She must have chosen a fragrance to match the Lilly's natural aroma.

How can I reciprocate?

"Secretary's Day is coming up very soon." She gave me a little wink with the eye. Thank you, Isabel; I will mark it on my calendar.

I researched the custom of recognizing a secretary on her special day: "Dinner, not flowers; the girls are always hungry."

******

Practice meals have now started the hands on training phase.

We invited the restaurant owner to participate. He sat at my table and made comments of various degrees, all good input. "Please do not be angry."

No, we do this amongst ourselves. That brings about perfection. A critique is directed toward improving the product. It is not personal and not meant to be criticized. Nothing is perfect from day one. Practice will get us there.

"Yes, wise. I must practice this from now on."

I asked him to keep me a lovely table for Secretary's Day once I had a private moment with him. "Ah, yes, a busy night. But you do not have your secretary here."

No, I don't, but I was recognized by a beautiful girl in the sales department on Boss's Day.

" Then you must reciprocate." She is a smart girl, for she would be left out since she is no longer a secretary."

I do not want it free, understood? I must pay for it. Otherwise, it will make me look cheap. I leave it up to you.

"Yes, in ten days on a Wednesday. You will do well with her, trust me!"

The GM invited me to his favorite restaurant.

He ordered for me, thinking my Spanish was insufficient. I let him go ahead, and then the reason was a surprise. The clams listed as almejas negras came on the half shell, "small and black and still alive, "just like oysters," he commented.

Only oysters do not bite back, I said. They still moved as I was biting the black clam. It's good tasting, a surprise, but not offensive to a Chef.

He was surprised; he must have expected a fuss from me spitting it out; instead, I bluffed and asked him for a second order.

15

"I cannot get more. One must call ahead to get them still alive. All others turn into ceviche."

We should have this on our menu. "There is not enough supply from these waters. We would be calling it out in a short time. I did not see it listed on other restaurant menus."

He made efforts to warm up our distant and cool relationship. "We are from the same blood. Let us become great colleagues!"

He had done his homework on me and found something that astonished him.

"The action in New York was gutsy. Aren't you afraid of them?"

I told them I took out life insurance, but not with an insurance company. My information on the union could have put them away under a federal formal accusation.

If I get a little scratch on my family or me, I will activate charges.

They realized that it was better to protect me than to hurt me.

Thank you for this exceptional treat and the rare taste of this delicatessen clam.

******

Test meals were done, and now the soft opening is at the doorsteps. We must make the final choice of employees. It will be Acapulco Déjà vu since only half of the trainees will be awarded a position.

The obvious front-runners found acceptance from the managers. I left about thirty, the rest to choose from. So many people made the daily journey and put in the utmost effort during this training program. English was a challenge at first, yet with the efforts and all the training, these individuals managed to adopt all the professional terminology and became cautiously fluent in communicating with the non-Spanish training staff.

Another very emotional day, tears in all eyes, and looks of, please pick me. I told them to call the Hotel often to see if any openings were available.

Bonus money would be awarded to all the trainees who did not make the cut, and they would be assured of being put on the waiting list for

Business is expected to pick up, allowing for additional hiring.

At first, the message was not understood, but more explanation to show increased determination would get them on the top of the list. "Si, Señor lo entiendo!"

******

Wednesday was approaching, and I called the restaurant to verify my reservation. "We have a VIP sign on it. It's a private table for you and your esteemed guest. Eight p.m., okay?"

Isabel passed a little note to me as a reminder as I walked past her desk. A slight nod and pointing to eight fingers confirmed the date and time.

A blink of an eye was enough on her part.

Meet me in the parking lot. I have a taxi ready.

"Oh no, no, I have a car. I will drive!"

In the car, I told her the name of the restaurant. "How did you get this reservation? They are booked way in advance, especially for this day. All the prominent people will be there; it's the best restaurant in town."

I just said I scratched his back, but this term was lost on her.

Then I told her the story of when we planned the menu and later invited her to preview the property and test meals. I also told her that she would be extended more courtesies to attend the grand opening.

"That is very smart, very smart."

Keep your eyes on the road and the way they drive here!

Greeted like a princess and escorted to the table by the hostess, Isabel felt like royalty. The private table gave her more status, and curious eyes from other women followed her.

A greeting by the owner, and then privacy.

He had chosen the menu and took my credit card discreetly as we walked to the table.

Food just appeared, course after course, in small portions, tasted teasers, and was a feast for the eyes as it was on the palate.

Wine from Chile was no doubt a unique choice. It was the perfect evening.

"He created this for me. I never saw it on the menu." She was impressed.

"All these ingredients are my favorite foods. He must have done the homework; it cannot just be a coincidence!'

"I had the most beautiful day in my life!" She kissed my cheek and said, "More to come."

"I have a problem now. The girls in this country live at home, so I cannot invite you there for my surprise. The hotel where you have your room is also off-limits to me as an employee. If I am seen, I get fired."

"The solution we have here is a hacienda, a motel-type with a garage door. Privacy is assured with a small payment, and the door opens and closes behind you. Access to the room is from the garage.

If you do not mind a place like this, it is a place where single girls take their boyfriends; it's not sleazy, it's spotless, just not a hotel room."

Okay, it will be fine with me for the surprise.

A waterbed in the room was a surprise. "Go slowly and be gentle. I do not have experience. I am only nineteen years old."

I slowly undressed her while I caressed her body for a long time. I will pay a little extra attention to areas for more stimulation if needed.

Her body smelled of delicate cologne, and her hair, I remembered from the last hug, was alluring, and stimulating like the lilies.

My reaction was rapid, hard, and pulsating. She wanted to get me to the same level when I reached the bra and panties. Surprised about the waterbed, I assured her it would work fine. She followed my lead, and once there, we climbed into the waterbed.

We kissed, caressing each other's body, simultaneously driving the desire to a peak.

Backing off and breathing and continuing the play to increase the sensation.' Then, a pause again, and finally, she reached her first orgasm. "Que hermosa," she called out.

It must be a different god, I was thinking.

Que Rico, with a moment to catch my breath. I am ready for the next stage.

Young and correspondingly tight, her inner flesh wrapped my best piece into a tight grip; the sensation was something new to me.

It must be like a virgin. She told me that I was her second lover. She had just lost her virginity a month ago and was hungry for more. The man who took her virginity was not coming back. He feared that his wife would find out. The perfume, they know it from the scent!

I reached my height and breathed while playing with her body. She loved it, and this led to another beautiful, loving experience. So tender and sweet, it was the crowning of an evening that should never end.

They dropped off at the hotel at a distance, a brief kiss, and she went on her drive home.

We needed to establish this tradition in the USA. It is definitely a day to celebrate and show our gratitude.

******

A letter was addressed to me at the office. It was personal and confidential, so extra glue was used, and a symbol across the seam in the back assured confidentiality.

I put it in my briefcase and went to attack the regular mail.

"Aren't you going to open it?" What? "This hot letter you received; did you not steam it open? I was kidding. "Hell no, privacy is sacred."

Yes, and for that reason, I will open it at home.

"Are you not curious who sent it? What if it is a letter bomb?"

I would endanger you, too. This way, it only gets the receiver.

"How was it in Panama? As difficult as expected?"

It worked better than I thought. Murphy's law took a break and must be for the Irish and Americans only.

The people have beautiful attitudes, and when this is fundamental, it all falls into place. I told her about the restaurateur, the Boss's Day, then followed up with Secretary's Day.

I was included.

"Tell me more." Not here. We need to be alone, and here are too many nosy ears.

"We are going to have a Secretary's Day next year. The movement makes the rounds, and many companies now endorse it."

When I opened the letter, I saw that it was from Amanda. She told me she had met a Southern gentleman years her senior. He was a luxury yacht builder and delivered a yacht to Fort Lauderdale. She fell in love with him, and she was hoping that he would propose soon.

His younger brother was now running his boatyard, which afforded him to stay in Fort Lauderdale.

He is staying in the business as an equity partner and looking to book new business. Settling in this town, he is already looking for houses. He knows about us since I am open and honest, and he is also open-minded. He wants us to get together and make our acquaintance. Just be friends. Call me at this number. I will arrange the date at your convenience.

CHAPTER 2

My father had an accident which put him in great pain. He had slipped and broken his knee. The doctors made every effort to set it and put it in a cast, But somehow, they must have hit a nerve that caused him intense pain.

He needed corrective surgery to set the nerve free, remove the pain, and freeze the knee. Waiting endlessly for a date with the surgeon, he was kept on narcotic drugs and painkillers, taking its toll on his health.

I went to visit him at his home and found the situation shocking. He had lost all his extra weight; sitting in a wheelchair, he was a skeleton only.

I could not understand this delay. Are hospitals overbooked, or was it the insurance?

In the US, this would be done on an emergency basis, and within days, we would be in an operating room.

Was it a problem with the social and medical system? Who gets priority, and why are privately insured people treated with less urgency?

I could only stay ten days and left with great sadness, despite his dominance in the past to control my life. I felt helpless and needed to get back to my job.

Shortly after I returned, my Mother called to inform me that he had finally received an appointment at the regional hospital.

"Call me and let me know how it went."

My older brother called instead to tell me that our father had died; he never came out of anesthesia.

I should not make the trip for his funeral as I had just been there to see him; it was better to see him alive than in a wooden box.

I told my son Martin that his Opa had passed away. He knew of the accident and how I found him in his vegetative status. He would pass on the information to his mother.

******

At the office, all seemed normal. Aggressive memos started to be disbursed by the Dobermans, a name they had since earned for their aggressive style.

The tone of his writing came through being abrasive. He did not use courtesies but went straight to the point and used angry words. He might add the "or else" at the ending instead of the name.

The grapevine was in full motion, and a secret plan to stage a coup was developing.

No one liked these guys; they made enemies on all levels, including the GM's RVPs, the department managers, and the corporate support staff.

Why is Charles putting up with them?

I talked to Andrea, Charles's secretary, during my visit to her home.

She was disgusted and ready for a transfer.

"New divisions are forming, and good secretaries are in demand."

Yes, I agree!

Cupid still did its magic with us and serve a dire need for her and a diversion to me, if just for a night.

At the meeting, the deficiency I found in the design of the mega hotel in Orlando took center stage. The rolling roaster ovens were not approved; instead, the main kitchen ovens would have to be engaged for a significant event.

Once the hotel is open, a healthy operating equipment budget split up over two years could purchase the equipment. Promises, promises!

The leadership picked me as the opening Director of Food and Beverage. "It will take a strong, experienced professional with problem-solving skills.

I was resolved not to accept the assignment for this mega hotel.

I had good reasons. In addition to the flaw in the banquet kitchen, and adding the General Manager from the New York hotel who served as Resident Manager during my attack on the union and cleaning out the crooks. He stood on the sideline during the activity and let the General Manager and F&B Director take on the task with the Union.

When the dust settled, he was first in line to take a share of the credit.

The Golden Boy was his claim to fame.

I could not work for a two-faced man like him.

Receiving equipment support would be measured against his bonus.

The deficiencies in the hotel will be corrected if the management team is pushing on a united front. The budget review is the forum to do battles over it.

Another month and another meeting at the headquarters will pressure me to accept the assignment for Orlando.

How do I defend my decision?

I have more than five years of experience working in a regional job. With six years, I qualify for a front placement to enter the cross-training program to become a general manager.

I took a copy of that memo to the meeting. Charles Brown had committed to supporting the move and not making the regional position a dead-end job.

The deficiencies are not backed sufficiently with corrective action. It could be years before it finds a final solution.

I could also mention the general manager, but caution is advisable. He has the EVP's backing.

Non-committal language from the Assistant VP can be an issue as a last resort.

During my visit with Andrea, I learned about the latest strategy the Doberman will use to force a decision.

I called the VP's office, but the AVP picked up the phone.

I wish to speak to Charles about personal issues. I do not share this with you.

"He is not in the office; you better talk to me if you want answers. You are in my region. If it deals with Orlando, we are running out of time. One way or another, a decision must be made this week." Here was the "or else" hidden in his words Then he realized that he had spoken too soon. The phone call gave me reasons to believe that he was on a mission. Take it or leave it. I will get you out of here, one way or another.

By the tone of his voice, he made the music.

At the meeting, all eyes are focused on me.

Immediately, Kumar went on the attack, labeling me as the reason this hotel project may be delayed. The demand for a change to the banquet kitchen and the delay in making a final decision became the focal point.

I brought forward the company's commitment to cross-train and enter a General Manager's career, but it was simply brushed aside. We must first resolve this staffing assignment.

Cross-training was not to be discussed now. Bigger issues are on the table.

I countered this with his lack of commitment and my lack of confidence in his commitment to support me. Problems are already there, and more will surface.

If you want to see me fail, then I better decide right now and resign.

I handed him my envelope and walked out.

A bomb must have hit him. His strategy did not go his way. He wanted to see me suffer and struggle. Eventually, he will be satisfied with firing me.

Relief came over me, and I flew home to think it over.

I left a great company. Could I have gone the grievance way to the top if necessary?

No, two steps up the ladder had been poisoned. Meanwhile, this Doberman would tear me apart like prey.

******

I signed up with a college from the Miami Hotel. He, too, was railroaded by the General manager and quit his job.

A project in Coconut Grove became available to convert a fast-food restaurant with minor renovations into a full-service restaurant. The cost is minor and involves a deck cascading to the street level.

My contribution amounted to half of the development cost, giving me fifty percent ownership in the project.

We opened a trendy place in the heart of the Grove.

Anticipation and excitement were building while we added a deck towards the sidewalk. With two hundred seats, the full liquor license was granted, and the menu offered a wide variety of trendy food. It had something for everyone living in this artistic corner of the city.

Management duties were shared on a rotation basis. Since both partners had strong culinary training, it was a logical solution, and neither was stuck doing the kitchen duty alone.

From the first day, we enjoyed the business of the residents in the Grove.

Through its high visibility, the restaurant became a place to be seen.

Friends sharing a meal and an evening of fun, couples on intimate tables on a date night, single men, and girls just on the lookout for a date or groups of girls celebrating a "girls' night out. The bar overlapping the inside bar counter had its following. Young men searching for a mate or conquest spent money on expensive drinks and showing the statue. Standing room only became the norm when drinks and snack food were passed overhead to those who could not get close to the bar, and payment was returned.

The casual environment was conducive to the benefit of the business.

Then there are those people looking to exploit a new business.

I had been on the lookout for the typical party of four in their sixties when a man tried to shove an oyster in my face, saying it smelled bad. He tried to get out of paying his bar tab.

When I looked at his bill, I learned he had his fill, and I called his bluff. Pay up or else. We have friends in the neighborhood. Have a look at the police patrol across the street.

Couples enjoyed an evening under the stars with a great bottle of wine and a creative meal. Then, on occasion, I offered free after-dinner drinks to the ladies.

A bottle of Absolut Vodka kept in the freezer with a block of ice around its belly, combined with Passion liquor, became the after-dinner drink.

The idea came to mind when the beverage sales representative offered Grand Passion Liquor at no cost to test market this new product.

With the first sip, I found it excessively sweet and unappealing.

If we could cut it with a straight shot, it would give me the idea of the Vodka.

The Vodka was set into a large metal can, filled with water, and frozen, forming a ring of ice around the bottle.

I took one lemon, peeled the rind, and dropped the rind into the bottle. The juice was then added.

Froze Absolut and the Grand Passion Liquor with four glasses in hand, I approached the table with two couples.

May I treat you ladies to an after-dinner drink on the house? Elated and honored, they gladly accepted. "What's the name?" We call it "Absolute Passion!"

The men felt left out and asked me," What about us?"

It's too much passion for the men; I was teasing.

I poured half of the Vodka with the Passion liquor and served the ladies. The men received a double shot of frozen vodka straight up, and the double shot charged to the men made up the price.

It caused commotion, earned praise, and attracted the attention of other tables. They wanted the same. Seldom did I return any of these items to the freezer.

******

Promotion at the Grove attracted thousands of visitors, and the organizers did not supply sufficient toilets.

The onslaught on our restrooms was overwhelming.

Long lines of all genders are waiting patiently. I needed to resupply paper goods and pick up debris on the floor.

******

The Coconut grove borders a seedy section of Miami. Crime-ridden and drug dealings make the daily headlines in the local paper.

We knew this and thought of ways to protect the property and ourselves when leaving the business after closing, often by 3 o'clock in the darkness of the night. My partner carried a weapon and encouraged me to do the same.

On a day when I was on kitchen duty, he came to me nervous and told me that a man from Boogie Town had spoken to him about providing protection. " You know this area and the risk of owning a busy restaurant. We know all the seedy characters and offer you protection from them for a modest weekly fee. Think about it! I will be back in a few days. Okay!"

"What are we going to do? Should we pay and have peace? What do you think?"

I told him to calm down. He is bluffing and will stage a minor break-in, taking what he fancies: bottles of alcohol and cigarettes and nothing else worth taking and carrying out in the dark of the night. Besides, we are on a busy road that never dies down.

Then we see his next move.

It came as I had predicted, only that he ripped out the stereo receiver, left minor damages behind, and took a few bottles and cigarettes. He had entered the building through the ceiling, gaining access by tearing the Soffit panels out and slipping inside. Is he a skinny man? "Yes, just bones and skin."

It was not long. Before he came back asking for my partner.

Since I was working the front and looking after the service, my partner was out shopping for supplies.

You can speak with me; I am his partner and authorized to negotiate with you. But doing this inside in front of our customers is not the optimal location. Let's go to the back of the parking lot. We can talk freely and not have others listen in on us. It is a delicate proposal from you.

He followed me through the kitchen while I motioned a muscular cook to follow us and took him to my car parking space. His back to a live Oak tree, I pointed to my car.

What?" Do you know who broke this small triangle window and stole my camera?

"Hmm, I might be able to find out this guy. I know that you have been broken in at the restaurant."

I see. You are well-informed! " It is our business to track these people and put a stop to it; that's why we offer you protection."

That's all good and fine, but it makes me angry. Extremely angry.

Let me tell you something about me. I am a butcher by trade, starting from life stock and slaughtering the animals. Never anger a butcher, for we have long knives, razor-sharp knives; with one move across the neck, the head will fall off. I gave him the sound and motion of the knife slicing the skin and then through the joints. ZZish - ZZish

This man turned white as I gave him my fist across his nose, causing his wire-rimmed glasses to fly to the ground. He broke loose from my hand, holding him against the tree, and ran for his life.

I told my partner about this episode, who was even more worried until two local policemen came for coffee and a check on the business.

I told them the story from beginning to end. They responded to us, "it is the absolute correct action to bring this kind of extorsion to an end. It is the language they understand. You will never see nor hear from them anymore. If we as Police were allowed this kind of treatment, we would not need guns, and these hoodlums would go away or get killed by the others for their failure."

******

When desperate customers were waiting, refreshing bathrooms was not the most enticing job. However, I found a way to have fun with it. I pulled desperate girls out of the line and let them use the men's bathroom while blocking the men from entering.

Stimulating conversation grew from the initial "thank you, so nice of you and the occasional kiss or hug." It was a marketing stroke in a personal manner that yielded romance.

I started to apply a performance rating to the cultures. Latinas, as a broad group, received the highest marks. It was amazing to see a melting pot of women who made themselves available so freely and without a hustle.

Never any demands for free restaurant service, only driven by their natural desire to hook up with a man.

My success made my married partner envious. I told him to take the front service duty on busy days like this, but he preferred the kitchen and hid from the masses.

Instead, he planned to oust me and make his wife a partner.

"We have the majority vote, and we are voting you out. You can stay on as a silent partner, but we will no longer allow you to work here."

The shock hit me like a slap in the face. I was at a loss for words and realized that until that day, I had been living off my savings.

Hiring an attorney was out of the question; I was almost broke.

I demanded my investment capital and was promised to receive it if the business could repay it.

29

Defeated, I went to my townhouse and talked it over with my girlfriend.

Days later, I went to look him up and confronted him about getting all the money in full.

He tried to change the subject and recited that his wife was putting him under pressure. He had to act to save his marriage. Okay, whatever reason, this is now a done deal, but you must pay back my investment money.

He committed to it and signed a letter to pay it in 3 installments over six months. I wrote it off to Karma to settle this score.

CHAPTER 3

While searching for a job, I contacted friends and co-workers from the past. A position comparable to my former regional Food & Beverage job was available in a company with numerous franchise hotels of different brands.

The interview was scheduled promptly at their headquarters in Pittsburg.

Three names with the Vice Presidents' ranks were on the interviewer's list.

Each Interviewer was given a minimum of one hour—enough time to probe on individual priorities.

With my resume in hand, I entered the first office. He introduced himself as the Regional Vice President. He stated his name and offered a seat on a comfortable chair across from him. It was a casual setting at the side of his desk.

"We already know a good amount about you. Your former employer was kind enough to send your credentials and add your accomplishments. We have a close working relationship with that corporation and run franchise properties. It gives us confidence. We must see if you fit the team we are forming on the model of your former position. We can forgo the skills and technical knowledge questions. Let's just have a casual chat and tell us how you live your life and what motivates you."

I was surprised at the novel approach; I know it has been a while since I sat for an interview. Has the world changed that much?

The places I lived and worked, my failed marriage, my hobbies, and my passion for classical music, art, and sculpture are important to my lifestyle. I could have added more, but I did not want to overwhelm him. He has a warm personality; a caring radiance came from his voice and choice of words. It became an easy conversation partner, showed interest in common subjects, gave open-ended questions, and kept the flow going.

He pointed to the city's cultural venues, sports enthusiasm, and the hotel location in his region.

He gave me a brief history and said that he comes from a General Manager's post at a Florida hotel. He was getting to a point where he was selling me on the position.

When I left his room, it felt like I had found a friend. He looked satisfied.

Next on the schedule was the Corporate Food & Beverage Vice President.

He got straight to the point. "What we want from you is the system of your former employer. We are behind with operating procedures, and you know how rigid they enforce them. There is no way to get any variances, no matter the location."

I smiled at this comment. "Why are you smiling? Is it possible? Can you deliver?"

I recently opened a four-star property that needed and called for variations. I fought for them, and we succeeded in implementing all programs.

"How did you get away with it?"

I had the backing of the hotel's developer, and I committed others in high-ranking positions to backing me.

He sat back in his big desk chair and put his fist to cover his mouth. I studied his body language.

He continued selling me on the position but never revealed his aims or how he runs his department.

It looked like he was consumed in thoughts and trying to impress me. I felt compelled to ask him the questions and turned the table. I was now interviewing him.

He spoke freely and was proud of his accomplishments in the hotels, the beverage department, entertainment, and bands, but he said nothing about catering, food, or kitchen procedures.

It felt strange.

I had 30 minutes in between the third interview. It gave me time to reflect on the last one. I found it grotesque that a Vice President was unprepared for a post they planned to fill. Should I have asked him more detailed questions on the subject he intentionally omitted or left out being pre-occupied?

He is undoubtedly a poor interviewer; I learned that much about him.

The following person was the Vice President of Marketing.

He was easy to communicate with and followed personal subjects and business interests.

Again, the interview flowed with questions and answers, and personal stories were mixed into the dialogue. He mastered the art of making the candidate comfortable and showed a wide array of personal interest in me.

He told me about his girlfriend and that he enjoyed the single life. He wanted me to open up about my personal life.

In my efforts to distract him from my personal life, I became engrossed in storytelling about the amusing episodes I experienced during my time in India.

That did capture the man's interest, and it consumed his allotted time. He had another appointment waiting, and his secretary, Mandi, came in to remind him of it.

"Meet Mandi; we will be sharing her secretarial service."

This is another indication of my acceptance as the candidate.

Mandi introduced herself outside his office and reflected on the office atmosphere, his travel schedule and what she is capable of in terms of secretarial skills. Another sign that they had decided before I set foot into the company's office space.

It is nice to meet you, Mandi! It is my pleasure. "It's Nice to see you are making progress. We look forward to seeing you in this office."

＊＊＊＊＊＊

I called Angela my girlfriend from the hotel and gave her a progress report. It gives her time to digest the news.

The phone call came from the Regional Vice President. He confirmed the consensus to hire me and offered the salary and benefits.

Another move: I had hoped to avoid this. I hated to move and uproot again.

My townhouse is free and clear and has no mortgage payments, and it will be good keep and not sell it. I can scrape together a down payment for a modest house in Pittsburg. The homes are moderately priced. I was not planning on starting a big family with kids and pets. I am not even sure if Angela will follow me.

A candidate who has already inquired about renting my townhouse was the Chef from the Beach Resort. He is looking to move in alone.

My reporting date is in two weeks; until then, I have time to sort out my life.

Angela can make her own decisions if and whenever she is ready.

Renting my house and organizing the move have priority. It will not involve furniture that must stay here in Florida. Suddenly, everything looked easy.

I loaded my Benz 190 D and said my farewell to Angela. She cried and promised to join me in due time. I sensed her pain; she was in love with me and hoped to get married once I settled the job and moved in the house.

The cold North, or was it Mid-West, came as a shock. I must acclimate to the four seasons once more.

I settled into a split-level house. The cul-de-sac provided a quiet area, and the commute to work was tolerable.

My work started with a briefing from the Regional Vice President. He explained the structure and introduced me to the other team members. My office is set up near Mandi's desk. She helped me organize the files and delivered supplies. I asked her about my penmanship. I will manage once we have worked together for a while. Bring me your notes; I will handle the rest.

My Girlfriend Angela stayed back and kept her job at the hotel. Our relationship became a long-distance connection, and we kept it alive with evening phone calls and emails.

The areas of responsibility were split between New England and Florida. The opportunity to connect on the Florida trips sounded promising.

First, a team visit to Florida introduced the new Regional Team, which will take oversight from this day forward. This was a new concept for the company and the hotels. It will take them a few visits before they accept the team's involvement. The same was planned for the New England hotels.

An emergency canceled that trip. It was never rescheduled.

"You are on your own; this is the kind of support you will get from him, the RVP. Better stick to me."

That comment came from Stu, the VP of Food & Beverage. Our expertise will bond us together.

"I count on you when you travel to the hotel to make them understand and establish a good working relationship. It was then followed with a brief overview of the most urgent priorities in each hotel. The profile of the management and the F&B man. No word about the Chef and Catering personalities."

His words made it clear that no love was lost between him and the RVP.

"Be careful and stick with me. You are an F&B man, "was his last word. I am once again in the middle of a power struggle. How bad can it be when reasonable people sit down to solve their problems?

Was I forced on him in the hopes of salvaging a franchise contract?

I shook it off and trusted my problem-solving skills and management style.

******

All my counterparts in the hotels looked young and light on experience. I quickly noticed strong loyalties to the Corporate F&B VP.

It can be expected since he had been the direct line to report to on their business. I will go easy and find a way to warm up to these boys.

"It's the new guy, and what does he know about my hotel?" That question was written on everyone's face. Short answers and minimal eye contact led me to believe such information must be kept in the dark.

I found it the same way in my former start-up trips in New Jersey, but the experience level was more mature.

Will my resume or at least a part of it help? I decided against it; it may be intimidating. I do not need more walls to conquer.

A tour of the property and shaking hands with employees came as a shock.

I had the duty in my former position to follow through on what was termed the people program.

I mentioned the company I had worked for and the region I was handling. A connection between the brand name and the hotels in the area has now made an impression. The Fort Lauderdale man opened up with endless questions on the Intercostal hotel lounge and, of course, the four-star resort property on the beach. I discussed my involvement in a low-key approach and re-directed to the work and priorities facing his hotel.

Remember, the purpose of my visit is to learn as much as possible from you about your operation. Now, we broke the ice and discussed his food and beverage operation.

I did not do a thorough inspection. I glanced at the critical locations to get a feel for sanitation while shaking hands with dishwashers, cooks, and servers. It gave me a feel for what I needed to know. The Chef had his day off. OK, I will meet him on the next trip.

I noticed that emphasis was placed on bar and liquor sales. Food was secondary, with boring menu choices. Catering worked on their own with minimal supervision.

Does Sales and marketing dominate them?

When I visited the hotels in South Florida, the same pattern followed in all the hotels: the same cold reception and tight-lipped young men and still green behind their ears. It reminded me of the interview at Florida International University.

Only the manager at Brickell Hotel tried to learn from me. He had been a Catering director at the former company. His knowledge gave him a leg up since he understood the team concept, and now he has found a person he can relate to professionally.

Igor gave me a warm welcome and took me around. He knew the routine from his past and took me to every area and the employees to make the introduction. The Chef was at work and stopped to talk. Inter-department relations showed friction. He explained the imminent problems; it was made clear that he was alone with little support from his superior, the General Manager. He is fighting a solitary battle.

My assurance of a swift follow-up visit put him at ease for now. Don't inflame the situation with the other departments. We will do a fact-finding exercise first, and from that, we plan our approach. Just let the fires burn. The more we know, the easier the solution.

We shook hands, and I made my way to Key West.

******

Three hours in the car, passing endless Islands connected by bridges, gave me time to form a game plan. My approach on the second visit will be an eye-opener. These boys are asleep and need a lesson in management.

I suspected the frequent phone calls to their Godfather had been sweet-talked and presented the actions with lipstick. You can disguise the ugliest face with make-up.

Key West is in sight, with the hotel facing the Gulf of Mexico. The building's architecture made it look like a Southern mansion. Massive Entrance doors, high ceilings, archways to shade the sun, and occasional rain showers made for an impressive property. When I saw this style of building, my expectations were high. Inside, the luxury decor repeated the luxurious architecture.

My guest room did not disappoint.

Let me see if Food & Beverage keeps pace with this classy resort. My RVP had been managing this property. I made assumptions and met with the Food & Beverage director. He greeted me in the restaurant and offered me water. I know the water in Florida; I have a house in Davie. Please, a bottled Perrier or Evian. He directed the server to follow this request.

We sat across a dining table. As it was between meals, I gave him a quick overview of my experience, thinking that I could set the tone since he was older than the others. He tried to answer the questions but had nothing to add. Don't you have any areas you may want to improve? I bring you a load of experience, I am at your disposal. I much prefer to build up than play the role of an inspector. We both know that in food and in service, there can always be improvement.

I can only offer it; I cannot force it on you. Immediately, he relaxed; the pressure was off, or was it?

When I met with the Chef, and later with the Catering director, he was upset about this direct contact and made a slanting comment.

Are you specialized in these areas? Are you sure you want me to stay out of these areas? I pressed him for an answer, but none came. I understand your protective nature, but it is to everyone's benefit to draw from my ability. I have done extensive work in both fields.

What are you hiding? Rest assured, if there is something hidden, I will find it! Do not underestimate my resourcefulness.

Alarm bells went off with an inflamed face; "I will talk to Stu on this. I am not comfortable with you."

That is your right for now, but remember, the solid line goes to the GM, and a reporting line also goes to me. With the Regional team, all this has changed. Before you become insubordinate, I want you to know about this new structure.

The conversation ended, and so did my visit. I did not stay over and made my point to the new General manager in the de-briefing

Able to catch a late flight with Allegheny Airlines, I made it home to my house by midnight.

The narrow leg space on this flight was painful for a six-foot-tall man. I nicknamed this airline "Agony Airline."

My first report from notes provided a general overview, which was shallow and shameful and certainly below my customary reports from the past.

Only Miami Brickell had an elaborate, detailed commentary focusing on the tensions and the need for a prompt follow-up.

Key West received my carefully worded statements about the Food and Beverage director's defensive posture and unwillingness to open up and discuss operating issues. It was a flat-out rejection of working with the new Regional structure. Every effort was made to prevent any interaction with the Chef and Director of Catering. I suspected efforts were made to hide problems from me. How can anyone be helped? Foolish and immature behavior.

A solo look around revealed numerous violations in cleanliness and service procedures. The banquet was dark, and the DOC took a day off.

My RVP wanted a verbal report. He read between the lines and sensed that my careful language was hiding solid feelings and findings of specific issues. He knew him all too well and used the direct pipeline to cover his butt with false information.

All hotels needed the same priorities and corrective actions. I opened up and described them in great detail. A candied information flow and, in some cases, resentment turned into complaints. It must be expected from the first go-around.

Mandi commented when she came to see me. Are you always that gentle in your reports? OK, I look forward to it. The cat is walking on the soft paws; the claws will be out on the following information.

Stu was finally off the phone. The boys had been calling him to get the first word in, and then he called me in to go over this report.

"The report does not accurately represent your visit and conduct with these people. I have heard from all, and they painted a different picture." I agree with your assessment but understand that the written word cannot be removed, which only shows preliminary findings.

If they feel different, I will tell you that my feelings and findings are also quite different. If you wish to hear my straight talk, I will give it to you.

It was not a good visit, with one exception. There is strong resentment toward the new setup; they defy it by calling you directly. I will overlook it since it is the first time, and neither has received an advance briefing. Like I told Mandy, the cat was walking on the soft paws, but the claws could come out as soon as needed.

I guess you will take the version from your hotline, and I don't need to go into details.

These words rang a bell: A new guy is not a yes man.

Leaving the office, he called me back. "I am sorry. I owe you to hear you out."

He received the true flavor and details of my visit to the hotels.

I do not go to the properties unless fires are burning!

I left his office with mixed feelings. To me, it looked like we are singing from two different songbooks. I went back to the RVP and filled him in on the tone of my meeting in the Food and Beverage office.

"I am not surprised; he does not play by the rules. You report to me directly. Yes, sometimes it gets technical, and his involvement will take priority, but it must include me."

The last comment did little to put me at ease.

******

I scheduled a visit to help my man in Miami settle his problems. His predicament calls for the imminent involvement of the Regional vice president.

Stu called and ordered me to go to Cambridge with him. The General manager had pointed out cost problems in food and beverage. They have exhausted the conventional audit process and are at a loss for solutions. Stu wanted me to do an indebted property review.

At first inclination, I saw it as a trap. Does he want to test my ability to sniff out issues? It will be my first visit, and I have no knowledge of the hotel's history, nor the players involved.

I asked Mandy for help. Do you have a file from Marketing pointing to food or beverage sales, and can you get me the personal file of the F&B and Chef?

She assembled a dossier with comprehensive information, resumes of every department manager and sales records spanning twelve months.

Great, Mandy. You have done a super job! I thought you could benefit from these files. Judging from the reports, you are thorough. They are making waves already and have set a new profile, which my marketing guy will also adopt. The top floor has already asked for the report.

******

We checked into the rooms and visited the General Manager. An attractive, college-educated woman in her early forties welcomed us to her office and went straight to the issues.

"You must solve this cost issue; it has been too long. You come with a partner to fix it and fix it for good. Those are the marching orders."

Stu took it offensively and looked at my reaction.

She is in charge; can you blame her? She comes from marketing and has an MBA! Let's give her our best efforts.

I want to start with an inspection. We will meet the managers on duty as we make our tour. Stu looked at me as if it was his first inspection. "Why? Don't you want to see the numbers first to point to the problems?"

41

I already have the numbers. The problems are generated on the floor, in the kitchen, the bar, banquets and wherever employees handle the product.

I pressed my point, and he went along. The F&B director wanted to start in the restaurant, but I told him to take us to the storeroom. I want to follow the product from receiving to the customer. This way, we will not miss any steps.

The storeroom was locked. What is this? It's the middle of the day. Was he out to lunch and just secured it?

"No, he is in there." There was a knock, and he opened up with a look as if we had just caught him looking at a Playboy magazine.

Don't you get visits from the Chef or F&B? He looked at all the faces and hesitated to answer. Not good, I thought. Well, is there an answer?

"Yes, they do come down here, but infrequent."

Please show us around and walk us through your procedures for receiving the wares. I see you have all the hotel supplies here, too. "Yes, Sir."

The room looked clean and orderly, and walk-in coolers and freezers also made a good impression.

Tell me about these liquor bottles. Are they from the bar requisition?

"Yes, Sir, I just completed the order and will make a delivery as soon as the bartender shows up."

Does he pick it up? "No, but:" he stopped at that point.

I let it go; I had an idea to follow this trail.

What is in these boxes here? Can you open them, please? The boxes contained expensive prime-cut meat that had already warmed from sitting out.

Why are these here? "The guy comes to pick it up."

Who is that guy? He is now getting nervous.

"Why are you asking? The meat guy, of course." He smiled.

OK, when is this pickup going to take place? This meat must get back in the cooler.

"He is delayed. I hope he makes it by 5 pm, traffic, you know."

Put it in the walk-in until such time.

We continued our walk while Stu questioned my actions. All I did was ask questions. Do you see anything wrong with it?

"No, of course not." Now, on to the kitchen.

It's nice to meet you, Chef. Please show us your kitchen. I'll give you another look as if I were making the most unusual request.

I quickly noticed the sloppy food handling, workstations were not cleaned after each use, waste cans showed too much thrown-out food, and the refrigerators had damaged gaskets with black mold.

Inside, I noticed blatant violations; raw fish and meat were kept on the top shelf while he had produce in open containers right underneath.

A look at the tiled floor did not fare better. I stopped and confronted the Chef.

Tell me if you find anything wrong here.

He pointed to the fish not being on the right shelve.

Is that it.? "It could be better organized, but we are prepping lunch."

I understand this. I have many years of experience in the culinary field, and I want to point out the violations the health inspector will find and the reasons to shut you down.

I pointed to the fish, the meat, the dairy product at the entrance, and lettuce with meat juices dropped on it. When I looked at the floor, I saw the round corners and weeks-old dirt.

Do you want me to go on? I received this blank look.

Can we go to a quiet place in banquets and grab a table to rehash this situation?

I want to know more about your training to get to this position.

"I went to the Culinary Institute and was looking to make back the money. This education had been draining my finances and my parents' bank account. I opted to work for individual restaurants since they paid better than anyone else. Eventually, I had enough experience for a resume to apply for this job."

Do you order the food and, in particular, the meats?

"I give the store guy the list; he then calls the vendor and receives it."

What about inspecting the food at the time of delivery? "I see it when it comes to the kitchen, and if it is not the quality, I scold him."

Let me tell you a little about myself to give you a reference for what I will say to you.

I grew up in the meat business, from live animals to the final meat cuts. Additionally, we produce sausages and smoked meats and sell them retail in our shop directly to the consumers.

Then, I started my culinary training. I worked all over the world in the best hotels and with high-caliber Chefs, emphasizing learning and adding to my knowledge and skills.

Today, I can carve ice sculptures, model tallow sculptures, produce pate en route, grand buffets, and cook a twelve-course meal in the style of Escoffier.

But I hang up my apron in favor of management; I am here to offer you my advice and share my knowledge.

The Chef is now relaxed and amazed.

I will tell you what you have missed while chasing the almighty dollar.

See, this lettuce you have in the walk-in looks wilted. You can bring it back to life again, and the same goes for all other leafy products. I will show it to you right after this meeting.

The meat is not to spec. The ends are cut at an angle; you lose yield, and each strip will lose you one steak.

The fish must be on shaved ice, in a bin or rack and placed in the back of the cooler where it is the coldest.

Get on engineering to replace these gaskets and set the temperature to the correct, safe temperature. Have a look at this fan. It is full of dirt and not running at full speed.

Clean as you go means that every workstation receives a thorough cleaning and sanitation after every use.

Sweep the floor. A clean floor is not violated; be sure to get into the corners. They are not rounded. Get spray bottles from Housekeeping and a gallon of bleach, and I will show you how to set up the sanitizing procedures.

There is more, and I will plan another visit to spend more time with you.

At the F&B's office, I told the manager and Stu that I saw a misguided young talent who had never gotten on the right track. But it's never too late.

I am not the man to hurt him. If he follows through, we will be OK.

The Chef took a deep breath and affirmed his efforts.

He invited us to his seafood lunch buffet lunch. Thank you, but we must first complete our tour.

A Maître'D was running the service. We spoke about his clientele and service staff. Is it difficult for people with minimum pay to live nearby?

We manage, and with the higher check averages, they do well.

What about the bartender? This bar has only a few barstools and a service station for the servers. I presume that most drinks are served at the tables.

"Yes, that is correct. Servers tip the bartender out nightly. We tell them that 5% is the requirement."

How do you get away with making it mandatory? It must be a discretionary amount. Long faces!

Who is in charge of the bar?

"The Maître'D keeps an eye on it and does the cash out at the end of the shift." Does the Maître'D have a bank-to-service change when the bartender needs to break large bills? "Yes."

Mr. F&B, could you please retrieve his bank from the safe and bring the keys to the bar cabinets?

I will go to the room and will be right back.

Please open the bank and the cabinet.

Stu did not say a word; he just looked at me with a question.

I asked the F&B man to count the bank while I went behind the bar to pull the pour brands out. At the same time, the Maître'D looked on. I pulled out my hydrometer to measure the alcohol.

One by one, I poured enough into the measuring glass until the scale floated. I made the Matre'd read it and record every measure: all the rums, Gin, Vodka, Tequila, and others of the light brown variety.

Meanwhile, the F&B man had a count and read it out loud.

I saw a rapid change in the man's behavior. He turned red, became fidgety, and moved his hair to the back despite the grease he used to keep it there.

Are you OK?

Tell me what this all means. "The alcohol is diluted, but only on the white alcohol." And you are way over on your bank count. Give me an explanation for it, please.

He was stuck and could hardly make a sound. Would you like to clarify this in the privacy of the office?

"What do you want from me?"

Let us start with the names involved in this theft. OK, the bartender is obvious; what about any service staff, the head waiter or Captain, as you call him? " No, not him and servers are not in; they do not know."

That leaves you and the bartender. When does the bartender come to work?

Another question! What's the method of keeping track of the drinks that don't get rung on the register? You better call the bartender to come early since we have an emergency.

We left the man in the office while we went to the secretary to draw up forms for documentation and confessions. Additionally, disclaimers kept the hotel and company harmless, and there was no defamatory language or slanderous talk after our departure from this employment.

With documents in hand, we ask him to write up his confession.

We are also asking that you sign this paper. We will not show this to anyone, but you are now dismissed. Pick up your last check tomorrow.

We ask that you keep it to yourself. HR will make employment references, which will be limited to your service time. Have a good life.

The bartender told us he was shifting coins from one side to the other. He has been using the empty bottles I had seen at the storeroom to cheat on his second job and throw off the par stock control. We called his other employer and informed them of this scam.

Again a termination and the usual paperwork.

Stu was at ahh.

We are not finished. The meat will be picked up soon. But first, I needed fresh air; it had gotten very sticky in here.

Outside, I looked for the loading dock. Already, I saw a pickup truck backing up to the dock. While I observed it, I noticed these meat boxes getting loaded.

Stop! I called the storekeeper. Who is this man? "He picks up grease and?" meat, and he will return it to the meatpacker?"

The packing plant is closed at this late hour. Workers start at five a.m. and finish shortly after lunch.

You have just been caught in the act.

I called the executive office and asked them to come down and bring security. Don't forget the papers and the secretary.

By the time they arrived, I had a confession from the storekeeper, but this guy with the truck was defiant. I asked security to lock him up in the office. Meanwhile, I ask the storekeeper to write a confession and name all participants.

"I was in a money squeeze from being unable to pay the hospital bills—the birth of my daughter.

This guy offered me a way to fast cash to escape my mess. He kept demanding, and then it became blackmail.

The storekeeper is now begging me: "Please, I have a family and a young child. I will make good on it, I promise. Take it out of the paycheck. It will hurt, but a clear mind is worth the pain. It has only been three weeks since we started."

I looked at Stu and the F&B man with a nod. With the confession, we have proof that this crook, the jobber, can be turned over to the law. A reprimand and stern warning will tarnish his employment record. A stern warning, and keep your nose clean from now on.

The jobber with his truck was arrested, and we received information about all the locations he was using for this criminal activity.

Before I forget. These empty liquor bottles must be destroyed when replaced with a requisition. "Yes, Sir, right away."

Mr. F&B, you will now buy us a great glass of wine.

We missed lunch and snacked on something the Chef supplied to hold us over to dinner. The GM briefing was a welcome relief to her, and I promised the Chef a return visit to share my experience with him.

******

Back at the ranch (my nickname for the office), I wrote up my report. I am accustomed to writing every detail, and nothing was getting whitewashed. Straight from the horse's mouth, I told Mandy.

Angela had changed jobs to get out of Miami. The city had become dangerous from the drug war. Killings had taken place near the hotel, and the way to work took her past hazardous neighborhoods. Her mom wanted her to take a job with an electronics company. The pay is that much better, and you may make new friends. Her underlying motive was to hook her up with a highly paid Tech man.

Mom wanted to drive a wedge between us; that much became clear. I was older, and I did not fit in with her culture. A phone call confirmed my suspicion. She informed me that she had changed her mind and would not join me in the North.

We drifted apart; the long-distance relationship was not working.

******

At one time, the RVP and Stu wanted me to join them on the same day in two different locations. Stu wanted to go to the New England area, and the RVP had a team visit scheduled for Florida

It had put me on the spot to take sides.

Kiddingly, I told the messenger to convey the question and preference of which part of me he wanted. Cutting straight down the middle gives each one half, but it is of little use. My humor was not appreciated.

You decide. Both of equal rank should be able to come to terms! This is just another sign of a power play from my bully, the F&B VP.

I ended up going to Miami. Great, the hotel had been my priority. I promised the F&B to help with the issues he was facing.

Communication was the core problem. Accusations had been made and countered with another charge. These managers did not communicate.

Igor, the F&B had a calm personality and managed his department with skill and deep knowledge of catering and wine.

We met and walked along the Miami River to talk. "How do you see this situation?"

My first feeling is how you communicate with each other when dealing with a problem.

I will give you the advice to turn the table in your favor.

You are creating an accusation if you point fingers at the other side's fault. He or she, in turn, will fire back in defense. An action provokes a reaction. In it is the biggest problem.

Remember this! Every problem has a solution. We are the creators of the problem or the employees or any outside sources. It is us humans doing it.

If you turn the issue into a question, you will receive an answer. It will be defensive, but the following questions will, in time, bring you to the point of a solution. You are no longer putting blame on others, but you are seeking answers. It will take away the emotions and arguments. Seeking a solution is to get to the bottom of the problem. Once you arrive there and agree, you will have the solution in front of your nose.

Igor thought about it and agreed." Can we practice together? I want to become fluent in this method. I see, in a way, how this defuses the fighting."

Yes, we start with the front office manager.

We set a time to meet on his turf, giving him a perceived advantage. I could sense the tension in the room.

We have come to solve a problem. It affects my cost of food and beverage. I cannot figure out why the revenue never matches the daily report from the night auditor. Has anything been done to adjust the numbers for these two revenue lines?

"It is your department; don't you know your numbers?"

We do, and we get them from the registers. Cashiers are checked out using this data, which we see as the correct information. The night auditors may adjust something, yet they take the reading at the end of the business.

Can you shed light on refunds that take place in the morning?

"Yes, right; this may alter the data by the amount we void due to complaints."

Where do these complaints originate? "There are few, but we get them in the rooms and before they leave, I make an adjustment to the bill." Are you correcting the room revenue to settle the disputes on the spot?

"No, the room charges have since been closed by the night auditor, but food and beverage are still open, and there is time to take the adjustment from there. It causes no questions from the controller or General Manager. Refunds should not affect your cost; they are booked on a different line."

We can clarify this with the controller, but you may be wrong. When revenues are reduced and costs stay the same, the results are affected.

Would you mind if we see the controller together to bring clarity and a solution?

They set a time and received the answer. It must be taken from the source of the complaint. Since the bar and restaurant had applied corrections on the spot, it was clear that the rooms department had to carry the refunds on their books.

Igor glowed with pride. You handled the situation masterfully, and you learned how a slight change in the dialog made a difference. Did you notice the shift in tone and body posture once the questions needed answers?

"You have solved my problems." No, I gave you the tools to become effective. Make it a habit.

Other nagging problems with engineering became his target to solve with the same method. He was proud and tried getting the management team to adopt this method.

******

Back at the Homefront again, Mandy told me the owners had called and wanted me at a meeting in the Executive suite. The recent report from Boston had caught their attention.

Mandy made the appointment and showed me to the office suite. I was welcomed with a warm welcome and received praise for my accomplishments during the hotel visit.

We also like your style of reports. They reveal details that provide us with insight into the operations.

Until now, we had the impression that the report from the F&B department received a whitewash from putting a good face on it.

It's nice to have you on our team. A fresh breeze was needed.

When I returned with a bright smile, Stu wanted to know.

He was jealous and showed anger but tried to suppress it. You are walking a tightrope, be careful.

I was confused by this warning. I'd been accustomed to having free access to superiors, and the Chairman had stopped to say hello, if only in passing. Never had there been a reaction like the one I had just received from Stu.

"He has a conflict with every person in this building." When I told the RVP, he was not surprised. They spoke of Stu openly and described him as a bully with inferiority complexes.

Another warning sign! Will there be consequences?

How can I survive in this working climate? I must find a way.

*****

I learned from a friend in my former company that the Dobermans had finally overstayed their welcome. General managers and Food & Beverage had formed a coalition and petitioned the EVP and company owner.

Short of a mutiny, Charles had no other choice than to ask for their resignation.

With this news, I settled down with a glass of Chardonnay and declared it victory day.

******

The RVP persuaded the owners to send out a memorandum clearly stating the function of this new regional team system.

A corporate Vice President heading a discipline like Hotel rooms and related Marketing, Finance, Human Resources and Food & Beverage will function to set the direction and policy for their respective division.

The Regional Vice President and his team will be the link to the hotel management team.

The Regional team will enforce control functions, standards, and policy compliance.

The Corporate VP team must play a supporting role to the Regional team.

For further clarification, feel free to contact this office.

******

A follow-up visit to the Florida hotels took on a different tone.

Suggestions to improve operations performance were welcomed. My F&B directors got the memo and started cooperating.

Suddenly, they wanted to learn more about my experience and apply my management methods to their benefit.

Problem-solving skills, the value of the people's program, and sales tools in restaurants, bars, and catering became desirable discussion points.

My visit became productive days in every hotel except the Key West resort.

The visit to Key West was expected to be hostile. Antagonism included the Food and Beverage director and filtered to the assistant managers.

My strategy from the earlier visit had to be changed. I went back to basics and asked to see the operation from the ground up.

A tour of the hotel to every area is now being examined with sharp eyes. I took my time and went through everything from the loading dock, kitchen, food handling, safety and sanitation procedures, and storage methods in the coolers, refrigerators, gaskets, and ice machines.

Every violation was recorded on a pocket-size tape recorder. To this date, I have never mentioned or commented on these violations.

Let's keep going to the restaurant. The Restaurant manager followed us while I looked over the carpet and under the tables to find food that had not been cleaned. An odor came from the area.

The side stations looked in disarray. Condiments like mustard jars and ketchup bottles had soiled neck closures, silverware and real silverplated eating utensils were tarnished, and forks showed black tips.

I asked the restaurant manager if he knew what caused these blackened tips. He had no answer. I left it and purposely bypassed his boss, the F&B..

His blood pressure was rising.

The indoor and outdoor bars carried yeast odor and fruit flies, another sign of poor cleaning.

This man was about to explode. I could tell this from his body language. He was searching for a subject he could defend. We had no luck, so we went to see catering.

The ballroom was, as expected, ornate and luxurious. Cleanliness was better, and the back storage areas were neat and organized.

The tables, chairs, and serving equipment needed to be replaced.

I looked at the F&B Director with a stern face. My look was not lost at the catering. She acknowledged it with a helpless hand gesture. I knew at once that the expenditure had been shortened in favor of the bonus. Requests for replacement were simply denied.

I told her on the sideline that I would check the budget and the numbers. I could not imagine that a stately hotel would be denied sufficient funding to keep the equipment first-class.

I thanked her for the time and received a smile. Then a remark: "I hope you have enough time to sit with me. I heard that you have substantial catering experience."

The F&B took this opportunity to protest. "She reports to me, and I must approve that."

Are you an expert in her field? "No, but the chain of command must be followed."

Does this chain of command apply to you as well? "I report to the General manager."

OK, and right after, aren't you calling your Godfather in Pittsburgh?

He gave me a dirty look for that remark. He knew that his standing would be on shaky ground from this day forward.

The tour took all morning.

I excused myself to go to my room and bring a notepad and a new tape. My bar visit will include an alcohol test despite the numbers not showing discrepancies.

"Do I need to go through all the areas where you found violations?"

How often do you get a health inspector in here? If he is due, you have your work cut out. My impression of these violations is that first, there is no management supervision, and second, there is delinquency and insufficient knowledge. The operation is managed amateurishly.

During this talk, I kept the recorder running.

Let me summarize my findings, which are recorded to keep the record straight since my last visit was reported to Pittsburg with false accusations.

Skills and knowledge can be learned. I can teach the skills down to the most elementary procedures.

I can share with you management tactics and am willing to invest my time in them. However, this effort requires a willing candidate and a positive attitude.

Then, let's see if anything can be done about the delinquency. I prefer to call it straight laziness.

I do not have a medicine for that. I am sorry; I must let you down. Don't you have anything to say?

"I want the General manager to attend this session about racking over hot coals."

Feel free to call him. But when I briefed him on the arrival, he wanted no part of it. This is your department; you must handle it.

If you wish me to go item by item, I will not have enough time, and the lady in catering requested time from me. Never mind the chain of command. Learn it first and then apply it.

All the points in my report are elementary procedures that have been neglected for months. A blind eye does not solve problems. Something must change, and change must be done with you leading the action. I do not tolerate sloppy operations due to a lazy manager.

It will not make you look good, but a reversal will come to your credit.

After receiving the report, I will give you one week to clean up this mess. Count on me returning for a follow-up. I may even request a health inspection to ensure compliance.

Take this as a stern warning.

******

"How nice of you to make the time. My name is Nancy. I know this is unusual, but I work here without support. I am sorry to say this."

I have seen the condition of your equipment; it speaks for itself. If you can get access to it, I want to know the budget.

At this moment, the F&B Director joined the table. Nancy asked him to show me the budget; she had never seen the book and was in the dark.

Reluctantly, he returned to his office and delivered the Catering part only.

For your benefit, Nancy, there is money in the budget; why is your equipment not being replaced? When I looked at the F&B, his blood pressure was rising.

Where is this money going? Is it being spent in other areas? Or is it simply not being spent to make the numbers look good?

He made an excuse to blame the controller. He is not approving any of our requests.

"Nancy was shaking her head; it was him who denied the requisition. I have my papers on file."

I saw Nancy's face express anger. She finds herself on the losing end of every debate over equipment replacement. It must be a perennial problem.

The F&B director left abruptly. "I have had enough of this interrogation."

Nancy and I spent three hours reviewing ideas for improving sales, wedding business, corporate meetings, coffee break upgrades, wine sales, and bar sales.

Nobody has ever spent quality time with me. I work from my best knowledge and do my utmost to present the banquets in a good light. She will need support, or she will be hired by another hotel. Nancy and I had spent a very productive time.

For my dinner at a resort hotel, the hostess seated me at a small table while all the other tables were filled with families. I opted to sit at the bar and asked the bartender if he could get me food. I was not in the mood for a lengthy dinner. I wanted appetizers from the menu and a good glass of wine. I was not in the mood to face another Lower Alabama experience.

"We usually do not serve food at the bar. I will talk to the Chef to get something prepared. I told him the situation and the day had been a bit frustrating. He understood. The conversation led to his bar operation.

"We get frequent complaints about weak drinks. The warm climate is melting the ice and watering down the drink in a warm glass. We would be served to increase the shot size and do away with these well brands."

He showed me they do not project the quality this hotel and its clientele deserve.

I will take it up with your F&B director.

"Forget him. These are corporate Policies. This man has little or no knowledge about the bar business."

He should count his blessings on having you behind the bar.

In the morning, I went to give the General Manager a briefing.

I told him I knew he was from the rooms division and had just taken the job from my RVP.

He was embarrassed when I described the violations. If the F&B does not get the work done, the deadline and consequences can have implications for him and the hotel. The health department may get a call to visit him.

I do not take prisoners. This man had misrepresented my first visit to his Godfather. This time I have it on tape.

Catering needs support. The F&B is not providing it. I asked the GM to talk with Nancy.

For the bar service, I will discuss it with Stu before I make changes.

In the morning, I received a phone call from the RVP. I want your opinion on the situation we have to settle. Can you stop by in Miami?

******

Entering the front door, I sensed tension. I had hoped to find this in-fighting resolved.

My counterpart, Igor, looked worried. I tried my best, but the rest of the group did not agree with my proposal.

We took a walk, and I asked him, do you like working like this: no, "I do not," then why are you in with the whole gang-fighting:

"I am not, I apply the method you showed me. With constant attacks, I get sucked in, and then I face them sabotaging my department.

I am not that good at it and fall back into my old track. Sorry."

We did a role-play and practiced this method with the front office manager.

When I sat down with my boss, I told him the process I had shown to Igor. "He said it's your personality," No! I told him it was my approach. Instead of speaking and accusing, I ask questions.

It is the right approach; I ask questions instead of making accusations, and in the process, I find the underlying cause of the issue.

"You must show this to me. I have an afternoon meeting with the department heads and assistant level.

I want to nip this issue in the bud. Let's do a little role-play, and I will open the meeting with this method. If I get stuck, please jump right in."

******

The meeting is ready to begin. A brief statement from the RVP opened the session.

"Recognize that you have a beautiful hotel. It can only become a warm place of hospitality when skilled professionals make it a home for our guests. We have hostilities here, something a guest will recognize when they enter the front door. You yell at each other and create bad blood within the management team.

I want to hear from you about specific issues, please."

The chief engineer said that his equipment is constantly abused, and nobody cares, causing breakdowns and repairs. Questions came one after another, and all needed an answer until a final solution was reached.

Next came Housekeeping. The same method of asking questions supplied answers to a solution.

This looks easy, and why can't you solve your problems on your own?

It came to him that a question will demand an answer, while an accusation brings a reaction. Action-reaction! Now that you have learned something, I want you to practice it right in this room; you will hash out all your differences.

We will have dinner in the restaurant together; we have a reason to celebrate. This guy has promised a special bottle or two of fine wine.

Superbly cooked and presented as a painting, the Chef pulled out all his tricks and earned uhhs and ahhs. In the morning, I left to fly home.

******

A letter from Hollywood, Florida, was in the mailbox. I took it inside to open it before dinner. By the handwriting, I could not decipher the origin, and no sender address was in the upper left corner.

Angela's mother wrote to me in a very straightforward and cold language that her daughter would no longer be able to see me. She has decided on her own to break up the relationship. Her desire to get married and start a family was now her utmost desire. She did not see that in you, and she wishes me good luck and health. It is over now!

I knew that the family pressured her. She had dropped hints lately but never came out that direct.

It is not her language and not her words. She is forced to break up with me. Mother is a dominating woman, a reason both daughters had moved out of the house. The same holds in the way she treated her husband.

I knew that I had just lost my girl. I loved her deeply.

She made a positive mark on me and opened my emotional side. These same emotions are now hurting as if my heart had been ripped out of my chest. Tears rolled down my face, and I drenched the kitchen towel; I put the food away. The "Joie de Vivre" has just left my life."

I want to hear it from her, I know she is strong enough to tell me, and if she feels OK with that decision, I shall accept it and move on. The pain will be there for a long time, fade, and come back, but time will heal the wounds.

A lousy night overshadowed a day when I could not hide my sorrow.

******

My training plan to teach these young managers management skills had become the project for the day. As I put myself into their shoes, I knew I was lost in my first management position. Yes, the need to train was there.

It is a skill that can be enhanced and be part of the seminar.

Other needs include hiring and interviewing techniques and putting candidates to the test before committing them to the payroll.

HR does only a screening; the manager does the interview by reviewing past jobs, technical skills, and character. It is as essential for the employee to like the workplace as much as it is for the hotel to like him or her.

I worked non-stop until I had it finally committed to paper.

Mandy is ready to get it typed.

She made it look official with everything organized inside an impressive folder.

I was pleased; this woman had skills beyond my imagination.

She titled the cover page: Food and Beverage, Training, Volume I.

The author, date, and company logo completed this document.

Must I write some more training modules since you numbered this volume 1? "It's a great start, can I leave it?" Yes, but I want copyrights. "Library of Congress?". Why not! She laughed;" I can apply for it."

Headline with the seminar title, then presented by, below my name and title, and then the company and address.

We went to lunch at a restaurant of her choice.

She told me about her life experiences with a failed marriage and no kids, but she was happy to be single. Life is less complicated this way. How about you?

I had the urge to tell her about the breakup, then decided against it.

I thought to tell her stories from my life when my brother from Germany came for a visit to Florida.

It was a lighthearted story that described our sailing adventure. It puzzled him to see how easily I floated the sailboat from the trailer. He needed safety instructions before I took the boat on a tack to make it out to the deep water.

With a distance from the beach, I changed course going north. The breeze was strong and steadfast, and that gave us good speed. After a distance, a turn to go south became a violent maneuver. I called him, duck your head now. The boom is about to come to your side. That was a close call when the main sail tore across to make the jibe. It scared him, and we sailed south and back to the launching ramp.

Another tricky maneuver, taking the wind from behind and capturing the energy by extending the sail to its maximum reach, proved easy. But a rogue wave had another idea and caused us to capsize near the beach.

To prevent the sails from filling with water, swimmers came to aid us with the efforts to right up the boat. We climbed on board to complete this adventure.

Don't you have to pay to use this ramp? No, this is not Germany, where boat owners must be members of the yacht club or own a house on the lake. The city provides this service for the taxes we pay. This way, anybody can launch her anytime with ease.

******

Stu got wind of another meeting at the CEO's office. He called me into his office and shut the door.

He used a loud voice that traveled past his office. "You report to me, and yes, as I was pointing in the other direction, but first of all me. You are in Food & Beverage; you have no right to go over my head."

I kept quiet and listened until the end of his rage. When it subsided, I asked permission to speak. I spoke softly, a whisper tactic to make him listen and calm him down.

I was asked to see them at their invitation.

I did not ask for it on my own, and again, I was with the RVP together. You can verify this over there. I pointed to the RVP office. The Gentlemen had read my report. All they did was congratulate me. They wanted to learn more about me; that is all. I know better! There was nothing earth-shattering, and there were no questions on the function of this department. If that had been asked, I would have referred them to you.

Are you not proud of all the accomplishments your department has achieved recently?

"Yes, but it is primarily yours."

These problems had existed for years, and nothing was done to resolve them. The department owns it, and the credit is spread throughout Food & Beverage. If you want all the credit for yourself, then do the work as I have done.

I am sorry, but I have emotions, and today they are a bit raw.

"Next time you go upstairs, you take me with you. Now, what is getting your nerves so sensitive?"

A private matter, I do not bring my personal life to work!

I asked him what he had on his schedule so I could plan my time.

"I must create a new restaurant concept for the new hotel in town."

Have fun, I smiled. It is not an easy task. What do you know about it?

I have seen it done once, and from this experience comes my knowledge. This project was levels above MacDonald's.

His body showed signs that he must be a regular and that restaurant level.

The hotel restaurants were two steps above fast food. The food was the same; only bar service and seating made the difference.

Back at my desk, I took another look at the seminar brochure. As I read through the pages, I must have shown a grin.

Mandy came to see me. "This is good material, and you pulled it out of your head."

Then I noticed the side notes reminding the presenter when to pause, raise the tone of the voice, and perform many other tricks. A mention of co-presenter plays a role in presenting this material to a group.

I have a session scheduled in Worcester, MA, and asked the Lowell and Cambridge managers to attend.

CHAPTER 4

I see this on your schedule. Whom are you taking to be your partner?

I don't have anybody yet, and the people at the hotel have not volunteered anybody.

"Would you teach me while I travel with you and co-teach? I have never done this kind of presentation, but I am a fast learner."

Great, can you get clearance from the office manager? Food and beverage will spring for the flight. The hotel room is complimentary; otherwise, we will have no extra charges.

"Yes, I will do so."

Then we talked about how I was introduced to this training seminar. I also told her I broke up with my girl; better said, her mother broke us. This is what got me worked up. But I don't want to burden you with my troubles.

"Do you like this city?"

I have found two venues that appeal to me: the Symphony and the Opera.

The icy light beer and sports fanatics do not interest me.

"That is amazing, I love the arts, but I can never go. Going alone is odd, and my sister does not go for that. I have the same dilemma. Do you want to go together to the next concert?"

Do you need a little black dress? "I know that every woman is supposed to have one, except me."

Let us go shopping in Massachusetts when we are there for the training; we get one there. I'll buy it.

"No, I pay for my dress."

Let it be my gift for everything you have done so far.

Mandy got the approval, and we made it to Worchester.

After checking with the General Manager and extending an invitation, we made our way to the meeting room.

Twelve managers were sitting in a half-moon arrangement on round tables.

Good morning, meet Mandy, and my name is Treb.

Let's start by writing down something you've done that makes you proud. It can be professional or personal.

A scramble started for pens. Only two managers carried a pen with them.

Who the gentlemen with the pens?

Thank you, you have done well, and a word of advice for all others. Carry a pen at all times. It serves to take short notes; you can always find something to write on. Okay?

The session is about training. Just call it out to me. Let me hear the training methods you have used yourself.

The usual methods came from the group, but they quickly faded out.

We all use the show and tell method, but have you ever thought that making mistakes is a learning tool? How about reading, mentoring, leading by example, and the trainee seeing the process and then doing a role reversal?

Suddenly I heard more ways to train an employee.

Let us not forget to train ourselves.

After a quick break, I handed the lead to Mandy. She wasted no time getting their attention.

Taking glances at the training manual, she carried on with training to become result oriented. Follow-up is as necessary and delivers every opportunity to extend praise. Whenever mistakes or failures come to light, remember that everybody learns at his own pace. Repeat and praise once more. Positive reinforcement will earn you rewards.

I noticed how the group became deeply involved in the presentation. Mandy used every trick to keep the attention span alive.

Then a lunch break.

Mandy looked relieved. I noticed that you are excited about this work.

"Yes I can involve myself in it and grow to a level when I conduct seminars. It looks complex on paper, but once you are in the subject, it flows on its own energy."

That is correct; the start is the hardest. Breaking the ice is an essential element.

"I noticed the simple trick with the pen and paper. You took control of the group at that moment."

For the afternoon session, Mandy took pages from the book, got them to answer questions, made them get up and walk around the table three times, and drove them crazy. I took turns shooting from the hip; I got a newspaper and a P&L statement.

From the magazine in the gift shop, I took current events and pointed out how all these daily instruments we take for granted are, in fact, learning tools.

Then, there is the obligation to pass on knowledge, engage in debates or discussions and seek common ground. "All this is learning, right in front of your face. Practice and apply it to every situation."

We called it a day once we had exhausted their brains.

Back at the GM's office, we filled him in on the enormous participation.

"I see I missed something instead of this boring budgeting."

Over a drink in the lounge, we discussed other training needs. How about interviewing skills, problem-solving methods, and time management?

"Can you do all of these?"

I have it on paper now; the rest is easy. Mandy wants to learn, and in time she can take over.

Dinner off the menu choices was good, a standard menu, but well prepared.

Mandy joined with a glass of wine.

When alcohol took hold of her, she wanted to get fresh air.

The wine stimulated her mood,

Then came the moment when a woman's heart was beating faster. She hooked her arm into mine while we walked the streets of Worcester. The little black dress in the window, That's it. Can we stop here before we travel back to Pittsburg?

Yes, we will; this one looks terrific.

The conversation touched on the working relations Stu was imposing on me. He sees me more as a threat than support.

She followed up with a comment. "He is a bully and has gotten away with it with these kids. Now he has a man to face with superior experience and is scared of his job. I believe the undercurrent has had enough of his bully style. That is my take. "

"The owners are contemplating a change, and I see you fit the mold."

How much blood does one have to give to this bullfight?

That is the million-dollar question. Corporate politics is not my favorite game. Politics are always a mud fight. I don't have an appetite to enter the dirty battles. I'd much rather preserve my health and sanity. I may never be a VP, but I know I have outperformed the ones I know personally.

Just a paycheck for my soul and self-esteem!

"You are easy to talk to, a refreshing experience for me, and a new breath of fresh air in the office."

"They are all in love with you!"

"Watch out!" Not to worry, I have experience. I prefer to be the hunter and enjoy the chase better than conquest. Becoming the prey is fun if the predator turns into a pussycat at the conquest.

"It is an exciting way to look at a relationship! Not that far in, just the start, after the role changes for good. Men have the pants on at home, you know?"

I agree!

After the walk, Mandy reminded me to finish the wine by the glass story.

Oh yes, I had forgotten about the story from Tampa and its aftereffects.

I want to brush my teeth quickly, and after, can I come over to hear it out?"

Innocent-faced, she went to her room and was back before I could finish my business.

She smiled, showed her white teeth, and sat on the bed.

Where was I? as I sat next to her.

She made sure that the bodies had contact. In German, we called it Tuchfühlung, meaning only enough of a touch to have the clothes be in contact but transfer the contact point to the skin.

The wine-by-the-glass sale had a surprising follow-up outside the company.

"Yes, I love it," sitting there like a child listening to Grandpa's stories."

I was invited to a high-class tasting, and while I thoroughly enjoyed the first Tasting of premium wines, red, white, and rose the second Tasting included a surprise.

It was one of these educational ones when one gets to smell the various components a wine has as its character, not all of them pleasant. The tannin is acidic and does not smell nice. Imagine sulfur which smells like rotten eggs.

The components are attractive when it comes to fruit to which the wines are often referenced, like blackberries, apricots, or chocolate.

I can tell you I have never looked at wine the same since. It was an effort to plant these individual components into our memory. I look for these items and find them now.

"The second one was a champagne tasting with Krug vintage champagne, which is not a well-known Champagne.

This is top-of-the-line for the connoisseur. They explained each vintage year and the blend of wines they had used to achieve the signature taste.

Then the dosage is always kept a secret. They served fine food in between the different Champagnes.

I kept wondering why I was being invited to these tastings.

I did not stand for a distributor or a wine and liquor store. Not even buying for the hotels fell under my responsibility.

The third tasting involved Remy Martin Cognac, from the VS, VSOP, XO, and the top level, Louis the XIII.

Again, the finest food from all over the world was served: goose liver pâté, exotic sushi, sashimi, graved Lachs, stone crabs, blue point oysters, and Maryland lump crab cakes.

It was an education to learn the distilling process, the care after that, and the aging in wood barrels.

At the end of the Tasting, a man pulled me aside. They knew my name, and I am now speaking with the head of the US team leader.

The head of this group of people said that I had changed their point of view in the way they wanted to market the premium wine.

They finally found a way to sell by the glass, which they knew. I started initially by pouring off dead inventory. Thereafter, we took it up to the next level, and that's when I tapped the category they had difficulty selling. It was a level of quality that fell between the grocery store's upper tiers and the well-known premium brands and vintages the connoisseur was buying.

They expressed their gratitude and proposed a promotion for the Beach resort.

The rest of you know already how the Beach Hotel received help from this generosity.

All the while I was telling the story, Mandy had moved closer, but I did not notice.

"I want to make love to you, not just sex but compassionate lovemaking."

She whispered it to me and then kissed me passionately.

The reaction was instant, and we wasted no time expressing our affection for each other.

It reached the height point, took a break and one good thing deserves an encore..

The rest of the night we cuddled and slept fully satisfied.

Returning to the office, I made separate appointments with Stu and the RVP.

Mandi and I presented the results of this seminar. I wanted Mandy to hear the different comments from these two men.

Stu questioned the money spent to take Mandy with me.

She was serving as the co-presenter. The difference in voices and gender keeps the audience alert. "Now I see why these presenters do that. It makes sense because my mind wanders in about two-minute times."

She made it work; none of them went to sleep, not with her. She has taken to this like a natural talent.

After a short time, she was no longer consulting this here book.

I gave Stu the book. This is a starter guideline, and once you get this group on a roll and involved, it calls for rolling with the punches.

I guarantee these kids will not forget this soon, if ever!

"I get it."

Now the RVP; I started by setting the scene and opened up with the textbook. I gave him a copy. "You wrote all this? You have studied these books?"

No, this is from the school of life's experiences. I have a master's in it.

He got the joke and laughed.

"I must use this line sometimes myself."

We used basic training methods such as the four-step army method, mentorship, and resume.

The biggest challenge in a setting is keeping everybody alert and engaged in taking part. We used every trick in the book to keep the attention span alive. That is where Mandy came in, with a different voice and a lower expectation, not as a structure but as a critical assumption from a woman presenter.

She is a fast learner and manages to control the group.

After lunch, we had them going nonstop until we finally ran out of time and had to stop. Sorry, we're out of time. More another time.

"This man can lead them in any direction by picking up on a word and showing it to his path to finish a point in progress."

Thank you, Mandy.

"It was easy. Once you shoot from the hips, it becomes a conversation; a debate will get out the facts and lead to an agreement. Fascinating stuff. I want to do more groups along these lines, expand my skill level, and be more versatile for the company."

"And more valuable," he added.

She is too humble to mention this. Imagine a corporate trainer to tech learning/training methods, team building, creative problem solving, a retreat to set the big-picture goals and conflict management. All are applicable to our hotels and can only improve management effectiveness.

"I fully agree, and I will get this idea to the heads upstairs."

Mandy was on cloud nine.

Here is a man who supports excellent ideas and has you leave his office on a high note. Stu can learn from him.

On the weekend Mandi came to visit me at home. Her parents are divorced, and caretaking was divided between the two sisters. Her father needed care since he lived alone. The closeness to her father was her choice to look after him.

******

Stu was still laboring over the restaurant concept for this new hotel.

I saw him studying all the latest restaurant types—Chili's, Bennigans, Friday's, and a brand-new one called Applebee's—and trying to extract ideas from each.

He called me in and asked me again how I developed this concept in Fort Lauderdale.

My theme was predetermined by the owner. It's not the same situation. I waved him off It could not be applied here.

If I may say something? "Okay, go ahead."

You go about it the wrong way. The stuff you pick is already in the marketplace. To copy anything will be seen as a poor copy of another concept. No one will fall for it. Do not take the public as fools. They all have their favorites and compare this concept against it. If they find the same food on your menu as in Friday's restaurant, the place becomes a failure.

"You have to start up from scratch, something unique, fresh idea, well prepared and catering to the hotel guest.

"But how? I am not a super creative man!" You do not have to be!

Go with a systematic buildup by going to the marketplace. Look at what people buy and see what is in the food bins.

Leaving his office, I could see how this project would fall into my lap.

"Just book yourself crazy busy with tons of priorities, building blocks to put departments on a solid foundation! These kids are all light in the loafers, meaning there has never been a solid experience base to build on. All superficial promotions on a "yes man" basis. It is high time to earn their keeps!"

******

The seminar in Miami was approved and scheduled for next week. Mandy was all excited and came to my house. Who is caring for your dad?

"My sister is covering both babies, reluctant and envious of the opportunity she is pulling doubles giving me the time."

That's absurd. It's your effort, and you have earned it. I am just the facilitator. Are you always that humble? "Only in front of you."

Next week we have a great opportunity again. "I cannot wait, my love."

******

Miami training was a breeze; Mandy took the reins and directed me to jump in to break the monotony. I kept it low-key. I did not want to steal her thunder. From time to time, I would interject a subject in a different direction which she picked up by reading my mind.

Involving managers to participate and presenting material to the other attendees and feeding more material, until the entire group was fully engaged with each other. It turned into a self-teaching seminar. All she needed to contribute was an occasional new subject and the group went on with the debates.

She wrapped up by 2:00 p.m. Exhausted, she took a deep breath and wanted fresh air.

******

A message was telling me that a young lady was waiting for me in the bar.

It was Angie. How are you, honey?

"Been better, and you?"

Doing well. I have success in the job and enjoy the work; just one of the two bosses is a jerk. Why do I have the honor of seeing you? Something urgent?

"It is not that I want to beg you to be back together. You have moved on, and I have too. I am dating again; just this raven mother is killing me.

73

My dad has died, and now she wants me to recognize her lover as my father and still keeps me hostage. I wonder if you can think of a way out. My mind is scrambled, and I can no longer think clearly."

Where is your sister? "She is at Fort Lauderdale or close to it off I-95.

Do they have a guest room?

"Yes, three-bedroom apartment?"

"Ask her to take you as a roommate for one month. Ask her to play the game with the mother that she will keep the leash on you so you would not run away to Pittsburg. She will release you in her custody, and you will find your place, an efficient or small apartment.

Tell your mother firmly that your father is and will forever remain your father even in death. Nothing and nobody will replace him. It will put this guy in his place, and he is on his own with your bossy mother.

"I have to tell you, the night I confronted her, I used your method. It was a charm. See, I learned that from you too. God, I have learned so much from you and the self-confidence it has given me. I will forever be in debt to you."

Drama queen. Just keep a little spot in your heart. That is enough payment for me. I will do the same for you, and on this basis, we stay friends. Deal?

Deal!" Kiss on the mouth, and off she went.

******

Back at the ranch, word had gotten back to the RVP on the seminar's success. He will take it to the owners. The owners are excited about this. Credit to you. Mandy pointed her finger at me; for getting the ball rolling.

Up until then, we only knew her as a terrific secretary.

Mandy discovered herself by reading the lesson script, found the need for a co-presenter, and took it to success.

Stu came to see me and asked me to look over what he had put on paper so far on the concept.

"I would give it to you, but you have started so many projects to stay super busy, and this would only take the second rank, and time is of the essence. The interior architects are pushing for a direction."

After reviewing it, it became clear that he would return to the old strategy of copying other restaurants.

Good restaurants are timeless. Look at the Pump Room in Chicago, Stall Mast Garden in Stockholm, the Hermitage in Arizona, Scalia in Los Angeles, and Tour d' Argent in Paris; they all have stood the test of time. Good Chefs make a name for themselves by branding their names. You don't want to buy a franchise.

I have an idea.

If you create a comfortable area and give the hotel guests a place to hang out, like they have at home, a family room, a den, a basement, or someplace he has a beer when he gets home. You will attract them to this room and serve upscale food and beverages.

Think of all the stuff you have at home. You build it from there. I can see a couple of easy chairs, overstuffed and wonderfully comfortable. This is a comfort zone you don't want to leave and do not have to because service comes to you. Food in small portions, enough for a good snack or two plates to make dinner.

Place board games, a desk with good light and stationery, TV, and play cards. A selection of books on a bookshelf, the latest business publications, magazines, and daily newspapers on a reader stick, and a source to look up the market results.

I guarantee it will be busy with hotel guests.

We will make money from premium alcohol, high-quality wine by the glass, food as I have already described, and what more one needs to wind down a busy day.

"Wow, this is awesome. How in the hell did you produce this?"

"Look, I am a traveler. I sit at the bar if I want to eat dinner when I am alone. This way, I have a TV or the bartender to talk sports or women. The drink comes faster, and so does the food.

Butt in our bars we do not serve food.

Would you go to such a place?" Call it "The Den."

"Yes, in a flash, this is a go."

Get its name protected as a company proprietary trademark.

"You are good. Do you want my job?" "No thanks, too much politics. Just the salary will do!"

******

Our newest hotel opened up in the company's hometown.

For the grand opening ribbon cutting, the chairman of my former company will be coming. All corporate staff is invited. The office will close for the day.

I was standing in the background of the lobby facing the entrance and waiting for the arrival of the chairman of my former company and the franchise name. Mandy stood by my side, all smiles and dressed up.

I had not seen him since I left his company!

When he entered the front door, he looked around the lobby, the decor, and the architecture, and when he spotted me standing in the background, he walked straight toward me, shook my hand, and said:

"Nice to see you again, Treb. We lost a good man in you. Best of fortune to you!"

The corporate VPs and Directors stood there with their mouths open. They could not hear what he said to me, but the mere gesture of making a beeline to shake my hand was symbolic.

Mandy shook his hand Nice to meet you, Sir!.

"Your wife?"

"No, my secretary, the best there is.

"Good to have a great person behind you!" Mandy was shaking in her boots.

"That is the most incredible event in my life so far. He is a great man to remember your name without a name tag. You must have made an impression on him."

Stu was so jealous; he unloaded on me for disrupting the procedures.

It was his will and his alone, so back off your childish play. I said it with a low voice. to make him come close to hearing it.

Stu was now on the warpath, and suddenly, he became the author of the new concept and told everybody how he came on to it.

He went so far as to quote my words to give it credibility. He included the fact that copy rights have protected the concept and name. He needed to be the hero in front of the hierarchy.

But in reality he wanted to discredit me and take the glory.

Do I need the credit? I have work to do and cannot waste my time with his child's play.

Stu is now ordering me to conduct training seminars and creative problem-solving in hotels outside my region.

I have enough to do. Have the respective regionals do it? It is their territory. Why do I have to neglect my region for their benefit?

" It is for the good of the company."

Are they incompetent? If so, why are they in this position? Why don't you train them and send them out into the field? Besides, I have a second boss who will also have something to say.

"Fuck him. He is an asshole. You report to me as the solid line. He is the dotted line and a secondary ranking."

I will confirm this, and then I'll let you know.

"He was steaming; how dare you disobey me?"

I am my own man. I will never kiss up to anyone!

The RVP had been taken by surprise by this statement from Stu. "First, he must clear this with me. You are on my team, clearly defined in the corporate SOP. He likes to forget and use his bully tactic to bluff his disciples."

It works with these two kids, too young and inexperienced, but blind obedience makes it work for him, but not for the company.

"If he comes at you again, give him this paper to read. Do not get into a shouting match. He and I will square off with the owners if need be."

He was still on a rampage, especially since word had gotten out that he was not the creator of this new concept.

Secretaries had let the word out about who had produced the ideas.

I have a feeling this is all about self-preservation. Something must have been said to the owners from the chairman about me.

The pressure is getting to him, and he cannot handle it. Bullies always have thin skin; I have seen it too many times.

Up front, the strong man behind, they need diapers. Mandy laughed out loud to attract attention.

Someone called, "Storytelling time." No, Mandy waved them off, "just a funny remark."

"You let me know when you make this decision." Mandy is reading my mind. The dark face gave it away.

"I hate the loss, but I understand it. You know best what is right for you.

I will come to visit if that is okay."

Anytime, I will be available for you; you are special to me.

Stu carries on with forcing the training on me in all hotels.

"I will shuffle the regions and give you these hotels, and he takes yours." It came like an order, an ultimatum.

Is this your strategy to clean up these hotels?

It will provide the kids the opportunity to mess up my hotels! I have not yet maximized the potential of my hotels.

I will have to ask my other boss about this; I disagree with it unless….

"You must obey me. I am the direct line of authority over you." At that point, I handed the SOP to him.

Can you read in this rage? It tells you the precise reporting line, which differs from your version.

"I never agreed to it."

Does it matter? The CEO and COO sign it. Good enough?" It infuriated him further.

"You son of a Bitch." He is yelling across the office floor.

My mother is a human being and not a dog in heat. I take exception to this and am deeply offended. You better take it back now.

"I am not taking anything back!"

That gives me grounds to file an official complaint on you.

I consider it verbal abuse. I do not think this company was founded on language like this and I turned and walked away.

His loud voice carried into the secretarial area and was heard by all. Shocked, they looked at me as if they wanted to know my action to follow.

I went to my RVP and said what had just happened.

My demand to have it taken it back was not met, and my promise to file an official complaint will be coming to you. I trust you will take it upstairs.

Stu had beaten him to the punch and went upstairs at once to report insubordination. I was accused of using foul language toward him, and he would not tolerate it.

Stu wanted to have me reprimanded with a stern warning.

The RVP had just arrived as Stu left the owners.

It was his word against hearsay. "We do not know what to make of it. We know he is a terrific guy, but this is going too far."

"He was insubordinate, and if there is any truth to this, we must act."

The RVP was too late to stem the tide against me. When he returned, he was honest and told me to be careful of him; he was out for blood.

Okay, been there. I know how to handle this.

I told Mandy, This is the moment of glory. She knew at once that the letter of resignation had been handwritten for her typing.

I took it to the RVP and said in the role of the solid line reporting, "I am submitting my resignation. It has reached the point where my health is affected, my dignity destroyed, and my family's name tarnished. To call my mother a bitch has gone too far.

I do not need these types of influences. I have a life to live and will do so on my terms. I give thirty days' notice. I will be returning back to Florida He was in shock and yet not surprised.

It takes an effort to get me to quit. Tell me if you have anything you want me to finish between now and my last day.

This copy was put in Stu's mailbox, not hand-delivered or sent by the secretary. He saw it the following day with the other mail.

He stopped and turned around when he came out of his office toward me. He did not know how to approach it.

Finally, he calmed down and, in a low voice, said, "Sorry to read this. We shall miss you!"

No, you will not. You have your will. Now get yourself another "yes" boy to take my place. Do you want me out today? "I would not mind.".

I informed the RVP that I was asked to vacate the F&B office space. Here is my contact information in Florida.

"Is there no way we can arrange for you to stay on?"

Not as long as I have to face the devil. I will see him in hell anyway. Joke. He laughed.

"Let me think on this, and now I have to go upstairs and tell them the bad news."

I packed my stuff, and Mandy helped me carry it to the car. In the parking lot, we said goodbye.

In German, we never say goodbye. We say, "Auf Wiedersehen" (until we meet again), never a definitive closure, always a way to leave the door open for the future.

"I like this, and this is what it has to be for us, my love."

A hot kiss and tears wiped off both faces, and I went to the house and called the realtor..

Never look back. A new door will open now. Just find it!

I had accomplishments in this job. It is the daily paycheck for my soul; nobody would ever take it away from me.

Such a belief is therapy and keeps me going. Uncertainty is an element I must now confront.

Uprooted once more, I started my journey to home base. The townhouse will be waiting for me and again give me shelter and solitude.

CHAPTER 5

I drove my Mercedes Diesel down the highway to the Interstate until I hooked up to the familiar I-95. A feeling of going home had taken over. The warmth of Florida was alluring and seductive, something that always lifted the spirit. The sun had the power to give life and energy. Ocean air and saltwater cleanse the mind. I will re-set my aims and find a way forward.

Driving fourteen hours straight in a Diesel Benz is not troublesome. The seats are comfortable, only the radio fades out, and a new channel must be found. I was at peace with no regrets.

I did not fit into this arrangement with my superiors' constant power struggle. The F&B guy is a bad apple in that group of fine people. It was visible. Why they picked him to start was a mystery to me. He had Limited Food and beverage knowledge, none in the most sensitive area, the kitchen. Only the bar was his comfort zone.

He may have been on his last threat. Is that why he was afraid of me? I did not seek his position. I wanted to find a way to become a General Manager.

******

The house in Davie, Florida, needs to be cleaned and aired. The friend who rented it during my time up North had moved in with his girlfriend, so the Timing was perfect for my return.

A shopping trip to stock up on food, beverages, and water. I had taken the excellent water in Pennsylvania for granted. Florida water is not the same quality.

Stay low-key, call Germany, speak to the parents and brothers and call Martin, they need to be updated.

I wanted to hear from Angela. I was concerned about her situation with her evil mother.

Bruno, the man with the pasta restaurant in Miami tracked me down two days later. He was still seeking me to help him with the reopening of the restaurant at the Four Senators in Miami.

He begged Mandy to get my home phone number. I decided to let it go to the voice recorder. He will call again. Right now, I want to savor my time in my home and decompress. A walk to the pool, then a few sunrays tanking vitamin D, and the sounds of birds and nature all contributed to the feel of home again.

Mandy had told him that I was on my way to Florida. He is excellent at his profession and fun. We will miss him.

It was not long before I received another call. Why the bother? Can't people leave me alone? I haven't even given any thought to my future. Give me time. I want a different direction, a new field of work and to leave kitchen, food, and beverage behind.

The move to and back from Pittsburg turned expensive. Despite the selling price matching the purchase price of the house, the cost of selling with the realtor's commission took money out of my wallet.

I want to collect my thoughts and start with a fresh slate.

It would be nice to have Angie here for comfort, but she has dumped me. Her mother has pitched me, and it still hurts me more than the attack by Stu..

The next day, I went to the mall to get household supplies and then ate Mexican food at a nearby restaurant. It was always a favorite place from the past, and it all spelled home once again to me. It made me realize how alien I felt in Pittsburgh. A fish out of water

A dip in the pool and just a drive around the area made me feel whole again.

Angela called the Pittsburg office number and found out from Mandy what had just happened. She knew my Florida number; I kept it alive for the tenant.

"Are you going to be OK?" Her voice, with the accustomed caring reflection, told me that she was still a friend with strong feelings.

Just like a cat, I land on my paws; you know that. "Can I come over? I have to tell you in person."

Right after work, she showed up by 6 pm, excited to tell me where she was working. It's the new hotel by the Airport in Fort Lauderdale.

The job is excellent, and the commute is less than 10 minutes.

My former job at this high-tech company was too impersonal. I found them to be weird Geeks from a different planet.

"She clung to me; you made me a woman; you taught me the way of life, and I am eternally grateful for that. Do you have a relationship going on right now?"

No, but I have numbers to call and announce my return.

"I bet you have; good luck, my friend, be well, and good luck with whatever comes your way now."

That was nice; she still needed to see me and touch my body. I can feel the eternal bond from the little signs of affection. It stayed at that distance. Her mother's influence carried her weight, keeping all connections at arm's length.

I called Nina, the secretary from the Beach Hotel; yes, the number was still ringing, but the voice recorder took my message.

I am in my house here in Davie, give me a call if you like. My number is!

In an hour, she was standing at the door, "Surprise!" A hot kiss and a hug like she had just seen me yesterday.

Have you eaten yet? I am just cooking.

"I like your cooking; go ahead; I have not had lunch and am hungry."

I gave her cheese, hard salami, and a glass of wine to snack on; it was like old times, and she said jubilantly, "I love it."

"I am also starved in other ways; Big Mo was my last engagement."

Your poor baby, this has to change at once.

"I did not call back just took the chance, and here I am. Please have a look; she is shaved and ready for Big Mo."

"Are you staying put now or at least for a while?".

I can see the urgency in you let's not wait any longer.

Intense lovemaking was her passion. She needed it desperately.

Dinner followed, and then you could take everything you wanted from me. This night belongs to you and will serve as the best medicine for both of you.

She went home for a change of clothes and went to work with her usual big smile. The boss will be happy to see her smiling again.

The GM had moved from the Causeway hotel to the beach. I liked him; he was always good at having fun conversations.

L' Elixir d' amour has now come back into my life. Nina will be a fine companion, reliable, and grateful for all she receives.

She had a difficult childhood and was adopted into a family with kids already her senior. Her adoptive mother loved and nurtured her to adulthood.

She got pregnant at the age of seventeen and then moved away. She keeps that a secret.

A dark history: she will forever carry this secret with her. She loved her son and cared for him the best way she could afford.

He grew into his teen years, an extra burden for a single mother. The connection with her mom in Minnesota remained constant, but her siblings never returned calls. Bad blood and rejection from her Steph siblings towards Nina had been a continued issue.

I learned this story after we had tender moments.

She will treasure a man in her life to help raise a teenager.

Two weeks later, she moved in with me.

Nina was good for me, and I was the right companion for her. She became my constant companion, going out for pizza and beer, fine dining, movies, the opera, symphony, outdoor concerts, or the beach, and I regret having sold my boat.

"Don't you have any relatives here?" I have a son in Colorado, brothers, parents in Germany, and a daughter in Barbados. She married into a good family.

I miss this perky girl; she is so fun to be around. One day I will visit her and see her children. Hopefully, it will be a girl, and I will have a granddaughter.

CHAPTER 6

I started looking for a job with the cruise lines and received an invitation for an interview within days.

"The job entails the food & beverage operation for one ship sailing out of Miami with eight hundred passengers; then we have two Vessels on the West coast in San Pedro. It's the harbor for Los Angeles.

"Two men had run them independently until now.

Policies and operating procedures are in desperate need of alignment.

Besides that, we serve meals and drinks, which you know well from your experience. Your resume is pretty impressive.

The salary is paid bi-weekly.

If this is agreeable to you, we will have an offer letter to you by this weekend."

******

"The protocol to go on board a ship will be shown to me came as a statement. You will not have a problem with the versatility of experience."

I was introduced to Daniel who runs the hotel side as my colleague in the hotel department..

The letter arrived as promised. I signed it and hand-delivered it to the Miami's cruise line office.

Today is a port visit to the ship and an excellent way to start your job.

Your predecessor will hand over the office. It will give you a head start.

*****

"Turquoise Seas:" I like this name; it looks proper to name a ship after the waters it navigates.

Large spaces supplied a vast dining room with four hundred seats, bars on the top deck, and between the Show lounge and the Casino. Another lounge is a dance lounge. There are game rooms for children, a pool, and cozy areas for privacy.

"Protocol meant to see the captain first, inform him of your mission and address him as the Master, then brief him when you leave the ship and if you found deficiencies, he wants to hear what will follow as corrective actions.

Any equipment changes must go through the home office and the chief engineer on board.

There's not much else; passenger ratings drive the ship's performance, and all charges from the bar are posted to the master folio of the cabin account."

"Food cost is dollars per Diem. You will see much of the food getting wasted."

"Breakfast is served in two sittings in the dining room.

Lunch is open sitting with the pool deck featuring a buffet lunch, and dinner service begins at six pm and 8 pm, again two sittings.

On embarkation day, the dining room manager assigns passengers a table, and no changes are allowed unless they would kill each other. Every table is filled.

The entertainers and so-called staff, like casinos and gift shops, are fed in the staff area in the back of the dining room."

All of this seemed well organized.

"When you sail with the ship as an officer from headquarter staff, you will receives a voucher from the office with an assigned stateroom. You take your meals at a passenger table.

That about covers all details."

"At the office, we have the last voyage statistics, cost, food list for next week's sailing, and passenger count."

"The HR department handles the crew rotation.

Look in on them, say hello, and do the same with the purchasing.

I will take you to the president, the marine folks, and that will do."

"Here is your office; get familiar with the forms; if you have any questions, see me."

The first day on any job is always confusing. I met people in uniform and in the office. The introduction was comprehensive.

In a pile of papers I found reports on revenues and cost as it is called "per Diem."

Personal profiles of the Chief Steward equal to the F&B manager, the Bar manager, the Chef, and the Dining room manager pointed to the vital role they play in the service of the ship. All of them showed substantial ship operation experience.

I had a starting point. It gives me a picture to go forward.

Once familiar with the office procedures, I will schedule a trip on the four-day cruise itinerary. Business takes place on board.

The office staff has the supporting mission to the ship.

The office was low-key, and no distinct hierarchy was felt.

Everybody is on a first-name basis. The dress code is encouraged to be comfortable but business-like and adapted to the climate.

On board, the officers' dress code is defined by season: blue in winter and white in summer. Officers wear their marine uniform with stripes on the sleeves or attached to the shoulder when a shirt is worn only.

Office staff dressed casually elegant in the evening, with long pants and a dress shirt during the day and a dark suit at the captain's gala night.

I was addressed by the crew respectfully as Mr. or Sir. The crew members are calling me Chief.

It felt like India; Deja vu.

From the resumes, I learned that the Chief Steward came from Canada and was born in France. The Chef is from India, and the Bar Manager's home is Singapore.

The kitchen revealed that nobody had cared about this working space. Inferior cookware, worn cutting boards, and low-quality knives could not cut a tomato.

What is going on here? I asked the Indian Chef.

"Sahib, we are the forgotten children. I notice how you look at this ware; you must be from the trade. The purchasing man has followed your predecessor's command to spend little or no money in this area. The office people see this as an area that consumes too much equipment."

I am a former Chef. I feel the pain you have. Changes will be coming very soon.

I cannot expect you, good people, to work under these conditions. Be patient; I am new and must find my way around the procedures.

It does not look right. The kitchen is at the heart of an operation. You produce three meals for eight hundred passengers daily. I cannot accept it.

Please make a "must-need list" for me. "Yes, Sahib, at once."

I met the ship's buyer. He is a young man who has been in this job for 12 months. He was following orders.

Hallo Karri, We have not had time to make an acquaintance, but here I am, and I wish to establish a close working relationship with you.

He had finished with the loading of food and supplies into the storage areas of the ship. Painstakingly feeding case by case by means of a conveyor belt inside the open hatch of the vessel.

Asked mil to meet in the kitchen while I spoke with the Chef.

I looked at the equipment and picked up a knife. What is going on here?

"I followed orders to buy the cheapest ware; it will only get destroyed by these; then he stopped."

Karri blushed, looked at the floor, and said that the former manager had tied his hands.

Let me open your eyes. If I had to work in this kitchen, I would throw everything overboard. It is inferior material and a waste of money to buy it. I am a Chef by trade; I know how a cook feels when he is degraded by materials like these.

"You are the boss now; I will follow your recommendations. The list is in the office. We can review it together after the trip."

Thank you, we start with the knives.

This kitchen must be challenging to clean. Do you have a power washer or a machine that scrubs the floor?

He showed me the water hose. Our power washer uses way too much water, and the chief engineers keep reminding us to use it sparingly.

Karri, we have work to do. Do you have the budget numbers?

We must find the money for this kitchen. We cannot allow this condition to carry on. The health department will hang us.

"It is named USPH, US Public Health, a section of the CDC."

Thank you, Karri; it tells me everything to watch out for.

The Assistant Chief Steward joined us in the kitchen. He had overheard the word USPH and quickly added that this ship was overdue for an inspection. A failure grade will trigger a re-inspection, and the cost to the company in the form of a fine will be in the thousands.

Karri here is money to protect; I see this as a high priority.

"Music to my ears, Sahib. I folded my hands and made a little bow towards the Chef. Namaste, I hope to have this right; it's been years since!

Have you been to India?"

Yes, I worked in New Delhi years ago.

"We must talk about this once; I want to hear more, Hatcha."

I notice your accent is from the Islands, but not Barbados. Is that right?

Yes Sir. How can you tell the difference?

I told him I had a daughter in Barbados.

How is it that you have family there?

I will tell you the story when we are at sea.

He smiled with a wicked grin. Island relations were on his mind.

I know what you are thinking, Benny, but I assure you it is different and will surprise you.

At dinner, I sat at a table of eight. Since I was solo, there was an open seat.

One couple and a family with two teenagers.

The daughter looked mature and may be out of high school or junior in college. The brother must be three years younger. Mid-West was my guess.

When people speak of Grinders and Pop, it is a dead giveaway.

Girls are always more mature than boys.

The other couple is from New Jersey; I can always tell when someone has a gum-chewing habit and snaps it.

The conversation was about the ship at first, the cabin, and the movement. I was asked where I was coming from; the question went at once to what country. "And where is your wife or girlfriend?"

She had to work, and we live here in Florida.

The daughter had to know everything.

At that moment, the dining room manager welcomed me to dinner and inquired if everybody was happy with the table. The special attention prompted more specific questions from the girl.

"How come he knows your name?" You are very curious, any guess?

"Is he a friend?"

No, I work for the line; this is my first voyage. I have just joined the company. Please do not ask me specifics about this cruise; I am green and need to learn it as you do.

"Do you have to work during the day, no time for sightseeing or shopping?"

I must see what is going on here. I have to support this ship from the office. Only when I sail with the vessel can I see the action? I must make every minute count.

"Now I understand it. I want to be in management someday, but I have no idea what a manager does or goes about finding out what the employees are hiding."

I need a half-hour to go over the dinner with the Chef and Manager; after that, it is my time. I can explain basic management skills to you.

More questions about the ship's operation and why it is called sailing when we don't have sails. I hear different names which I do not know.

Ships language is a professional communication tool to find items and locations in precise terms. It makes communication more efficient. In an emergency, this is most important since every second counts.

"You know so much; I want to talk to you more; is that OK, Dad? Yes, but don't stay up too late."

We agreed to meet on the promenade deck starboard side.

I was complimentary to the Chef and the cooks when I took a peek into the Galley after the meal service.

The meal is not sophisticated, but the passengers would not know what to do with a high-class meal.

Food came out hot and well-seasoned. Do you come from India?

"Yes, Sir; hatcha!"

Tell me from which state, please, Bengal.

I worked as a Sous Chef at the Intercontinental.

My visits to your country took me to Kashmir and also to Agra to see this magnificent Taj Mahal.

"I worked there too and learned to cook from the expatriates.

It was, of course, during later years."

I have a curious question: We promoted a cook to a soup cook position. Is he still there? His name is Anil!

"Yes, he survived. The other cooks made trouble and sometimes sabotaged his work. He fought them and still keeps his new status. He often spoke about a German Sous Chef who gave him Face."

He learned on his own by watching me.

"Was it you? So glad to meet you; I always had that secret desire from Karma to put me together with you. I must write him that we have connected."

Tell him hello; I often think of him and tell people the story.

"If you wish for something special, I will gladly cook for you."

That is kind, another voyage; this time, I must see everything as a passenger does.

Towards the end of the voyage, you must tell me how the menu fits the cooking space.

Yes, Sir, we have our challenge here. I thought so.

"Breakfast is critical, and I must be present. A la carte orders and these crazy Americans with the egg orders, up, over, over easy, poached, basted.

I still do not know how to do basted."

You are a testimony of our cook's training in New Delhi. The Government's efforts to educate and create a productive hotel workforce have come to fruition. You are living proof as the Chef on a cruise ship. It speaks to the success of the program.

European training at the Intercontinental helped to land this job. I am grateful for the opportunity.

******

"Amanda is my name. I am so excited to get this chance to speak with you. I can see your confidence projecting from you, and you must have immense experience."

Here is what we are going to do. I will give you an overview of management.

Are you still in school and holding a part-time job?

"Yes, I will graduate in a month. I turned eighteen last month and want to go to management school."

Good, think about what your manager is doing wrong or what you think he could be doing better. The stuff that rubs you the wrong way but he or she won't tell me. Make notes to keep it fresh in your mind.

I am going to list a manager's attributes and skill requirements. Check mark once you can match it.

Leadership, be a trainer, a mentor, a counselor, a teacher, a problem solver, a visionary, a team builder, a controller, an inspector, and a motivator.

Yes, we hear that in school. It is a tall order for managers, especially when it is their first job.

The primary responsibility of a manager is to handle people!

Of course, generating profit is also high on the list.

Let's forget about school for now.

Through the people, commerce is created, and when business is handled correctly, it will bring sales and profit.

All that sounds simple if the manager does his job and hires the right person.

Train the employee, give guidance, follow up, and keep efficient work in progress, it must come together as a harmonious workplace.

Hiring the right person does not mean the most skilled.

The employee may bring bad habits and a superior attitude towards others. It will create tension and disrupt the workflow.

An employee with a great attitude and the hunger to learn will be by far the better employee.

It will be easy to train this employee and have a loyal and productive person who will work and perform with minimal supervision.

Please do not take it for granted. Check on it, it presents an opportunity to give a pad on the back or should they make a mistake, you can correct it on the spot and avoid negative consequences.

You can measure how training plays an important role. Most managers avoid it because they do not know how to train or ignore it for convenience.

I have written a training manual on various training methods. A seminar was conducted by Mandy and me in Massachusetts.

"Was Mandy your secretary?"

Yes, she was and took it to heart to learn and to stage a seminar.

"I also want to learn this; I think it will be fun."

Fun is earned when the seminar is managed with skills. You find yourself in situations where conflict arises. Then you reach deep inside your experience to solve the conflict. It sounds and looks easy when everything goes as planned.

"Don't you have to go to bed. I can stay longer, My brother shares the room, and we keep our secrets close to the chest."

I see that you are partners in crime, or better said, in malice.

Amanda smiled and cozied up to me. I was waiting for it, and it came as expected.

"Will you make love to me? You have privacy, and I want to learn that skill, also. I am a beginner, and until now, I have not had the full service of a man. I read it and watch videos; it tells me there must be much more to sex. A mature man's skill level must be much higher to help satisfaction and bonding for friendship."

You are correct in your description, but you have just come of age. Do you have protection, an IUD, or the pills? You want to be protected and not get pregnant if you are active.

"I have been on the pill for a few weeks"

OK, but please be discrete. I am not sure if I should do this. It may be against company policy. I will give you the room number and leave the door ajar. It must look as if you are returning to your room.

Conquering a foreign man with anticipation of the unexpected was the desire and hunger for a new experience. The accent may play a role in it. Are girls aggressive, or is it motivated by being away from home? The sense of adventure and new-found freedom?

She did spend the night and returned to her room to get a change of cloth.

The first port day is in Nassau the Bahamas.

******

I walked around a town with too many liquor stores and crafts markets on every street corner. Men approached tourists to buy pot and hustled them to no end. I found this offensive.

These passengers come here for an enjoyable day. Why would the government tolerate this behavior?

Coconut pie lured me to a restaurant. It was midday, and I was getting hungry. I ordered Conch fritters, seafood chowder, and, to crown this meal, a coconut pie. It did not disappoint me. I asked the server girl if I could get the recipe for the coconut pie; it was the best I had ever tasted.

"It is my mom's recipe, but she is at home. Come back tomorrow, and she will decide if she wants to share the recipe."

On my return to the ship, I passed street vendors selling black coral. Is this coral not protected?

Not in our waters, we have to harvest; it may come to the point when the government puts restrictions on quantities. Buy it now; it will become more expensive when we get controlled.

I was confident that this could not be the truth. Authorities preferred the sale of corals over drug pushers. With every sale it puts food on the table at home.

******

I saw the cooks preparing the food for the first sitting in the kitchen.

Nervous at first when they saw me in the kitchen observing. Then the Chef explained my mission.

"He is a Chef and wants to check on the equipment needs. New replacements may be coming our way."

I received smiles from the Asian crew. Salamat Chief.

Dinner conversation is now about the adventure on a foreign and exotic Caribbean Island. "Did you see this item? It was so cheap, and did you get your T-shirt?".

The dinner would have put me to sleep if it were not for Amanda to carry on an intelligent conversation. Never mind the continuous questions, she at least showed a sincere interest in the functions of a cruise ship.

She carried a smile on her face, which her mother had noticed.

A frequent look at her face made me aware that Mom had suspicions about her little girl. Amanda kept her cool, engaged other people in small talk, and then returned to continue our dialog. She had chosen the chair next to me by switching with her brother.

After dinner, she asked me for more classes. Am I giving you a semester of schooling you aren't receiving from your teacher?

"You are a much more attractive teacher, and it also includes benefits." It was a hint for more midnight classes.

We talked about the need to spend time with employees and be visible and accessible. This spreads confidence and provides opportunities to administer praise or corrective actions.

Either way, the manager enhances the harmony in his department. It may look as if you are not working,

The CEO of a particular hotel company does this every time he visits a hotel.

"Tell me about problem-solving."

It starts with the conclusion that every problem has a solution.

It can be done by a person alone or by applying the knowledge of a group. You start at the problem and work your way back to find out who is involved and how it began. Once you arrive at the source of the problem, you have the key to solving it in front of you.

There are training booklets available for purchase. It is an easy subject when you apply a systematic approach.

Grand Bahamas is the largest of the Bahama Islands.

The day sailing got us to the pier by 6 pm.

I want to watch the action in the kitchen again.

I stood in the corner and told the Chef that the flow did not move the product forward to the pickup point.

I compared it to the kitchen layout in Zurich as the best kitchen. Life is easy when a professional configuration eases a natural flow. I will fight an uphill battle since the Marine Department was holding the purse strings.

In between sittings, I had a look at the bartenders. He was a bit nervous when the big gun was there.

I ordered a Campari; make it a Negroni, please. He knew the drink at once. Up and chilled, please. Thank you. This drink is in perfect proportion. I do get this seldom done so well. He smiled and eased up on the tension.

Where did you learn bartending?

"The Manila Hotel Chief: I live in the mountains outside the city with my family."

Did you get to call Mama and Papa yesterday? "How do you know what we call our parents?" Smile!

"I am the oldest, and I must help with paying for food and house expenses."

Good that you do, Danilo; families must stick together.

The bar manager told me that I had just made a friend for life.

I know it from reading up on Asian customs. I also worked with other Asians in India. I have never been to Singapore or Manila.

It is a coincidence that the Chef on this ship is from India. He learned the trade at the same hotel, the Intercontinental in New Delhi. We still have a friend in common at the hotel.

During dinner, I told Amanda about the places I had worked and lived. I have done things and worn different hats.

The hats I have worn come with a story but telling stories will take a week or longer. I will mention it when the opportunity is presented.

I had taken a confession four months ago, played investigator, judge, and jury when I caught people stealing. It taught my boss a lesson while I investigated it.

Educator, a mentor, a lecturer, and a college professor for just one day all gets added to the list.

I walked on water twice and also had a out of body experience as a child. All of these stories make for a long list to fill long winter nights with the Grand Children.

"Can I listen to his stories and management class again, please, Daddy?

Oh, but he needs sleep like anybody else."

I do breathing exercises. It helps to fall asleep in minutes. It's OK with me; I get enough sleep, even when it turns into a late night.

I had the whole table's attention. People are asking me to prove it. I can do that but will not make it to the room before I am asleep. Here are the instructions.

Take a deep breath through the nose on a count of five, go slowly, and fill these lungs.

Hold it for five counts; it will take a little practice. Then breathe out thru the mouth again slowly and count to five.

Do this; yes, five times, and you are done; close your eyes and have sweet dreams.

I will try this tonight the father announced. These people found this method exciting and will test it tonight.

I got myself into something; what will I do if it does not work, Amanda?

Dinner was steak, and I knew it would be a little overcooked. The meat had to be cooked in two batches, as the equipment did not supply enough cooking space.

The first batch must now be re-heated, which causes overcooking. Secondly, the meat is cut from a large loin and ends up thin. I will find a solution to this problem.

Dessert offerings included a flan. The presentation will need color and not just whipped cream.

Amanda wanted to see the show first and then meet at the same place again. That's OK; I will watch the show from the back by the bar.

A company team has produced the show, with dancers and singers with exerts from West Side Story. great voices were delivered by the soundtrack and the surround sound speaker system. It had a professional look and supplied great entertainment. It surprised me.

After the show, I met Lynda, the stage manager and shoreside assistant Director. She projected a perky personality, which fits the mold for this line of profession.

As expected, Amanda was already waiting for me and full of anticipation.

"Tell me first how you walked on water. I am fascinated by it!"

Mother Nature supplied the opportunity by an atmospheric condition that had not happened in more than one hundred years. I was in school doing my theoretical learning as a cook apprentice. In a seasonal resort location, schooling is scheduled during the off-season; in my case, it was Winter.

The temperature dropped to twenty degrees Fahrenheit and stayed there for weeks. This was a rare occurrence that slowed the current from the river that traveled through the lake. This allowed the water to freeze into a very thick ice crust. Cars drove on it, private planes landed and took off, and everyone walked across the lake.

It turned into a tourist attraction and lasted three months.

The school is located across the lake, which prompted me to walk on the water.

"Bravo, yes, you did."

It has not happened since, and now I have a unique experience telling a story to the grandchildren and also to a college student.

After graduation, I went straight to Zurich, Switzerland. I was fortunate to land a great job and avoided serving in the German military.

With this job, I began my learning on the fast track. The Chef was a genius.

He taught me so much; I have to thank him. He was a great man who followed my career until his passing.

******

Breakfast was in full swing as I watched them cook the egg orders.

A basted egg order caused the cook to throw his hand up in the air. He started to cuss about the egg orders in the US. "If I only knew what this is."

"Eggs should be eaten fried, sunny side up as they call it here!"

Let me show you if you do not mind; I am a Chef too; I can show you.

You start like you would a sunny-side-up order and then place the lid on it. When the butter is nicely heated, add a little water so the steam from the pan will turn the tops of the eggs white. That's all there is to basted eggs.

I noticed that the skillets are all beaten up. These must be replaced at once.

Good day and keep them eggs basting! I will order it for myself.

I needed to see the pool lunch buffet and the people patronizing it.

I'm making a mental note to ask questions! Why is there a lunch menu and a buffet with two different food offerings? The buffet served all passengers, and the dining room was empty except for two tables. Why are we doing this? It seems inefficient and wastes food.

In port is considered a day out for a few selected crewmembers, and it is done on a rotation. In reality, it provides the workers with time to re-supply for their personal needs. Most every crewmember takes a siesta in the afternoon. An early start, late nights, and never an entire day off make for an exhausting work schedule.

The Captain's Gala night is promoted as the night to dress up. I put on my tuxedo to look the part and walked the receiving line, shaking the Captain's hand.

Greeted by the captain, "Are things going your way?" Yes, thank you; very much so!

Then a glass of cheap champagne that is not worth drinking.

Krug champagne had spoiled my palate, which made me switch to another Negroni cocktail.

A short welcome address by the captain following the introduction of all officers, and the party was over. There was no party, no get-together to meet other passengers. It gave me something to think about; what is the hype about?

Lobster took center stage at dinner. I knew it was crayfish, lobster from warm water, the one without the claws. I did not see the hype for this choice either and asked for an alternative. Pork roast with a vigorous spice rub from a Jamaican recipe suited me simply fine.

The Chief Steward later asks me about my dinner. "Did you have the lobster?"

You are a Frenchman, and you know great food. The Italians introduced it to French cooks, who then taught it to them.

"Yes, Catherine de Medici, mercy, Catherine!"

I can be polite and take the passengers' comments, and everything is OK, but I am not this kind of guy.

It is a high-cost dinner, and nobody gets a great meal due to the texture of the Langouste.

The only time I enjoyed a Langouste was on a tiny island called San Blas. When he received the order, the cook harvested the live lobster. He cut it into bite-sized pieces, sauteed it with tender vegetables and spices, and served it piping hot on a primitive serving dish, with a banana leaf as the tablecloth.

In this method, I see a possibility to bring out the flavor of the crustation.

The way we do it right now causes the crustacean to dehydrate and end up chewy and bland.

For dessert came a Baked Alaska paraded with fire from burning alcohol. It is ice-only plain cream and covered with raw meringue. If it were not for the fire, it would not be noticeable. Sorry, but I must be honest.

In good time I see this menu to be changed for a better selection.

After dinner, most passengers went to see the show.

I needed to think. It is labeled a Gala, and there is nothing that delivers a Gala night.

It should be a party with white uniforms mingling. A ball with people dancing, great drinks, and nonstop music.

Amused and entertained passengers settled in the casino to spend their hard earned money.

I watched the action with Amanda standing by my side. They throw money and dice on the crab's table and then call it fun. Can you understand how they throw hard-earned money away?

******

Amanda would not leave my side; she had become a constant companion.

We went to my room to follow up on the last time.

I instructed her how to arouse a man and take him to heights he had never experienced. It works both ways, as you have already experienced. It intensifies the final reward. It must be done with patients and allow a waiting period, especially when the imminent urgency goes for the climax.

I have to shower and take a look at the midnight buffet! Come with me. First cool down in the shower. You look red and hot. Don't raise suspicion with your Mom. We are letting her believe that it is lectures and stories.

Amanda came to the buffet alone. Her parents arrived and asked me to explain the display pieces. Platers of seafood, various salads, and roasts of meat are decorated and coated with aspic. Watermelon carving, Ice carving, and other sculptures are displayed for the cameras. The cooks are displaying the culinary arts for buffets. It was meant to be consumed, but who can still eat after a big dinner?

"You said you were a Chef?" Yes, once a Chef, always a Chef!

I had done work like this in my time when I worked as a cook and Chef.

I have learned from the best in the culinary field.

"He told me that last night and has more to teach me. I want to learn; I may never get this opportunity again. Is that OK with you, Mom?"

"Just remember he has a life, too and needs his sleep. Yes, Mom, I will be considered. I am your child; I just want to learn."

You know how to handle her to your advantage. Girls learn these skills early on in life, and competition is fierce in school and at home.

Amanda wants to get my professional opinion on the Gala buffet.

I see this as the first feature that spells "Gala." Culinary skills are showcased from artistic talents and pride is reflected. 'For practical purposes, it is one feature. It could be more if it were staged as a party. Music, dancing, and beverages make people happy. Dancing and singing do that.

This buffet does not receive the full effect. It is my humble opinion.

"You said at the beginning of the cruise that you are new in this business. Yet, I hear you bring suggestions to light that are great ideas. I hope that you are given free hands to implement them."

I come from the outside and do not have pre-conceived thinking. Do you understand the proverb, "too close to the forest to see the trees?" I see it with fresh eyes.

"I get it. Yes, it's like walking past a soiled area; if it never receives a cleaning, one does not see it any longer."

Correct, you are brilliant. You will make a great manager someday.

I will to be busy on the island and want to see the facility, equipment, sanitation, and service flow at the buffet. The crew must have this down to a routine since they do it weekly.

Passengers had ample choices spending the day in the sun. Paddle boats, table tennis, volleyball, soccer, and women had to work on the tan.

A dip into the salt water where children frolicked on the water's edge made for a fun day.

Lunch was served on makeshift buffet settings, with disposable plates and plastic cutlery. Charcoal-grilled chicken, various salads, rolls, and fresh fruits ready to eat completed the menu. Drinks were offered in fresh coconuts, and the coconut juice became the base for the rum punch.

I complimented the cooks for the efficient organization and the delicious chicken. It had a mixture of dry-rubbed spices, which I expected from the Indian Chef. I tried to list the items from the tasting but could not find all of them.

The Chef would not tell me first and made me guess.

OK, I will tell you the missing spices: Graham Masala and Cardamom. I listed them: cumin, garlic, onion, turmeric, allspice, cloves, coriander, pepper and salt, ginger, ground bay leaves, herbal choices, chilies, and lemon juice, and then I got stuck. I knew it had to be more.

To blend spices, one must be a Master of it, and he proved his Indian cooking skills with this blend.

As soon as I was back on board the ship, Amanda's parents cornered me and asked me to tell them stories.

Since I had been talking to the crew about the Indian connection, I chose this story.

Did you see the Chef with the tallest hat; "Yes, why is this man so dark?"

Amanda made a face; this man comes from India. He is from New Delhi.

I explained that I was given the Sous chef job at the Intercontinental Hotel. I was a newlywed with a child in the making when we came to New Delhi to this modern high-rise hotel.

Five hundred plus rooms and my job was the second in command in this kitchen with 150 cooks.

The hotel had a coffee shop like we know here as a family restaurant, a fine dining Continental cuisine like a grand salon with three hundred seats. This room was elegant and decorated with a curtain made from beets in the form that displayed a peacock in its most delicate plumage.

Servers wore formal attire, the manager wore a tuxedo, and it catered to foreign dignitaries and local prominence.

Additionally an Indian restaurant with flair and flavors of fine local cuisine. An Indian Chef took charge of this operation.

On the rooftop was a Chinese restaurant with a Chinese Chef and cooks.

The Executive Chef, the Sauce Chef, a Cold Food Prep Chef, the Pastry Chef, and I were called expatriates.

We were allowed to work on a special visa for two years.

In addition to managing the food operation, we had to train local cooks to become skilled enough to eventually take over our position.

The cooks took pride in preparing our lunch in their style. The food was simple: rice, a little meat or fish, onions, garlic, and hot chili peppers cooked up in liquids topped with a bowl of plain white rice.

The first bite was torture and produced blood, sweat, and tears.

Amanda visualized me and started laughing loudly to attract people's attention. We had to eat this food, for Asians have this thing about giving Faces. You cannot insult them; you must make them look proud and be appreciated!

We had this fire in our mouths which these cute boys knew and had fun with.

Finally, the office boy delivered us salt and hot tea. Take the salt and rub it against your gum with the tongue. It will loosen the oils from the chili and wash it down with hot tea.

The salt will help you retain water in your body. Dehydration is always a danger in hot climates with little humidity.

We did not understand that part until we all felt like wilted flowers one day.

The dry heat in April and May, the hottest month there, dehydrated us. The 130 degrees Fahrenheit inside the kitchen made us sweat without feeling it. It had us fooled. We needed to take salt tablets to hold the water in the body and, yes, hot Darjeeling tea with sugar for energy.

******

A pot washer helped me with my work while he learned cooking skills. He was keen and hungry and learned by observing me at every step; he would then repeat it strictly as he had seen me do the task before.

Anil impressed the Chef and me with his efforts, so we decided to promote him to a cook position. We had a vacancy because one cook needed to retire due to illness.

With this action, we broke the Caste system.

CHAPTER 7

"Wonderful storyteller; is he not fantastic? I have heard all kinds of his stories during these days; I treasure them and learned so much from him."

She is a quick learner and will go places and make it big in life. Mama has raised a very clever girl.

Amanda said, wait a couple of minutes; this was an underhanded compliment.

Let's have a beer and then go to dinner; It is a casual dress code tonight.

Danilo, the bartender, asked if he could make me another Negroni.

No, Danilo, thanks for asking; I will join my dinner companions, and we are all very thirsty. A beer for the men; the young lady will have a glass of Chardonnay, please. Thank you, Danilo.

Amanda just remarked it is nice that you call him by his name.

He told me about his family and siblings and how they grew up on their farm. They live outside Manila, and he is the oldest son.

Greet him in his language, "Magandang Hapon."

Danilo smiled and said," I did not teach the Chief this, but he is brilliant and observant."

"He has taught me management and knowing your employee is the highest order."

"He is right! Management 101; first semester!"

Amanda laughs, "102; the second semester and starting now.

You can graduate soon if you take extra credits! This earned me a kick under the bar!

Dinner is served, and I will choose chicken in a curry sauce. Tell the Chef I want it, and he can turn up the spices for me; he knows.

Amanda was talking with me and telling me all kinds of stuff in a low voice, namely the reactions to my stories. "Dad said you two seem to hit off very well and asked me if I would like to have a daughter?"

I do have a daughter already, and she lives in Barbados. She is married and has a good husband.

"But how did you get a daughter in Barbados?"

That is another story, and the cruise is over tomorrow.

I like little girls aged three to eight. After that, the terrible teen years and the cost is twice as much as a boy!

A fist was raised from the girl sitting next to me!

My turn to place the order: For an appetizer, just a soup, followed by the salad, and leave it with me; I will eat the salad at the same time as the chicken.

Amanda remembered the unfinished story from the restaurant concept study.

"I need to finish my course to get the diploma tomorrow." There goes another sleepless night!

I was commissioned to put a seafood restaurant concept together, but not for money.

It was destined to make history in this four-star hotel. I went to about twenty places until I found a direction. This man referred me to a fisherman for the most delicate fresh fish in the area.

When I went to see this fisherman on the recommendation of this restaurant owners recommendation, he showed me around his old plant.

His fish came directly off the fishing boats packed in sea ice. The fish had been a week since taken off the hook but was as fresh as if caught right this minute.

"I have engineered an ice machine to freeze salt water from the sea. It keeps the fish at 28F and does not freeze their fish. A double-size compressor and controls are all it took to make it work. I have these machines on every fishing vessel, which makes a difference in the quality and also in the cash register.

With this superior supplier, I had my concept completed.

" It's a short story. There is more to it. We have more work to do."

We will do analytical work and then complete the course to graduate.

"OK, Professor "

I gave her a way out and an excuse! She smiled and caressed my knee under the table.

Everybody went to the show, and we put on our show one more time doing the whole gamut from day one to last night.

There was so much variety that she did not know if she was coming or going until total exhaustion.

You need to go to your room tonight. I must get up early and will not see you in the morning. We say now, "Auf Wiedersehen," until we meet again.

"It is wonderful when two lovers take pride in giving pleasures as much as receiving them!"

Don't cry; count the great times we had and savor them for as long as they last.

Smile again and kiss this fool, you have made my time incredibly special, and I will savor it forever.

She smiled and went to her room.

I thought about this girl for a while, lying awake. Did I harm her in any way, or will she manage the emotional turmoil? Will she carry it as an experience and use it to guide her life?

She is a little actress cunningly redirecting conversations from hot topics.

I must credit her smarts and personality for turning this into a permanent inner smile and keeping it a secret from her brother.

******

The morning came too quickly; the ship cleared after the Agriculture officer finished the inspection.

The loading can now start. Delivery trucks are lined up, waiting to unload the orders.

I quickly noticed that the produce had been ordered from four companies: meat from three and groceries from two.

Additionally, all hotel cleaning supplies, and paper goods are split up among multiple suppliers.

Is there logic to this, or is it to get the best price? It does prolong the transfer to the ship by at least 2 hours, by my estimate. Every time a new truck pulled up, time was lost getting him ready to unload the pallets, which were then fed into the ship by a conveyor belt.

 The inefficiency is so clear; why has this not been seen and corrected?

The young buyer, Karri, came to the dock, greeted me, and asked how the cruise was. I said thank you; all was OK, but as I looked at the truck lineup, I just shook my head. We must talk about it.

"We do it by bidding and picking the best price!"

How do you know that is the best price? "I see it on the bid sheet by comparison!"

It was not the question; every stop and time delay for a truck does cost the purveyor money. These trucks had been here before the ship tied up.

Yes, everyone wants to be first in line. That is precisely my point; Karri was not catching on; is it youth, ignorance, or plain stupidity?

We'll talk later.

I went to collect my passport. The Purser had it cleared as part of the crew.

By this time, only managers were in the office. There was no clerical staff, and the top brass were late. Rank has its privileges; there is nothing to worry about when the lower levels carry the workload. Oversight is the best term!

I finished my report but realized this is a different culture when I read it. Multinational personalities include the Brits with their noses up high, Norwegians and a German heading up the Captains, a French man on the technical side, and a token American.

I must tone down my direct approach; it may ruffle feathers. I do not need to make enemies the first week.

From the first day, I had probed the secretary about how she wanted my reports.

"Better no report, but it must be hand-printed; I cannot read this European-style cursive."

What am I going to do? I neither write print style nor am I writing neatly. Dictaphone she refuses, and verbal dictation is not my preference.

She left me hanging with a question on my mind.

A bad start in an area where I had such success and excellent service left me wondering how this would work.

I waited for Karri to return with the ship's orders for the following week.

Let me look this over, or better yet, let me have a copy; this way, I do not occupy your time; it is a busy day for you!

With a highlighter and marked the items I had seen inferior quality. Knives are on the priority list, spoons, whips, serving pans, egg pans, and chlorine test strips.

Do we have quality criteria? I noted all items and looked at the food order. The fruit and produce seem a random pick; no USDA grades are specified. I noticed at once that she is a ton of work ahead of me.

Karri came to me to see what he could do and discuss the loading procedures.

I got time, Karri; It will take a little longer than I had first estimated. I showed him the highlighted items. I see things wrong with these supplies.

There may be reasons for it, but if you think you are saving money, you are wrong.

I come from a different background and have only worked with high-quality cookware, knives, and all we need, and this stuff lasts a lifetime.

What you are buying is a cut above disposable, and seeing the quantities they are asking, it is in fact disposable ware.

Remember the dialog we had at the Pier? "Yes, but I am still confused. I still have questions and want to clear this up for both of us."

Let me start with the economics of the business in general.

With this, he received a lecture on produce and the margins the distributors work to make a profit. Then the trucking cost, the drivers' wages, and the schedule they must keep.

Every business must turn a profit!

Highlight the best prices on your bid sheet, and now you must consider the quality!

The vendor with the lowest prices will be chosen as the primary one you award the order to, provided he delivers top quality.

Take a second one known for its quality and give him a small order. If the first delivers good quality and is as good as the second, then you can rotate weekly and keep two produce houses happy.

Call him and inform him that the next order will be significantly more. Can you do something about the price?

Take what he offers, don't haggle. He will lower his prices the next week to score the high volume delivery again.

You tell the other manager the same and inform them that in months, we will do a weekly rotation. We recommend that they plan their supply needs accordingly.

Follow up on the meat and grocery but stay with one good vendor. Quality has its price, but yield makes the food cost. I know this may sound strange, but I will show it to you in time.

We are earning benefits by the speed at which we load the ship. I bet we can shave off two or more hours on the total time.

In total, you will not spend more money. The purveyor will consider this account as his premium customer and will never do anything to jeopardize the relationship. Do you want to give it a try?

"Yes, I will let you know, boss."

These highlighted equipment items! I had seen enough pain in watching them work. We will short the order and start buying quality products in its place. Again we will buy it only once, you must trust me. I was a cook, and I understand the thinking.

We start with high-quality Solingen knives. Two per cook will be good. We will get them to sign for it, and if they damage it, or throw it away, then the cook will pay for it twice our cost.

When we do this together, deliver these knives, I want you to see the cook's eyes.

There is a French proverb: "You must be rich to buy cheap." Are we rich because we keep on buying?

Then there is one more thing on the meat specs, but not today; this is enough for you to chew.

Thank God this day is over.

******

The rush hour traffic on I 95 to Alligator Alley, which is now a construction zone. will get me home in time for dinner. Hopefully, Nina has a meal ready.

This girl is on fire! Something simple, yes, your famous fried pork chops. Let us first eat; I am sick of the rich food from the trip.

She made great chops, potatoes, salad, and a Heineken. Then I will be ready for you.

I am too direct with my report. I must soften my language. I will type it as I soften the wording.

"Why, don't you have a Secretary?"

Yes, and no, she is putting me as the lowest-ranking person. I am used to excellent service.

"Let me do the typing as you rewrite the words, and I can help you with that too."

I am thinking about how I can turn this around. I will not take her bossy attitude. I am used to efficiency and getting the report out on the same day.

"What if I take it to work and do it on the computer? We have great software. I can do a number with this; I will do it at lunch or when the bosses are out of the office. Besides, my boss likes you, which you know from other hotels. He speaks highly about you.

He won't mind if he sees me doing this for you. Tell them your better half will issue an invoice for services rendered. "

"You will get action with that, I guarantee."

You are brilliant, Nina, just a doll and so love dove all the time!

"I got to take care of my man; he is precious too; I have not been so happy since I can remember."

With dinner done and her son fed, I thought to have a conversation with him about electronics.

Fundamental knowledge was insufficient to venture to a high-tech store and buy a computer. Derek would be great to aid in the choice of such an investment.

I mentioned it to Nina if she supported this idea.

"There is an angle to warm up with him. We must take him shopping to tech stores; he will be in his element."

Good, we make it a joint project, a family affair. It put a big smile on Nina's face. Her concern about having her son bonding with her new boyfriend was a worry. We may have the key to it with this purchase. He can set up the software and instruct us on the function of this machine.

I need training but never find the time to take classes in a community college.

Nina was ready for a roll in the hay; when she got hot, nothing's stopping her.

She takes the initiative, works all the tricks she knows, and brings total happiness to both partners.

What a woman, one for keeps, and yet she never makes any sign of wanting to be married. A smile had been the only signal when I mentioned a family affair going shopping with her son.

A platonic relationship and sticking together through thick and thin can be as close a bond if not better. I wonder if she is seeking this type of arrangement. Someday when her tongue loosens after wine, she may be in the mood to talk.

Finally, a good night's sleep on the waterbed; I had missed the comfort and the steady temperature it provides.

We did manage to write the report on the IBM writer, but she was not happy with the looks; she will rewrite it at work.

An uncooperative secretary can be blamed for two days delay of the report. If my boss wanted to read the report, I had a draught on hand. I typed on an old IBM typewriter myself; please excuse the errors.

******

Today I want to take the time to go over food specs. The meat first, then produce and grocery brands. We will do beverage at the end, OK, Karri?

Karri finished his work and waited to get any comments before giving the order.

"A woman by the name of Mary is doing this work."

Listen to this, please; we will buy only choice-grade meat with a yield grade three. Ask the meat purveyor to select the smaller strip loins. The beef is from a younger animal and is a little lighter in color. We can cut a thicker steak, and I plan to cut back on the portion. I see too much food left on the plates; It only ends up feeding the fish.

Money will be saved in the portion reduction, less fatty loins, and even a lower price. These loins are often set aside since hotels and restaurants seek large loins. You will be the nice guy to take this inventory off their hands.

The product must be choice quality at the minimum; green-tipped Bananas, SK or Sunkist citrus fruit, apples 90 counts, and Baking potatoes we take from the eighty to one hundred counts. I have everything marked on the order sheet.

When Mary received the paperwork, she had expected the multiple orders to be split between 3 or 4 vendors.

"It makes my life easier and makes sense, your idea Karri, or the new director?"

"His directive, I should say suggestion, but I took it as an order. I did not think to fool around with him, but he laid it on me gently. "

Mary said," Talk softly but carry a big stick! I like this guy. I am taking him as a doer and straight talker, but still a Gentleman."

"Bring him here to introduce me as your right and left hand." One down and more to go.

While Karri and I were reviewing, I saw the former manager sticking his redhead into the door.

"Just a week and already all these changes? What for, we did fine all these years."

OK, no doubt, but I have a separate set of tools and want to use them to the company's benefit. There are always better roadways leading to Rome!

After this redhead left, Karri confessed that he was under strict orders and never allowed any suggestions for a better way.

"When the Chef had comments on food quality, which I conveyed to him I was told to leave this to him. What do they know? They come from underdeveloped countries."

He will get used to it; we have nothing to fear. His comment makes me think. Where does he get this information so fast? It must be from the vendors we are cutting out. We have ample good reasons, and quality is the primary cause for the cut.

If he causes a stink, then something will surface, and that will be his sticky hands.

Meanwhile, we will prove ourselves right with results. Nobody can argue about a better product for less money spent.

We will take the blame for now and If it gets too hot, this guy better has a clean slate, or I will sniff out the rats. I am good at it.

Back to the task at hand: The Chicken you buy as a whole bird, you can supplement with breasts. We don't need all these bones for soup. It saves on handling. Ask the vendor to deliver the chicken in shaved ice with a scale stub telling us the weight.

The fish must be delivered the same way. I want a saltwater ice machine, but it will take time.

"Did you see all this on one trip?" I pointed to my eyes.

"Mary wants to meet you. She places the orders and confirms all the invoices for payment."

Let us meet this lady; she is an important spoke in this wheel.

Hello Mary, "I know your name; it gets thrown around already." Is that good or bad?

"From my point of view, it is about time we get a new broom in here!"

That is quite the statement; yes, we are making changes. We keep going in this direction and get better with every order.

"Oh, my, I like you already! Nice to meet you. We will work well together."

******

Have lunch? Where and what? "Cuban sandwich down this street? Come along." My treat!

Downtown Miami is buzzing. We have a community with mom-and-pop shops. Latin blood is now the domineering economy in this city; it saved Miami from deteriorating in the late sixties. The sign says " Habla Española." It would be more appropriate to say," English is still spoken;" it would be more applicable.

119

The fast-food stand making our sandwich had a line. We better know our choice beforehand.

Pork sandwich with garlic sauce for flavor and grilled top and bottom. Add two Cervezas, and lunch is served al fresco. After a Cuban coffee, we are set for the second half of this day.

We will meet with the seafood vendor, a fast-talking Cuban man. Alberto was on time, an adjustment from Cuban time. Manana would be too late.

Tell me about the availability of fresh fish. We have always used frozen fish, but I want to look into fresh. We can make a change. I have ideas and want to run them by you!

I told him about the fish restaurant at the Beach in Fort Lauderdale.

"Yes, I know, super wonderful place. I wonder where they get their fish."

All are super fresh and packed in saltwater ice! "I have not heard of that."

I gave him the basic needs to get this going and then stirred the conversation to the ship's needs. This had intensely captivated my thinking.

The problem with fish is not that it cannot be delivered fresh from the fisherman, but the challenge is its storage. Once the fish has been frozen, it loses texture, and its juices quickly absorb the odor.

"You know your fish."

I put this concept together at the Beach. I did the research and set up the idea. The restaurant was the owner's vision.

"That explains your indebt knowledge!

I am going to lay out my thinking. I can do business if I get fresh fish delivered in finely shaved ice and a weight label. It will help us in minimizing the handling of these tender fillets. The fillets must be cut to the specified weight. The idea is to take the fish from the ice into the frying pan.

The second item is this awful crayfish, but we will discuss it later. For now, we are stuck with tradition.

Karri, we can do this fresh fish on the first night out. The lobster follows on the second night, and on the third, we do shrimp. It will cut out all frozen fish fillets.

Karri's eyes are about to fall out of his head, and finally, his comment. "If we pull this off right, the ratings will go through the roof."

It is precisely what the passengers are expecting.

"You don't miss a thing; he was on the ship for the first time last week and came home with all these ideas."

"He calls it two eyes wide open despite only four hours of sleep."

My report is coming tomorrow; it is being typed by my secretary at home. Why does our secretary not do it? It would be the weekend at best if she showed up every day. My girlfriend is a super secretary, and she is waiting to see the presentation.

Take this copy; look at my equipment and machinery comments and give me your opinion.

Before I forget, can you get me the story on San Pedro?

I have to get out there very soon; this guy is packing up and gone. There will not be a handover.

"A sharp girl is doing what Mary does here; she will hold things together." That's good to know.

******

Jim went to see Karri after he left my office. I saw it from the corner of my eye. He will undoubtedly exercise influence over him, one more push with either a promise or a threat.

If Karri is honest, he will tell me then I know if I can count on him.

I was looking for the best approach to take the equipment to the other side, the Marine Department Chief.

"Can I count on the support of my boss? "

I see little or no chance. He is strictly rooms, entertainment, Purser, and administrative staff. He does not have sympathy for the back side of the operation.

******

Karri came to see me as soon as he knew Jim had left the building. Let's hear the conversation.

Karri looked a bit shaken and started talking fast and nervously. Please slow down, close the door, and tell me from the beginning.

"He came and asked me if I liked the new guy already labeled as a new broom. I told him there was a fresh breeze blowing, fresh air, and fresh ideas, all very logical. Don't screw up more than once, but he is a fair man from what I have seen so far, and yes, I do like him."

"Best of all, I am learning already."

"Be careful with this type; they come in, turn everything upside down and leave a big mess. I am not convinced the new guy can back all the claims I had seen on his resume."

"Please keep your eyes open and listen to old Jim here; he is your Mentor. But if you cross me, you will pay dearly, understood?"

OK, not surprising to me, jalousie, envy, an inferiority complex, or only plain ignorance, I shall put it to the test! Just do your job the best you can.

Loyalty has to be earned, just like respect has to be achieved. Your excellent work will earn you my respect, which is a given.

If you make a mistake, remember that we learn by making mistakes, I will show you the correct way and move on. Do nothing against Jim, be cautious, and let him believe you are still in his corner. We do this until we have tangible success.

Sometimes you have to play the game for a brief time. The tide turns, and Jim will find himself in hot water with his bully tactics. Then his ammunition is no longer hot.

I have taken on bigger guns in NYC with the Union! A story of them whenever we get the opportunity.

CHAPTER 8

The office is finally organized, and it made me feel much better. I started a list to track development and achievements.

Fish and menu changes are pending.

Equipment list, whereto? pending

Meat, follow-up on board, imminent

Chefs knives, control paper, done, instruct on board.

Canned fruits in syrup for pastry use, pending.

Meat trimming demo on board, pending.

The fresh fish program, input from onboard managers, pending.

Brief the captain on the idea of fresh fish, pending the next visit.

Find the money for new equipment purchases, pending.

The list can grow endless.

The knives will take two weeks or longer. They must be ordered now.

Karri had already done his homework and sourced Henkel brand knives. Let's do this Chef's knife and a smaller one, which will be a set.

We need a form to sign for receiving the set of knives. The crew purser will handle it at sign-on and sign-off times. Get this ready for delivery in two weeks. By then, I will be back from California.

I will work with the butcher on the meat trim. Then, the pastry man and I will discuss the dessert concept. I see him as an experienced professional.

Karri, look for a crunchy cookie that will not get soggy from high humidity and become a part of the dessert presentation. How about Florentine cookies, Great!

It is late, and can we call it a day? We achieved a good amount today.

At home, Priscilla had a formal letter announcing the birth of her daughter, who has yet to be named. Would I like to be her Godfather and come to the baptism?

I answered that I was honored for this influential appointment.

Priscila answered back. She misses me and is very much looking forward to my visit. The paper had a water stain that also moved me to tears.

Nina wanted to know what just moved me to tears.

She has that effect on me. She is a wonderful daughter; you know Priscilla in Barbados. I understand; she has a special place in your heart; she has an entire seat.

I have you there too. A passionate kiss followed that revelation.

I received a piece of fish as a sample; I will do the cooking tonight.

 It looks like we will fly to Barbados to attend the baptism.

"Great, I have never been there and am dying to meet your exceptional daughter."

I hope you're not jealous. "Since I know the whole story, I understand your affection for her."

Can I ask you to research the customs of baptism and the godfather's role in a girl's life as a child?

"We have a server in the restaurant from Barbados; he will give me the scoops."

My son checked in and told me that he had landed a job with a builder. This man had seen him work in the lumber yard, and the builder saw a future for me in this field.

You are a natural; I will teach you how to build high-quality houses. I was hired on the spot.

He needed that since he had given up school toward an architectural career and was depressed.

It excited me as well. I feared Martin could get in with the wrong people.

He has made rapid progress in renovating his house. He can rent an attached apartment and has extra income.

Hunting season yielded a sizable buck and set him up for a while with meat. He is doing well. He knows how to take care of himself. With this job, he can grow into the building business.

It put my mind at ease.

A good day calls for celebration. I have a bottle of bubbly already cold in the refrigerator. I reserved it for a special occasion. This weekend, we are going shopping for a computer.

Your report, wow, this looks like it's for the White House! It will be most impressive.

"How is your illustrate secretary doing?"

I have not spoken to her; the purchasing woman does the little stuff. I won't give her the satisfaction of rejection.

I will set off a bomb with this document and then I have the upper hand.

I will not give this magnificent report to her to pass it on to the boss. I will hand-carry each to the recipients.

"It is a good move; she cannot destroy it or do something to put her signature on it."

"Notice the font, a rare font the GM likes, which is hard to get and costs money."

"The GM was asking about you, then saw the report, laughed, and said no problem, this guy never runs out of solutions. We gladly help him out. We should invite you both to have dinner with my wife and me. Will you set it up, please? He must have ship stories by now!"

In a week you have to go to California; "can I come with you?"

Not on this trip, it is strictly business, and it's my first visit to the office and two ships.

I can arrange a companion ticket when I go sailing as a follow-up. How does Alaska sound?

"A cruise and then Alaska in addition; you are the best!"

******

The fish was ready, and we both had a buzz from the champagne taken to our empty stomachs. Great fresh fish is so much better than meat! "Even my famous pork chops?" Yes, taste this. "Fantastic, I never knew what to do with fish."

The first rule on fish is freshness; nothing else matters; you cannot go wrong.

******

As she predicted, the report was a bomb! She had done the ultimate job on this document and spent the hotel's money to create it.

The secretary just looked at it. Is this possible, this kind of skills, who has them these days?"

"She knew from school that this was an expected format for official government documents, but for a cruise line. What has become of this new guy? Is he teaching me a lesson?"

While distributing this report, I ran into the President.

He greeted me casually and called me the new guy he had heard about already: " All good, nothing to worry about. What do you have here? Let me see. Can I take this copy?"

Of course, I have mine in a plain format and as a draught backup. I can work from my copy and use it as a working paper.

"It will never reach my desk. The presentation is formidable. Put me on the list for your reports, please. I must stay in touch and want it straight from the horse's mouth. Send it as a blind copy; it keeps these guys honest and does not rattle the cages too bad."

Your secretary did this?"

No, my girlfriend; "keep her; she is precious."

The boss was embarrassed, knowing all too well her moods and lack of effort of the women we needed for the secretarial services

"I apologize, I know I should have let her go some time ago, but she was demoted and forced on me. Let us see her reaction; she must be seeing this as competition."

My girlfriend works for the GM at the Beach Hotel in Fort Lauderdale; he knows about this work and consented to have it done at the hotel. We are old friends from way back from my hotel time as a regional.

"If our secretary has one decent bone left in her body, we can turn her around. She has a life to support, and at her age, it is too early to retire and too late to get another job unless she wants to be a cashier at Publix."

"You have been around! Are you sure you want to give it a chance?" What is to lose? I have a safety net.

She came to me and told me she was embarrassed by how she had treated me so far. She now realizes that I am a professional man with mountains of experience. She had a peek at my resume.

"I read this report and made a copy as a reference and style; please use your handwriting, and I will correct any grammar. I have a long history too and want to show what I have as skills at my age. It took me back to my glory days. Forgive me, please!"

She ran out of my office with tears in her eyes and went to the bathroom.

When she came back, she waved her hand and thumbs up.

The next day, Mark came to me and asked me what I had done to her. She is a changed person.

I woke her from her sleep like a Fairy Tale Princess.

No serious, take a look at the report. I placed it on the boss's desk. He is going to frame it as a picture.

"My God, who does work like this today?"

My girlfriend did it for a worthy cause! Then I filled him in on the strategy, and he was in Ahhh!

"You have made your point; she has awakened her old skills, recognized that there is competition out there and being grumpy only hurts herself."

I never did give her the time of day to shut me down or control me. From this day forward, we have to feed her ego, take her to lunch, and don't forget to praise her for her work.

I am sure she will appreciate a little souvenir from the trip. She never gets to go anywhere.

It has lifted the mood in the entire office. We need to set up a secretary's and boss's days.

I remember that day in Panama, and I was not even on staff then.

******

Angela sent a letter to the office.

Dear Love!

With sadness, I have to tell you that I have lost my Mother to Cancer. I am going to move into the house. You do know the address. Can you come by for a quick visit? I need your hug badly. My boyfriend has left me, and I have to start over again. But this is not the biggest issue. My sister, brother, and I have to settle the estate and split the assets. I need your advice!

Ok, I will be a little late and call Nina and after I will call Angie. I'll stop by on my way home tonight.

******

Karri, are we ready on Friday for the dog and pony show? "I have the knives here, and the Pastry stuff is all set."

Is the bread baked on board? Yes, we do; you never get to see the baker; he works at night.

I have to catch up with him on a short sailing!

******

Jim was now openly lobbying against anything and everything I was doing.

The food cost has decreased by a small margin, and the fresh fish program has become a resounding success. The captain is delighted he is promoting the fish to the passengers.

He asked me if fresh fish could be served every night. I said ice and pointed to the sea! "Do you mean ice from salt water?"

Yes, captain, I know a fisherman that figured it out and now has his boats equipped with ice machines making saltwater ice. At 29 F, it is like powder snow if you remember your childhood.

It takes a double-size compressor and more juice, serving all the ice they need until the boat is full.

The best part is that the fish is packed in this snow which goes into every cavity, keeps a 28 F temperature, and stops decay.

He delivers the fish packed in this snow from his plant to his customers. He has a lock on the market and also commands a fair price.

"An intelligent fisherman can think beyond hook, line, and sinker."

Do you think the onboard engineers can convert an old machine into a saltwater ice maker?

"I know they are great engineers, and I will challenge them. Will we have fresh fish on our vessel seven days a week?" Yes, master, then we can do fresh fish every night.

"I will keep this under wraps and not leak it out. This red-headed Jim will put a stop to it."

******

That afternoon, the secretary came to my office for the first time and sat down. Point-blank she asks me, "who are you? I have to get more information about you, where are you from?"

I came from the land down under

Where women glow and men plunder

Can't you hear, can't you hear the thunder?

You better run; you better take cover.

I said it loud enough to make the office wondering about her barging in on me like this.

They all screamed and applauded. She finally got it, the song, yes, the song!

I told her that it has now been the 2,249,000 ½ times I had been asked where I come from, I thought of making a joke about it, and this time is the ½.

She laughed wholeheartedly after I told her, I am from Davie, but I was born in Germany.

We talked about Germany and the way I entered the US.

"Do you know that you have changed my life around? For years I had been depressed, taken medication, thoughts about suicide, and all this dark stuff. You cured me with a report that took me to the glory days of my career."

My girlfriend is a live-in secretary and a top-notch person, amongst other attributes. She did that for you. She typed the report for me since I got the cold shoulder from you.

Everybody in the office is now bearing witness to this talk!

Nina figured out that this is the medicine that will turn you around. She had a similar experience at one time. I pulled her out of her depression, and this was her payback.

"I took the report from Mark and replaced it with a copy. I will treasure this document and give it a proper place in my home. Hug me now, and we shall live happily after. "

Rousing applause and a hug that lasted ten minutes.

Nina broke out in tears; I am so happy for her and my humble contribution to her recovery.

******

Off we go to Barbados. Pack your Bikini and the little black dress you love so much. I ask your boss for the time off to attend my granddaughter's baptism and take on the duty of a godfather. It will be a two-day affair. We fly Wednesday and return Saturday in time to meet the ship before I go to California. It will ease the travel itch a bit.

"You know best what eases my itch!" All in good times and take it slow and easy. To make it to the mountain top, one has to climb.

******

The butcher watched me with great interest;" I can tell you have done this a few times."

"I praise the Lord for these new knives; my prayers just got answered." Are you from Jamaica?

"Ya man! Have u been there?" Yes, in Negril and had a fun time!

"Went to Hedonism?" No, but next door and sneaked to the nude breach when the girlfriend was taking a nap. She never did figure out why I had no tan lines, I told her it was my natural skin tone, and she took it completely. These people there have fun.

"I worked there once; girls drive you crazy, you know, the employees, seeing all these bones and boners all day got them so horny, I could have done them in the deep freezer, and they still are hot."

He was laughing and listening to my explicit instructions.

These strip loins are selected to be on the light side, small eye, but we can still cut a thick steak and save 2 oz on each portion.

"People are wasting this good meat, it breaks my heart, and I am with you, Chief."

It will also be done on the tenderloin with one oz less, and these tenders are from the same animal and smaller, I mean thinner; just give it a little push down with the palm of your hand.

"Right on, Chief". We bought chicken breast. All you need to do is take them out a day ahead and keep them in the cooler; this way, they thaw slowly and do not bleed so much.

The rest of the birdies do as you have done.

Now pay attention. Do the chicken as the very last job. Then wash the tables and the floor. You know to get into the corners, they are not round!

When all is clean, take one of these spray bottles, fill it with warm water and top it off with two tablespoons of bleach, then spray all areas and let it sit.

"That little bleach?" Yes, any more will get you sick; we do not want you sick; there are bitches waiting for you in Negril. Laughing and the Yes Chief sealed the deal.

Karri will sail with you in a week, and then you make the switch; We keep it a secret until that day.

Back to the office: "The provision loading was done by 10 am. The kids get time off and love you for it."

******

She was more composed when I stopped at Angi's House after work. She came running like a toddler the minute I opened the door. Hugs and kisses like in old times. Have you missed me?

"I am so lost with all this stuff, I never had to do this, and my older sister is busy at work. My brother is in school for another couple of months; it is left for me to do. The funeral is over; the emotions are settling down. With the trust, the estate has been cleared."

Two down, so far, it's good. Neither of the siblings wants the belongings mother left behind."

Except for sentimental keepsakes, place an ad in the paper to sell it. Call it an "Estate sale."

The people who visit Garage sales will show up. Have it out to see.

No need to make any display; take pictures of all and then have a price in mind.

It will be pennies and dollars, no big money, yet when all is gone, you have cash. Keep it, share it, or give it to the student; they always need money.

Just ask them for an offer, then bargain and sell. A sale is a sale; there may never be another one.

The other choice is to sell it to People who buy the contents of a house. It's called an Estate sale!

They offer you what seems like little money but is likely more than a garage sale will generate. These people will clean the house out, and you won't have a problem disposing of stuff.

Rent the house through a real estate agency. They will do a credit check and take the first and two-month security deposits. The last month's rent is permanently lost, as tenants always see this as the last month's rent.

You live close by to keep an eye on it.

Once you've rented, find a Handyman and pay him a retainer fee. The rent you ask for must cover tax, insurance, maintenance material, and the monthly retainer fee. This ensures someone is coming to fix stuff and get to know your house.

He will love it as it supplies him with a steady income.

You put the security money into a savings account. Rent money goes into a checking account at the same bank. Get a debit card to pay bills. Utility power, water, phone, internet, and TV are the tenant's costs.

Property tax and major renovation fall on the home owner. A fresher up of paint and minor repairs are needed in between tenants.

Set parameters that are allowed in terms of decoration; color changes must be approved in advance. The lease will have language on leaving as they found with normal wear and tear excluded.

You will have an added income since there is no bank loan to pay. Do not distribute the receipts to your sister or brother. Allow the money to accumulate and build a nice balance in the account.

She kissed, thanked me, and told me she still loved me. I want you to know this.

I know you have a girlfriend living with you.

******

I see more resorts on the list of hotels on the arrival console offering transportation. Of course, the famous Castle is a part of this choice. The Barbados Airport has been modernized. It is vastly different and has so much more traffic.

I still have feelings for this place. It made my heart beat a little faster, and good memories will remain embedded in my heart. A limousine picked us up in grand style; the business must be doing well. It all works this way with more resorts, food, and imports.

"What are these green stalks growing here?" It is a sugar cane for Appleton Rum. This island gets its share of rain; therefore, the sugar cane does well here.

The house has been enlarged and refinished on the outside. Warehouses had been added, and delivery trucks of all sizes were waiting to make deliveries.

Priscilla greeted us in the doorway. She looked radiant and showed a touch of maturity. It gives her a stately lady look. Long hugs and kisses are her trademarks.

Our luggage and a box are taken to the house.

"What is this?

"I do not have a name yet; we are counting on you to name our little princess. She is sleeping right now, but soon you will make her acquaintance."

Meet Nina, my girlfriend and resident secretary. "You are joking again; I know you too well."

Nina was impressed with how she was handling me. "The comment is yet another hint to a story, but of course, always a delightful story and never a dull moment."

"I invited Maya, but she could not get the time off. She is in a convention hotel and has the top job handling the big groups."

My secretary in Hartford, these two met in training in Washington. I explained to Nina.

Nina works for the hotel at the beach and is the best Secretary in Florida and beyond. In there is the story or part of it.

"So, you are playing a big part in his story? It gets more mysterious s by the minute."

I have fresh juice; you must be thirsty. Help yourself to snacks if you are hungry.

"You must tell me what is in this mystery box."

Nina said I researched the customs in Barbados, and I learned from a hotel server that a godfather must bring a giant candle and light it when the child receives the baptism.

The family shall keep the candle lit until the girl gets married.

"My God, it is so pointed correct, an age-old custom."

"But, when there is a hurricane, and the flame is blown out, then the tradition is interrupted. The candle cannot be relit. It can be taken as bad luck or good luck. It is a personal choice."

"In my case, it was blown out by my fifth year. My mom decided to take it as good luck because I was always smiling, and in my smile, she saw the candle burning eternally."

A great story: you see, you have your own stories and are collecting more daily.

"We have a remarkable story about Maya and Priscilla in Washington. We can do this one later."

"First, we need to give you the tour, and by then, the baby girl will be ready to meet Gran Pa and Godfather."

Here is a candle that will not blow out in a hurricane. It's an oil candle and requires a refill four times a year. Nina will do the honor of lighting it as the water flows over Kyra's head.

"Kyra," how lovely, how beautiful a name this is!"

I thought of it and felt that a name reflects a person's character. We are planting this seed for her to grow into a woman with an independent spirit, compassionate, self-assured, and determined to make her way.

Kyra is a journalist who brings news and stories on television in her own words. She makes it her story. She takes the heading and ignores the prompter script. I received my inspiration from her.

Kyra already has her mother's fine qualities, Grand Ma's genes, and Daddy's determination.

"Wow, amazing. That is big and grand, and I am so proud of you and considerate of Nina for researching our tradition.

"Before I forget, I made a reservation at the Castle for the Pirates dinner for the two of you. You have never sat down for it, and Nina will be amused tomorrow night."

"Tonight, we do a Bajan Barbeque catered by my sister, and Mom cannot wait to see you again."

The tour took us through the house, the library, a bar with all the finest rum from the family.

Then there was the business side, with the office, storage, and coolers as big as a house. For the freezers, we had to put on heavy coats.

After, we reached an area labeled food bank.

Alex explained: "We need to give food to the underprivileged. The groceries that are approaching expiration date, fruit that is still good but will not last three days in the store and dented canned goods go to these people. The government forgets these people, and social services are corrupt. We decided to handle it in-house and under our control.

Meats are the same story: Packaging damaged and eatable food, which others throw away. We give it to the poor. "

"They sign in, and this way, we get to know them, and the families have food. It gives us an outstanding reputation and a warm heart to feel good. We would suffer the loss anyway. There is no extra cost, just the work to hand it out. Priscilla has much to do with it. She knows firsthand what it means to go hungry."

It's a beautiful gesture; our big guys should learn from it.

The US Agriculture Department is the biggest food waste.

"Meet our Princess "Kyra"! The girl smiled, hearing her name for the first time."

Babies are much more advanced than we know; they absorb everything. Languages are learned by listening and never need to give feedback. "If you see the child, you will notice the tongue moving, eye contact changes, facial expressions, and a smile. The eyes move around to watch the surroundings, and the sense of smell is noticed when a strong odor or perfume reaches the tiny nose."

That evening we met up with Mom. Her biggest smile needed no commentary but a big hug.

I introduced Nina to her, and she started to talk. The fact that a food critic from the New York Times wrote such a detailed review, every tourist from the North had to see my humble food stand. " I cannot call it a restaurant, but a stand will do."

"Your man told me never to change this to a full-service restaurant. It is so perfect for the area, an Icon he called it, and I still do not know if he meant it to be a landmark. Let them drool; he meant having saliva accumulate before a savory meal: Yes, take the profits and build yourself a model kitchen with the latest machines and refrigeration. You will have so much business, a waiting line, and turn business away. And that is your best advertising.

This will make life easier, and now you have the younger daughter all ready for takeover. I followed his advice, and he was correct to the last penny.

The stand is still the same, with rotten wood replaced, and kept the same Island charm.

"Now I have a son working it, and I socialize with the customers and tell the Priscilla story! And all this had started with this man's visit."

"It marked the start when you released Priscilla to work at the Castle. Then came the recipes nicely handwritten, and this tale was the test coking to the crown."

"Mama saw her daughter in a brand new kitchen employed by a huge company. Where will this take my precious Priscilla and me?"

"At the grand opening, I met all these dignitaries attending the Party and this show with the captain pirate displays so much showmanship! Priscilla glowed with pride, and so did I. I stood in the back, not wanting to be in the spotlight"

When the Pirate captain pointed to Priscilla and told the guests that her family had roots in his castle, let me tell you; I must have stopped my heart for a minute."

"Of course, I knew all about it, kept it a secret for I was ashamed to tell it to my children."

"Nina smiled; you have such an excellent relationship."

I received a precious gift when Priscilla asked me to be her surrogate father.

Receiving a daughter without diapers and teenage tantrums is enormous.

Grandma laughed so loud that the associates came running to see the reason for the laugh.

******

The BBQ was island-style. Nina labeled it exotic since she had never seen tropical fruits and smelled these aromas from the dishes. Fresh seafood choice and scotch bonnet peppers, excellent and hot and served with lime aioli. Then came the curries and stews, chicken in a variety, fresh fruit, breadfruit chips, plantains, Mango, bananas, and coconut. It was lavish.

Friends and family attended.

I met Alex's father and the son who is now entering the rum business.

"He pulled us aside and described that our business had grown significantly since you promoted our brand at the Castle and all these custom drinks with copyrights.

Then came the contest, which is still going and involves other islands; it gave us free publicity, contributing to the success. Even our friends and competitors from Bacardi came to see this spectacle."

Nina was amazed.

The open-air breakfast had a variety of fruits and bread. An omelet and strong coffee set us up to go sightseeing.

With chauffeur and limousine, we went into town. Elegant buildings that had been a reminder of the colonization of the English, are now housing well-known fashion and jewelry stores.

The tiny wooden houses had been torn down and taken away the island's charm.

Typical tourists want us to see these primitive housing and forego the comfort of today's style. I heard that comment at times when locals hear tourists making derogatory remarks. Is modernizing an exclusive right to those who visit?

Barbadians had been keen to put British oppression behind them and wipe out the past.

We had lunch at Mom's place, the landmark for local cuisine.

Restaurants are trying to copy Mom's recipe and calling it their own. Original this and that, a lie, of course, yet it works for her. She is super busy.

A waiting line in front of the window to place the order made us see her success. Lunch was al fresco to savor this food.

Mom pulled us out of the line and straight to the kitchen.

Shining stainless steel equipment, tiled walls, and floors are all very modern. The equipment is arranged to ease an efficient workflow. Architects could learn from her.

When a cook designs a kitchen, I told Nina, they place themself in the center of it and then decide the equipment's placement.

"Why did you not tell me yesterday? I would have cooked you something special!" All your food is exceptional, and I wanted Nina to see the heart and Soul of Bridgeport as it is today. Nina savored the food. There is so much going on here, all the spices and aromas; where does it come from?

"You are speaking like a Chef." This woman is the master of blending flavors to make them work together. She knows every trick!

Mom refused to take payment. The server received a generous tip.

Late afternoon, we made our way to the Castle. The driver was still raving about the food. I told him the story's beginning when Priscilla joined the Castle.

I am honored to work for the family of Miss's Priscilla.

We took the driver with us on the tour of the Castle. Looked around the lobby and front desk.

I pointed to the large wooden table and began to describe the Pirate's dinner.

Then came the entire history lecture from the start of piracy and development to the present time.

Nina was feeling the genuine emotions what this historic place projected.

She would have never made the same connection if she had never seen this Castle.

At the beach, a young man has now replaced the woman. My inquiry about her told me his mom has retired and is looking after the grandchildren.

You have a great tradition, a heritage to carry on. I am fully aware and shall do honor to this special place.

Beers please, a burger, we are attending the Pirate's dinner. Incredible for you; how did you get the tickets?

We have connections in the highest places; the driver smiled and said something in the native dialect. An explanation!

The restaurant had new staff and smiling faces, with name tags engraved with "Associate." I like it. I has become a widely used definition of a worthy employee.

The Chef's voice told me that he was still there.

"How nice to see you; I was hoping you looked me up; I had seen the name on the dinner guest list. This dinner is going more vital than ever.

It made me famous, and solicitations from fancy resorts are becoming a bother."

"Here is my comfort zone and teaching factory. I am proud to be awarded a charter from the State to educate cooks and allowed to issue a diploma at graduation."

That must be rewarding to you. "It certainly is, and I stay here for as long as this company keeps me.

Other resorts took notice of this place with this little restaurant and the castle dinner. It is your entire fault! Hahaha. The General Managers wanted to expand the specialty restaurant. The demand had grown to a long waitlist, but the State will not issue a building permit. It is perfect now. Why mess with success?"

You are right. I am pleased to find all this undisturbed and in pristine condition.

"Can I buy you a drink? The bartender is waiting for you."

Eddy made a big name for himself too. He is well known and heads up a rum council to preserve the sugar cane fields. The quality standards of Barbados rum are receiving state protection.

He loves to glow in his glory, and he still loves to shake his cups with ice. First the drink and then I will tell you what I am doing now.

"Our soil on this island has minerals not found in any other places. It is the reason for the unique quality of our rum.

Developers are tempting farmers to sell the land for so-called land preservation. Who knows what their actual plans are? They cannot be trusted to be good stewards of our land.

You can see how this rum contest brought not only fame and fortune; it placed the limelight on our land. What else can be the contributor to our famous rum? We have become the star in the Caribbean."

"Is she your girlfriend? Yes, meet Nina. You have good taste!" A thank you from Nina, and her eyes glowed with fire.

This guy has not aged a bit and is still the charmer.

"I have a new drink, and now I have a name for it too, "Nina"! I like the sound of it." A bartender is much like a woman, always a secret here and there.

In record time, Nina drank this new drink which had just been named after her, but a refill would have gotten her drunk. We are attending the Pirate's dinner. I want you to be alert.

Tomorrow is the baptism; do you have any advice?

"Yes, wear shorts, it will be here at the beach. Wear shorts: you will be standing in the water holding the Baby's hand." "Kyra" is her name. I love this name; it's an excellent choice! "

"Priscilla stops by here and keeps me up on the latest."

People on a waiting list attended the dinner. They had traveled to Barbados to attend the Pirates dinner and combine it with a vacation.

******

Anticipation was building when the lobby lit up with red flame torches. A spooky atmosphere was now complete.

Male and female guests are seated around the big wooden table. Mingling with strangers became part of the myth. I saw it as an excellent refinement!

Wenches filled everybody's tankard with either beer or rum punch. It was still the same girls that helped bring this dinner to life again. She recognized me and told me how much this event helped her in her acting career.

Servers in sailor attire began serving the first course. It was delicious seafood presented so beautifully that the guests hesitated to start eating.

More drinks are served to get the guests in a talkative mood. Soft Island music played in the background.

Ready for the main course. A whole baby pig came out on a six-foot-long wooden pallet.

Aromatic spices filled the air. The sailors placed this pallet in the center of the dinner table, where the pig would be carved and distributed.

Loud pounding on the wooden floor announced the pirate captain's arrival.

Black beard limped to the table, wearing an eye patch, and carrying a parrot on his shoulder.

"Greeting to my honored guest. I had hosted fine dinners in my days. It has been too long to have a fine table to host. I am banned from the outer world, except when I see a hosted table in grand style. Eat heartily and drink, for life must be celebrated. Thank you for doing me the honors. I bid you farewell, God's speed, and fair winds."

The Pirate disappeared in a cloud of smoke!

Spotlighting and music made this presentation complete.

Finger bananas set in an alcohol flame were served as dessert. Champagne and a shot of Appleton rum completed the evening.

Everybody was filled up with food and drinks.

Nina sat across the table, and I saw her interacting with both men to her sides.

She was complimented and did not blink an eye about the spicy meat.

"How can you handle this hot food? Women are usually so sensitive."

I get to eat a wide variety of food. My husband is a Chef. He is the man who developed this dinner years ago, and it's the first time he gets to attend this table. She flirted and teased the two men and enjoyed her dominance over them.

Arriving back at the mansion, Priscilla was feeding the infant while Nina went to the room.

Come and sit with me and let's chat a little.

We revisited our lives, got updated, and ended up with Maya in our conversation.

"I am still wondering why she has not settled down with a man. She wants a man that is simple; she sets the bar high. She has worked with you the years of maturing."

"The boy's manhood is not measuring up every time she is dating. Secretly she would have wanted to get you in bed with her."

"She overheard you talk about orgasm at the office, and she knew that you had a secret affair with a German woman. Yes, she did not miss anything, which makes her so good."

"She knew that a night with you would set a benchmark for satisfaction. She wanted it, but office protocol made it impossible, and she lived at home with her parents. It was too many obstacles to overcome."

"When we shared a room during training, we talked about it and would have done a three-way if possible."

"But once again, too many office staff to keep an eye on the rooms. They made sure that everybody stayed in the rooms and then the Curfew! We both wanted you so bad, and her misfortune not to find a person to give her fulfillment makes me sad."

"You know the thing about sex is control. I was lucky; my man took charge at once and took matters into his power. He serviced me with multiple orgasms the very first time."

"If a man does not take control, then the woman takes over; she knows at once, he will be a weak man."

"Women settle for it for the lack of a real man. Others are frustrated all their life or go elsewhere to get a one-night stand. The search for the real man continues in secret. If this man is found and available by chance, a divorce will happen the next day! That is the raw truth about life."

"If young girls would trust their virginity to an experienced mature man and reach the pinnacle with the first intimate experience, they would take this as a benchmark of performance."

"Young men will succeed in their chase only if they can deliver the goods."

"I will teach that to Kyra when she is mature enough to enter a sexual relationship. It makes the foundation for healthier families."

******

The baptism was at sunrise on the beach. The waves are the calmest in the morning at this most symbolic location.

Shorts and dress shirt with the sleeves rolled up. You will be standing in the water, holding Kyra's hand. Godfather and Godmother are doing their duty and pledge to be the guardian should the girl ever need help. My younger sister will be the Godmother. The priest does all the rest.

It will be carried out in a short time. During that time, Nina will light the candle.

Breakfast follows at the restaurant, and you will need to catch a plane home soon after.

"My little princess will sleep well tonight. She has a busy day tomorrow. I am so happy to have had this time with you again. Hug and kiss and good night! Visit any time and do it often. I miss you, my love!"

The baptism was a wet affair and over within 20 minutes, just as Priscilla had described it.

******

On the flight back, Nina started to count the people we met these three days and the affects you made on their lives. "Do you plan this ahead of time?" No, honey, this can never be planned; if you did, it would not go this way.

"Then what is it that sets all this in motion?" Good question; let me say this! Positive reactions come from success. When you set out to do something, do it with the best efforts, then the fruits of your labor show results. Action brings good or bad reactions; the results will be there.

In my case, it was a chain reaction of good actions. It's the best answer I can give you.

CHAPTER 9

The flight to California leaves at ten and arrives after 11:30 am, and it will give me the whole day to meet with the Office Staff. Alexander Is the Vice President and is in charge of the West Coast operation.

Angela runs the onboard hotel department, and Greta is my contact person for food and beverage purchasing. Greta has been holding the food department together since the former Director left.

We have two ships on this side, the smaller one is the Columbia, and the giant vessel is called the Moon Dancer. A seven-day itinerary for this one, while the Columbia makes three days on weekends and four-weekday trips to Ensenada and back.

Alexander greeted me and welcomed me to his team. A nice touch from an experienced shipping man who knows everything about the two ships.

I liked this from the moment we met.

Angela looked energetic, a multitasker; her accent is unmistakably Southern German. "I did my internship at the Seehof Hotel in Meersburg."

My hometown is 15 miles away from Meersburg. "My family is near Heidelberg; I did it for two years am See in Meersburg, accidentally switching to German. The Bodensee is still my favorite place!" We'll talk later at lunch. Your predecessor had complete control over Greta, I tell more later."

A quick introduction with Greta; she looked busy placing orders for the second ship returning to port in two days.

I'll let you get back to your work; deadlines are looming, I understand. Can we meet after you are finished with these orders?

"Yes, by 3 pm, I am OK."

A desk was set up for me with minimal supplies and only pencils: "You have a place to hang your hat," Alex mentioned.

From the eraser part of the pencils, I concluded that this man took only brief notes and erased them afterward. The desk was empty, but a crumpled note was left behind. "Next week, max load with plus $."

Interesting. Let me keep this; Angela or Greta can shed light on it. It made me suspicious.

Nobody had revealed the reason for this man's departure. My predecessor, why did he leave? "We'll talk at lunch, OK? "

Angela took me to a waterfront restaurant with outside seating.

Sitting in the sun at the waterfront took me back to San Diego. I had lived in San Diego in the late sixty's., A Chef's job at the hotel on Mission Bay.

"I stayed there once; it was a charming hotel, but there were too many Los Angeles people, and you could not get breakfast in that small coffee shop."

I am all too familiar with the problem. But these details at another time.

Tell me about the character of the man who vacated the job.

"You use a nice word, vacated; he got his ass kicked out of here. He was abusing Filipino boys on the ship and always had his favorites. They would not say a word for fear of being sent home. He tried a new boy when his choice was on leave, and he picked an aggressive boy who did not tolerate his sick game. This boy came right to the top in here.

We learned about the cruelty and insatiable drive to abuse young boys. The story was collaborated by a dozen others he had tried, which sealed his faith. The police took him away, and in days, he made bail and left the country. Your boss liked him; he is still complaining about the harsh treatment the scum received."

Good to know when I write the report, I will keep him out of the distribution.

What was his relationship with Greta?

"Do the job for which we hired you. You have no authority to question my work."

Greta is a great person but was restricted. Her suggestions were ignored, and he cussed her out. He treated her harshly and almost made her quit. Alexander talked her into staying.

"She will be a bit cautious until she knows you. She knows that you are German, and with me being from the same race, she will extend her trust as she does to me. She likes a straight shooter."

"Treat her respectfully, and she will run the show for you here. We have money in the budget from the terminated man's salary. We need to upgrade her to a management position. She is worthy of it and will be your assistant on this side of the US."

"Alexander and your boss are at odds. A sort of power struggle. Now this joker you replaced in Miami wants to push his weight around to run the dry docks. Alex stopped it."

"You are sailing for three days tomorrow. We have everything ready for you to go on board; we just need to copy the passport. I see you still have your German passport and the green card."

"I will introduce you to the Captain and officers. He is a Greek captain. You will like him. He is fun."

"The ship has a long history of transporting the unwanted from England to Australia. The penal colony was set up at that time. The ship changed hands with a new name each time until it landed here with us as a cruise ship. She is sturdy and seaworthy for long voyages. With ample space for storage and provisions, you can well imagine what they had to load for a six-week journey. We do have our challenges, but you will see this for yourself."

Lunch at this restaurant was a fresh and good fish sandwich made with Seabass. My favorite from San Diego! By two pm, we made it back, and Greta was ready for me.

Please explain the process. We can take it from there, and you walk me through the operation.

"I had been doing what was dictated by this departing man.

I noticed her disgust in her tone of voice. "Please do not think that I do not know better."

Angela filled me in on this; you are friends. I know it will change quickly, but I want your feedback. We will make these changes together.

"This guy had called the vendors and set the price. The same goes for quality, and there is room for improvement. I have set up visits with the produce, fish, and meat vendor. Meanwhile, I am taking bids and screening as best I know. With your fresh eyes you can form an unbiased impression, this is most important."

"The deliveries did not get checked at the dock when we received the goods. He claimed to have done either at the plant or on the truck."

I get the drift. "I thought you would not waste time."

"I am checking the invoices and giving them for payment. We do that right here. Miami is not involved at all. He tripled the lobster order to the Moon Dancer, claiming the upcoming price hike due to shortages."

We don't know of an impending price hike on the East Coast. It is a warm-water Caribbean Lobster, also known as Crayfish. Please cancel this delivery and stick with the one-week consumption.

"OK, this makes my day." I showed her the handwritten note. "Yes, that's the day he ordered me to place this large order."

"The Chief Steward on the Moon Dancer also has dirty hands. Keep this in mind when you sail and watch your back."

"We are ok in the bar. This man did not know much about the bar business. He relied on the bar manager, and this he is a good manager."

We are off to a good start. I want you to think inclusive. We work together and decide together. You are my trusted partner. I need to rely on your observation and feedback. Since I cannot be in two locations at once, communication is vital.

I am thinking of appointing you Purchasing manager. It requires approval from Alex, and the same goes for the proper salary increase. You have earned it and been the stable Icon in the department.

"I love it and am happy to finally be included in a team!"

She had tears in her eyes and came to hug me. What could be better than this expression; I knew I had a trusted partner.

Angela watched the scene and laughed; "you are suckers for hugs;" it sounds like you want one too?

Angela told me as we left the building, " You had made considerable headway with her. She likes your approach to being inclusive, which was a key element that lifted her commitment."

Alexander wants to have dinner with the two of us. Does he speak German? "No, but he can swear in German."

We met at the Greek restaurant. First, we had cocktails and made small talk, and then Alex told me that he had called friends to get the scoop on me.

"You had hot actions in Pittsburgh with your boss and in NYC with the Union. You took a big chance in New York; you know they own a shoe store!"

I was factoring this in when it came time to face the Union. I gave them a choice either face the law or stand down.

"You can play hardball!" I play to win; if this takes down the Union, so be it.

"No fear?" Yes, Angela, but this was a calculated risk, and since I had gone so far already, I had to follow through. It's like taking half an aspirin for a headache; the headache will return.

I delivered a second blow with the Maître D. I set up this one, so the hotel management had to follow through. They learned the scenario the first time. It made for a double whammy, and the Union begged not to get the law involved this time.

The Union turned back the clock on ten years of past practice. That was the best of all, chasing them back into the foxhole and throwing dirt on top.

"Someday, we sail together. I want to hear the entire story and your strategy."

"You are the right man for us. I knew this when I saw your background and diverse experiences. I see a little bit of a Pirate in a captain. The Captain has full authority on his ship."

I am familiar with Pirates; I brought one back from his grave in Barbados. Do I have you guessing?

Alexander had ordered from the Greek menu.

Fried Saganaki, shrimp, octopus marinated in lemon and oregano, Kalamata olives, eggplant salad, and sea urchins!

"Do you eat these?" Alex was pointing to the Urchins.

A Chef must try it. I like them, but I know you fancy them; go ahead; you don't need to share.

Any restaurant daring to serve Urchins has fresh fish. That speaks for itself.

******

While working for this Hotel corporation as a Regional Director, I had the hotel in Barbados. It is built like a Castle, and the original builder was a Captain turned Pirate.

He lived from the same spot where he crashed his ship, a coral reef just before the beach where the castle stands high on a cliff.

He would lure other ships to the reef with lanterns, making it look like the Harbor channel. When the ship crashed, he captured the sailors and the Captain and plundered the goods. It is a true story!

The company added a wing of hotel rooms and a specialty restaurant. That one is a story in itself, and it has to do with my adoption, but first, this.

As we approached the opening of the rooms and restaurant, I was there for Grand opening preparations and looked at this majestic dinner table sitting in the lobby. The table was used as a decorative furnishing.

The night auditors observed me behind the front desk.

They did not know me but noticed a man snooping around this table and looking at it from all sides.

Two attractive girls are now asking. "Can we help you?"

Yes, is this table from the original owner, and has this table ever been used to serve dinner?

"No, but we are missing a fantastic opportunity." I looked at this table and thought twelve people could eat at it and make the hotel money. But it must be something special.

An entrepreneur in her, I thought. I already had the idea of a theme dinner in the format of the king holding court, but in this case, it will be the Captain to host the table.

I asked the girls if they had anything particular in mind. The other girl said she fantasized about dining with a pirate.

It became the starting point of a Pirates dinner we staged with the help of these two girls.

They were in drama school and looked at it as a stage production. We can help secure costume lighting, a producer, and an actor to play the pirated role. We want to take part as wenches pouring drinks to the guests."

Turning back the clock to Captain Pirates' time. He used to host such lavish dinners. I was surprised at the detail these girls had presented. Yes, I will support it and give it to the General Manager.

This can become a signature item for the resort. If we can pull this off shortly before the grand opening, what better way to impress the dignitaries and get free press?

Further planning with the girls surfaced the actor as the professor, stage lighting, and about everything a Broadway production presents. The girls will be wearing an old costume dress with a low-cut top. Their blessed proportions will serve this role perfectly.

It's a go, and I told the girls. They went to work to sign up everyone needed.

I secured a menu, servers, and table appointments with old-fashioned pewter tankards; the setting is perfect.

The grand opening took place, and everybody was accommodated in the restaurant with a lavish dinner.

The Captain's Table had been rehearsed. We are ready for showtime.

I was a bit nervous at first, but my nerves settled down once the guests were seated, and the torches were lit.

Out comes the seafood appetizers. The girls are busy filling the tankards with either beer or rum punch, and the men get a little peek into the cleavage.

The main course came out on wooden stretchers. The server carved it, and then the moment! A whole pig was placed in the middle of the table.

Smoke, dimmed lights, and a pounding noise on the wooden floor: the Pirate made his entrance. Wearing head scarves, an eye patch, and a parrot on his shoulder, he continued striking his wooden leg.

"Greetings, my honored Guests. It has been a while since I enjoyed being with such good company. Ladies, you look delightful. I am Lord and Captain Samuel.

I used these dinners in the past to influence the local politicians. You know, love and influence go through the stomach. It gave me prestige and respect. I had come a long way from when I crashed my schooner on the reef. I have no regrets; my life has been good. I had my pleasure with fair maidens, but I never abused any. They had fun with me also.

Eat well and drink, for I must go; my time is up. God's speed and calm seas."

A stretcher filled with flaming bananas came as dessert to crown the feast.

We received ample press coverage, and this dinner is sold out months in advance.

******

Our dinner at the restaurant came to the table. A whole fish on a platter came to our table. Roast potatoes, a sauce made from the pan juices and fennel as the vegetable,

Simple and most delicious, they know their fish. Herbal aromas filled the air while the senior server took it skillfully apart.

Dessert at a Greek restaurant is always the honey-drenched baklava with walnuts.

Thank you, Alex; this meal was a treat.

"What is the deal with a daughter on the Island?" Angela, it will be too late; we must postpone this to another day, OK?

Sailing with Columbia felt like being on a Schooner. Slowly cutting the water, a little wake, and a quiet engine with just a hum was noticeable.

The Greek Captain with an Asian crew had sailed the ship for the last five years.

After rigorous schooling and technical training in electronics, he became captain and joined this company with the acquisition of this ship.

Safety is his highest priority; the crew comes right after. He knows that nothing goes right if the staff is not happy.

At my first meeting with the Captain, he wanted to learn everything from me.

I must have recited my resume. I told the Captain my family background and how I came to sign on with this company. He thought I sold out too cheap. You should have held out for more money. I understand the position was the only opening at that time.

He described the predecessor's activities and what he was suspected of doing to young Filipino boys.

"He was on this ship sailing a whole week, meaning the three-plus, four-day voyage under the pretense of training the crew. My night watchman walked by his cabin and heard noises like a crying child.

Knowing that this man was in it, he became suspicious. It could not be him, a grown man; something strange must be happening. He came to the bridge and spoke to the senior officer, who went with him to verify it, and there was still the same crying noise.

This officer woke the staff captain, and he took a security officer with him and knocked at the door, but he would not open it. The bypass key opened the security lock, and they found this boy naked on the bed, bloody at his buttocks, and the Food Director standing over the boy.

"We caught a child abuser in the act. The staff captain called me to see the scene, and I ordered his arrest. Port police came on board the ship and took him away.

He was interrogated, and bail was set. It made him a free man when he made bail with a bond until the court set a trial date. The next day, Alexander fired him. He packed his desk and fled to Manila."

"Can you imagine how he damaged this kid's life? He was only eighteen. I was sick and swore to screen everyone coming on my ship. My crew is my family, aside from my land-locked attorney wife. She is working on the papers for a green card."

"I see we have an honorable man in you. The girls will benefit from you the way I see it."

Smiles, and that was my acceptance interview.

Mike, an American citizen who lives in California, shares his house with his daughter. Years ago, he lost his wife to illness and decided to try life at sea. The Chief Steward Mike looked like he had been at sea all his life. His bald head and stark white beard gave him the salty look of a seafarer.

"I need to be around people and stay busy. He fits the profile of a social host and with his hospitality experience, he combines his work with social skills."

His crew members are his kids. He refers to a drink as a "toddy."

I like Mike. He is a doer, listens to instructions, and comes forward with suggestions. Mike gets involved with the workers, and I noticed he is generous with praise.

It's refreshing to have a manager of his caliber being my contact person. It makes life easy and fun.

He introduced me to Chef Danny while the Kitchen was preparing the evening meal.

We will do a buffet that night since we leave late, and the embarkation will continue. The Chef and his cooks are from the Philippines.

"Hello, Chief! This familiar greeting by the chorus of cooks makes me feel welcome. Hello, Magandang Gabi!. "Thank you for your honor; you try to speak our language."

Mike told them I was German and let them think I had just arrived from Germany.

I told them that I had also worked in large kitchens at an early age and was a Chef like Danny. I live in Florida and have been in the US for years.

The introduction was received with great respect. "You can teach us German food, all smiling."

First, I want to be spoiled by your fine cooking, and then I will write to all your families about your great job here.

"Thank you, Chief, thank you for thinking of our families!"

The bar manager is from Ireland. Meet Mark, who was recently promoted and transferred from the Moon Dancer.

Mark stood erect and formal, shook hands, and asked me what I wanted to see.

 Nothing, this is not an inspection. I will ask when I have questions. Other than that, follow your routine. That is all I wish to see: your daily work cycle, your practice, and the business flow.

If you can show me the storeroom, I'd be interested. I am told it is spacious!

"Down at the bottom of the ship, we are just above the Kiel, and we have the place where it is always calm and the most stable. You will not feel any rocking and sound. The waterline is above, and the wake that creates the sound is just above.

We have ample room, as one would have expected. The ship was used for long voyages as a transport vessel to Australia. It helps us now."

I noticed the maintenance was far superior as compared to the Turquoise seas. Money was being spent to renew those worn-out parts, and the cleaning was superb. I did not see any debris. The paper, cardboard, and wooden crates are burned, and all food waste is flushed out to sea.

Plastic stuff got crushed and bagged and landed in the home port of San Pedro.

"USPH was here just this morning. We got a ninety-eight. We are good for six months, but we never let our guard down. It's best to run on their standards. The Captain does a weekly inspection, and sometimes we argue over little details."

"Can you settle an argument we face with the Captain on his inspection? He wants the cooks to wear gloves at all times. He is citing food safety."

Gloves must be worn when a cook handles the food during plating and anything ready to be eaten. I want them to wear gloves when they handle raw fish and chicken.

All food items that go into a cooking process do not need gloves. Use your hands and wash them every time a task is completed. The same goes for the workstation, cutting boards, and knives.

Keep a spray bottle strategically to follow up on the cleaning and kill the bacteria with a 100m part bleach solution. That will keep everybody safe.

"Clean as you go" is the slogan. I would encourage you to post this slogan around the area.

I want you to get a power spray washer and clean the kitchen from top to bottom. The machine uses small amounts of water, but the water's power will reach every corner.

What do you serve if I order a glass of white wine? "We have these 1.5-liter house wines."

I know you oversee the wine sales, and the wine stewards report to you on the sales while the dining manager guides the service. Please ask them to make a list of the best-selling wines and the ones that never sell.

I want to say hello to the service crew.

"Tread carefully. The servers are a group of boys that have been constantly abused. Tell them you are from Germany. They all have dreams of going there and becoming German. They hold this country in high regard. The boys all worked in big hotels with German management."

That is excellent advice from you.

"The Chief has a word with you; pay attention." We have a new boss from the office in Miami. He will sail with us on this voyage. He is German!"

Applause broke out, and everyone had big smiles on their faces. I started with my full name and said I had worked in Asia but never reached Manila.

I will go there one day, and then I will visit your families and wish them well.

"Thank you for thinking of our families."

Go about your work as if I don't exist; I want to be incognito and treat me like any other passenger. Otherwise, I have to come in disguise and be a ghost!

"You are kidding, good sense of humor, typical Germany."

Please seat me with lovely people; they do not have to be the oldest or ugliest. " Yes, Chief, I take care of it."

"It was a good introduction. How did you know about the family angle?"

My boss in Miami is married to a Filipina, and she gave me instructions. Know your workers; management 102!

A wine merchant had made this wine list. I could have guessed the outcome; it was always the same scenario.

Mark, let me explain some ideas on wine sales. The inventory must be sold soon. Wine does not like to be rocked like a baby. You may know what the Greeks did in the early days of warfare to preserve wine. They added tree sap, also referred to as Resin, to the wine. Thus, the name Retsina.

One needs to get used to it since they still do it today but with a lesser amount.

We have a better choice. We can sell the wine by the glass and stop buying the house wine. You can start tonight. Calculate the sales price as one-fourth of the bottles' selling price. If you measure tightly, it will give you a fifth glass, but I want to be generous. The remnant can be used as a taster to convince the passengers to buy it or poured off to the ones still nursing the wine.

Bartenders and wine servers will make recommendations from the wines that are already open for that day.

We have 45 minutes to dinner; can I get a Negroni, please?

"Drinking habits are like fashion; they go in and out of favors. We have more demand for the white alcohol, and still, the office keeps sending the routine brown stuff."

I need a complete inventory. I will instruct Gracie on the adjustments. Hang tight with the Appleton rum. I have a plan for that product. "Will selling these expensive wines in this fashion impact the bar cost?"

Let me explain it this way. Every bottle sitting idle is at a one hundred percent cost.

Once a glass of this wine is sold, the cost is reduced by the sale. You keep selling, and the price decreases in proportion to the sales. When all the inventory is depleted on account of the deal, the cost is zero, the money is returned to the company, and a profit will top it.

The bar cost measures revenue to purchase cost. We often get hung up on a percentage and forget the dollar amounts. More dollars mean more company profits.

"I see it now from a different angle. We have no risk when we sell the wine by the glass. To sell it is our aim by the bottle or glass; a sale is a sale, and money is trading places. I got it now!"

I will call this illuminating because I saw the light go on in your head! Good joke!

The wine steward overheard this conversation and added.

"Thank you, Chief, it will also expand our market. The person sitting at a large table with strangers hesitates to buy a wine bottle. We offer to hold it over to the next dinner, but the hesitation is a tall order to overcome. The sale by the glass gives him a chance to select his preferred choice, and he won't have to share. The same goes for couples who drink different wines. Women tend to prefer whites, and the husband who wants a red wine will now have the selection of a fine wine for himself."

At the bar, you will see that a good quality wine will be consumed faster than the current house wine. A second order is likely, and so goes the sales and compiling revenues.

We still serve a glass of cheap Champagne at the Captain's Gala party. "Yes, it's free; we don't get revenue."

You just said the keyword: no revenue! Here comes another method or doctrine.

If you were to serve a good quality wine, Champagne, or cocktail for free and limit it to one glass, you would run a higher cost. However, you are introducing a beverage of your choice to feature as a promotional item and whet the appetite by giving it away.

This beverage will continue to sell throughout the cruise and make the cost back. What do you think about this idea?

"You are testing me, I can tell."

It's not a trick question; I have it in mind with the Appleton rum. I am not ready to go with it. I need an ingredient to make the drink, but you can do a fantastic Margarita. Bring it out after the Ensenada Senior Frog party and make it an excellent drink. Do it for the Captain's Gala. The first one is free; all orders after that are for the money.

I have a connection in Barbados to get Falernum shipped to the office. Regular supplies will soon become available from a liquor purveyor.

She is my daughter. "How come? Have been married in Barbados?" No, it's a long story for a sea day, we need a couple of hours.

"What is Falernum?" It is a liqueur with an intriguing spice flavor. On the island, it is an ingredient in rum punch, which is the best there is. My daughter is married to the Appleton family.

I must go to meet my table mates. "Don't forget; the Captain wants you at his table tomorrow night."

I was seated with six other people, two couples and two single women.

The dining room manager introduced everybody around the table.

This was a nice touch to break the ice. It gave away my mystery status as a single passenger.

Molly and Daniela are from Bakersville, California; the others, I did not get their town. They told me it was some valley inland from Los Angeles.

Daniela sat next to me and became an interesting conversation partner. A talker that had to know every personal detail, private or professional. The routine questions can turn me off. But I am on the job and must be hospitable.

I answered them, and in the process, I learned that she was here with her aunt and Bakerville is a hick town close to the mountains. She stated her name again as Daniela, and she was traveling with Aunt Molly.

It was their first vacation and was seen as an adventure. ' From that conversation, I drew my conclusions. It will be small talk until I change the subject and engage her in a more substantive discussion.

She saw the crew and placed them as Asians; she had seen the Captain's picture at the check-in desk, and he was from Greece.

I am originally from Germany and years ago, I made a voyage by ship across the Atlantic from Europe to New York. I live in Florida, and the company's office is in Miami. I hoped to have settled the questions by volunteering my heritage.

"I wanted to go to Europe after graduation but had no money." Did you not have any savings? No, I was hoping that my parents would pay for the trip."

You should have planned for it and put money aside in a savings account. You pay the bills last and pay yourself first by setting a fixed amount aside.

It will force you to curtail your spending habits. Only this way will you ever accumulate any wealth.

"What do you mean by it? " When you get your paycheck or cash, put money aside into an account you do not want to touch; restrict it if the bank supplies such a thing, but you let it accumulate in a fund and collect interest. Never touching the principal is the first rule; invest it as if this money does not exist.

"Are you an investment advisor?" No, I was given this advice once and followed it to buy a house.

The dinner service was friendly and discrete while we conversed. Her questions became more substantive. I was not able to tell stories and purposely shot my answers. Mark had already started to press me for stories.

The dessert was uneventful, and I need to fix this. The end of a meal must be a highlight.

I remembered this company I used in San Diego called Fantasia Confectioners. The same goes for crusty bread. Gracie can do the homework next week.

Aunt Molly announced that she had driven and was ready for bed. "I want to talk to this fine man a bit more; he is worldly and exciting. I never meet people like him in our hick town."

"Can we have a nightcap in the bar?"

She rubbed elbows and guided the conversation toward spending the night together. "You must have a private room; can we go there?"

She had me undressed and started to work me over while I was doing the same to her. The slender body of a 20-year-old girl is undoubtedly worth a sin. I stimulated her senses and worked my way from the head down to the toes.

She was surprised that a man was doing this to her. It is called foreplay, but she tried to rush me. I had her under my control, and she gave her body to my caressing.

Slowly and calculated, I drove her close to the high point and serviced her as no man had done so far.

Oh, ah, oh God, oh God, screaming sounds, and then she was out of breath.

"Was this an orgasm? I have never had it so strong." Yes, Daniela, it must have been your first.

"I never even got close to it! The boys at home finish within three minutes and then go limp. Then they want to leave."

It gets better the second time around. "Tomorrow?" No, right now, you are still warmed up, and it is the best time to carry on.

The night we carried on until early morning. Did I awaken a sleeping Nympho?

****

"Captains Gala Night"

Mark already had drink service going, and people lined up for the handshake on the receiving line. He announced to me that he was serving Margaritas and Champagne.

Margarita, for the Captain, was pleased to see a change.

The guest list at the Captain's table included the two single women, Molly, and Daniela.

The Captain must have instructed the hostess to seat the younger of the two single women next to him.

He was on a mission; that was obvious. He looked at Aunt Molly and signaled with his eyes for me to look after her.

He was working with Daniela with charm; of course, the uniform worked every time to impress a young girl. His stories as the Captain captivated Daniela. Her eyes told the story, and she intended to go to bed with this vital man. It will be like a trophy and make friends at home envious.

Daniela felt important. He gave her an espresso and his favorite Anisette and took her by her hand to his room.

Molly will not be left out of this action. She grabbed me by my private part and dragged me to my room. It may have been a fantasy to have sex while on vacation, a form of conquest, judging by her actions.

The night, I turned out raw and satisfying to her. It was too feral, just not my style. A woman must feel this way when a man takes pleasure in himself and walks away after that.

The following evening, Daniela sat next to me for dinner.

"Can I have an encore with you? The Captain was OK but did not come close to your service."

With it, a short three-day weekend ended. Two happy women returned to their boring town and would like to brag about their adventures at sea.

I bid the Captain Fair wind and calm seas and disappeared to make my call to Barbados from the office.

Priscilla! "Hello, Dad, what a pleasant surprise. What gets you to call this morning?"

How's the little princess and your good man? "She is growing too fast, and he is super busy."

I have an idea! I have promised the bar manager a couple of bottles of Falernum.

"You could not call at a better time. My brother-in-law is going to Miami to settle a contract with Bacardi.

A distribution arrangement will be signed, including the high-end quality of the Appleton rum.

He will have the product with him. I will ask him to mail it to UPS to the Los Angeles office. Please give me the address! The Falernum should be available in a month from any Bacardi distributor.

Isn't it great how two fierce competitors have come together?" Excellent, you are an angel; I love you forever.

I had a little time to write notes and kept them in my desk drawer.

When I return from the next voyage, which is in seven days, I must follow up on pending items. Ideas tend to pile up, and we have paper for this.

Pending:

Dessert, Fantasia.

The wine list and sales techniques

The leafy products treatment, shame on me, I forgot it.

Bar sales

Rum Punch at Captain Gala

Purveyors visit and meats specs.

The lobster situation

******

The ship came in early and will be sailing before noon to make the long stretch to Mexico's famous resort city, Acapulco.

One-stop in Ensenada and San Diego may get canceled.

Weather and strong northbound currants are the reason to cancel San Diego.

The Captain was busy giving orders to push off. He welcomed me and promised to catch up later.

"The Chief Steward Niguel is from the UK. He is a close friend of the former Director and has the same preference as bed partners."

He avoided contacting me. We never even said hello; he looked cold and aloof. The first day, he disappeared whenever he saw me in the area.

I met the bar manager, Ari, from Greece. He gave me a tour to meet the dining room manager from Manila and the Chef from Thailand with an unpronounceable name. He was simply called Chef Bobby.

Ari took me to the bar and introduced me to his crew. After, we went to the staff mess room and had lunch.

The timing was great to meet all the staff personnel: casino dealers, Hairdressers, Entertainers, the doctor with the nurse, and the resident priest.

It is a busy place; the food looks good, and these people are well-fed. The Chef must be great.

"Yes, the man is excellent. He worked in major hotels in Bangkok. His English is improving, but it takes one to adjust to his pronunciation of the English language. With time, we know what he is saying."

Tell me about this, Chief Steward Niguel!

"He is heartbroken because the other Malacca has left. Niguel does not even know the circumstances. The office is very secretive, but my source is the German woman Angela. She told me in confidence." I do know the details about crew abuse. The man is a violent sexual predator and needs to be in jail. But I hear he left the country and bought a house in Manila."

"Niguel will be leaving since his contract is ending. I hope that the company will not bring him back anymore. He is the same predator and has tried it on this ship. The Chef and dining room manager are protecting the boys."

"Niguel is hiding and told me he had no desire to meet you."

The dual reporting. The wine stewards use the same system as we do on the Columbia. Please have them write up a list of wines that do not sell poorly or well.

I have an... "Yes, Mark told me already, and we can do the same and will start tomorrow. I must speak to the yeoman to make a little list of today's wine choices for the bar and the stewards."

Thank you, Mark; I like you even more. He is a good man.

" I trained him, a good boy! Did he also tell you what we discussed at the Captain's champagne reception?

"Yes, also a great idea. I always wanted to do it, but the Malacca would not approve it."

The latest, which Mark does not yet know! I called my daughter in Barbados to see if the rum company could get me Falernum.

"I know this stuff; it makes the most incredible rum punch. You said your daughter, yes, but how? "

It's a long story and involves a castle.

"The Pirate's place? I used to sail to Barbados on another ship and went to see this famous place. They have the best drinks on all the islands. Sadly, I could not see the Pirate's dinner. The bartender bragged about personally knowing this company executive who started all these promotional programs."

The girl working as the Chef in the specialty restaurant is my daughter by adoption.

As he told you, Priscilla is my daughter. She is married to the Appleton son. They have a darling girl, Kyra, whom I was privileged to name.

We will get the Falernum from a Bacardi distributor. Meanwhile, a case is being shipped to the office in San Pedro.

I am planning to introduce the rum punch only after the Captain has introduced his officers. With this, I am mulling over an idea that will involve the Captain as the person to make the introduction.

I expect to sell this rum punch throughout the week and hope it will become a bestseller. We give the first drink free; any added orders are for the money. This will be the method of recovering the cost.

Dinnertime food had a distinctly Asian flair. Soy sauce, lemon grass, and Thai chilies were added to the American menu.

I know the Chef means well and wants to show his Asian cooking skills. We can feature both cuisines separately but stay authentic. I must explain this to him.

Desserts are on the dull side, and the soft rolls are even worse. The bakers know good European bread. I noticed it in the staff mess room. An addition to my list is to increase the hard wheat flour. To catch the bakers, I must stay up past midnight.

OK. The Captain party will feature the Gala buffet. It will be late at night to see this presentation.

The first night's entertainment program featured the cruise director introducing his staff.

A juggler, magician, and comedian followed it. In all, it was a dismal performance. I wondered what they would offer on the following night.

My agenda called for a full night's sleep

At the breakfast buffet, I found pleasant surprises.

Fresh crusty rolls, French croissants, Danish pastries, fresh fruits peeled and cut, eggs to order, and watermelon carvings.

The coffee was disappointing. It was a simple American brand that was highly acidic and lacked aroma—another item for the purveyor's meeting list.

All provisions were put away in the storeroom. I was about to show them how to revive the leafy products when Chief Steward Niguel arrived.

He did not see me since I had been in the big cooler.

Suddenly he started to raise holy hell. "Why is the lobster order not on board?"

Are you short? I directed the question to the storekeeper.

"No, we have enough supply for at least four cruises."

Then why the big order, Niguel?

"The price had been rising lately, and we wanted to load up on the current price."

When the storekeeper told me the price per pound, I knew that approximately three dollars had been overstated.

OK, I will tell you a secret. Greta showed me this massive order and informed me of the overstocking this amount of lobster would cause. I asked her to cancel it; it's that simple!

"Thank you so much; it would not fit into the freezer."

Are there any other items on which we are overstocked? "The meat had been building up over weeks now. Strip loins and tenderloins, all the expensive cuts."

"Produce quality is inconsistent. Rotten oranges, apples, and lemons come in different sizes and never have a brand name quality. Lettuce is wilted, which I do not understand; These products are growing here in California. Berries, we have given up on those. The berries will be gone the next day when they come wet from the produce truck. We had to stop ordering."

Meanwhile, I noticed that Niguel had disappeared. The issue must have been too hot to argue.

Thank you for your time. I will visit all these suppliers and have a review of all the products. You should see a difference in freshness.

After all this commotion, I almost forgot to show the crew how to revive this lettuce.

I took it to the Kitchen to do the procedure. The Chef looked at me with a question on his mind.

First, we must deal with this; what I have done will bring it back to a crisp product. Then I promise you that these products will be of top quality in the future.

You will continue this process, for you must work with it for seven days. Tomorrow, you will see that this lettuce has grown in volume.

"Can I offer you a special Thai dish tonight?"

Thank you, Chef. I must see the same food that passengers receive. Otherwise, I do not have a starting point. "I want to cook something special for you."

Please do not be offended. Another time, I gladly accept your gracious offer.

"Can you help me to upgrade the desserts?"

I have a plan and will get back to you with the details. Without a pastry Chef, it is a challenge, and I know that you have seen the best in the business from your Thai hotel experience.

"I am happy to have a professional working with me, and I hope that Mr. Niguel does not return. He is a terror, always hits on the boys, and they come to me for protection. Sometimes I have four boys sharing my cabin."

It's his very last voyage, I guarantee. "Thank you, Chief."

I can tell that it is going to be a testy week. At one time, I will have to confront and ask Niguel questions.

Hostess duties for this ship included entertaining a group of passengers with a separate dinner.

When the Captain cannot place every VIP on his gala dinner table, the Hostess must fill as the host on a different night. High-volume-producing travel agencies must be recognized.

Eva found herself in a predicament. All her dinner guests were women. She needs men to mix the guests.

A young officer volunteered, and with my volunteering, we were the only men at the table.

The conversation is about the travel location each one has been to. One wants to outshine the other. It turns into a contest.

I once saw this kind of contest at a hotel cocktail party. Travel agents were complaining and talking down the hotels.

I was wondering how they can successfully sell a vacation or a cruise.

Are the brochures and colorful posters doing the job for them?

I was seated to the right of Eva, the Hostess. Two women followed, and a man was between another pair of women. Three men, six women, and the Hostess filled the table of ten.

Eva introduced herself to the guest. Then, she named the officer and, after me, the name and position in the company.

The officer received the attention of the women. What is your rank, and what do the stripes stand for?

I was relieved and thought that I would be overlooked.

Fat chance: here come the questions when I speak my first words.

"Where are you from, and where are your stripes?"

I told them that I am from Miami and the stripes are on the flag along with fifty stars. "Funny, but you have a good sense of humor."

"You speak with an accent; tell us your home country."

Now, you are asking a specific question. I will tell you that I grew up in Germany but not in Berlin, Munich, Frankfurt, or Heidelberg.

My hometown is near the Swiss border. It is a small village that is not visible on a map.

It could have been a brilliant stroke of Hostess Eva. She had my undivided attention, and we had an exciting conversation about the ship's history, company, and characters she usually gets to meet.

The wine had been pre-selected and was on the fruity side.

Do you like the wine this light? "No, but the wine steward made a choice; since I do not know much about wines, I rely on him."

You can tell him whether you like red, white, sweet, or dry.

We can have a tasting during happy hour. We are selling fine wines by the glass starting tonight.

It's attractive, and I would love it. It will help me make a good impression on the guests.

Tell me something of interest about you!

I am a country boy who grew up in a small village with nine hundred people.

"I would have expected you to have grown up in a city. You are so worldly."

I worked in Switzerland, visited Washington, D.C., Montreal, and New Delhi, and returned to the USA by ship.

I landed in San Francisco and then flew to Miami. I had a job waiting for me, and I needed to hurry.

My job took me to Key Biscayne, Florida; Buffalo, Minneapolis, San Diego; Hartford; Bethesda, MD; Fort Lauderdale again; Pittsburgh; and back to Davie, near Fort Lauderdale.

"Wow! That is a mouth full, and that explains it."

Dessert was on the table, and she had to make a little speech.

Ladies and gentlemen, welcome again to our ship and this voyage. She continued by telling how much the company valued its contribution to a successful cruise line. Keep them coming and do come again for the pleasure of your company.

The young girl across the table had been watching us and eavesdropping. She motioned to me her interest in talking to me after dinner. OK, the diver's thumb up to signal a yes. We waited for Eva to finish her speech and met at the bar.

We have a wine lecture and tasting date tomorrow at 5 pm.

The girl told me she had overheard my conversation with Eva and would like to hear more.

She is traveling with an agent in her office. Her manager is introducing her to the cruise business as a newly hired person.

"My background is also from a small village. People have a level of naivete towards our country's heritage.

Despite my newly hired status, I sold the most cruises in the office."

"Of course, my manager would never admit this! I see this cruise as a reward for excellent work and recognition from the owners. And that is the real reason I was given this cruise as a thank you.

I heard you telling the Hostess all the places you had lived. Have you lived there and held a job?"

Yes, dear, what is your name? "Nicole," nice to meet you.

"Do you run this ship? Yes, and two more, but only Food & Beverage service. I manage from a distance; I come on board to implement, control, and see to the crew's welfare. It is a tough job.

"You came on board with us, and is this your first voyage? What have you found out in the first two days?"

I have a list of items already.

The desserts are excellent and tasty but bland. The lettuce came on board in awful condition. We are now regenerating the lettuce and all the leafy stuff to get it crisp again. We don't have berries on board because they don't know how to keep them fresh.

The wine we drank was the wrong choice. The sweetness did not pair with or complement the food.

On the contrary, it overpowered the dinner.

I will give you tips that you can use at home. When you buy a head of lettuce, it is already a week old.

The time from the field to your table will cause moisture loss in the green leaves and wilt.

The plant preserves itself by extracting the water from the outer layer to feed it to the heart.

The same way your body reacts to the cold. Nature takes the blood and pulls it inside to preserve the organs.

The heart is the last organ to give up. To preserve the core, all other organs may be damaged.

We cut the stem of the lettuce a little to show a fresh cut, then submerged the lettuce in cold water. After fifteen minutes, you can remove the lettuce and let it drip dry. The lettuce will still have ample moisture between the leaves; with this, you place it in a cloth-lined box or bowl.

Wrap the extra cloth on top and cover the container.

The fabric will recycle the moisture and make it crip again. In a day, you will see a larger heads of greens, and it will be fresh and crisp.

If you don't believe me, try it; you will eat crispy lettuce all week long. The berries are simple. The moisture is the devil here.

She was so excited and kissed me on the cheek.

We had a glass of wine. Do you like this wine? It is the house wine. By the second glass, she had a buzz on. I knew where this would lead. "Do you have your cabin? I mean, you do not have to share."

Yes, I have my private room.

"I want to show you my appreciation. Can we go there?"

She was not a beginner and told me she had lost her virginity on her eighteenth birthday. She had a plan to prove that a mature man is the better lover.

"All my friends had a disappointing experience with young men!"

Her expectations had been high. I did my best to deliver to her satisfaction. She let me do my preparation and patiently expected the excitement until she reached her first high point. Her body moved in the same rhythm, making it much better. This method had worked so well, and now she was soaked wet.

The sheets need a change. I am not sleeping in a wet bed.

Housekeeping had the foresight to place extra sheets in the linen closet. She stayed the night and slept in late.

We met again for breakfast on the deck.

She looked embarrassed;" how do I explain this to my colleague? "

Tell her the truth: what is wrong with making love? It was not just raw sex; we did it with emotions and great satisfaction. She will be envious, but such is life.

When we reached Mexican waters came an announcement from the Captain. The first visit to explore this foreign country made these Mid-westerners act like little children.

"Do not bring drugs on board. Do not drink the water!" A warning followed and was repeated at the gangway.

Senior Frogs in Ensenada are popular and patronized by the crew.

Women and girls are enticed with giant margaritas while the crew lures around, hoping to aid a woman back to the ship.

His reward served a mutual need.

Nicole's colleague fell into this trap.

Eva had a date to learn and sample wines to expand her knowledge. It was her day off.

For taster portions only, I instructed the bartender and continued with the lecture on how to choose and where to get information about in the wine.

Then, there is the need to match it with the main course; remember this: Wine will taste a little different when food is consumed. A wine that seems too acidic or high in alcohol will adapt to the food.

Look for certain characters and flavors and relate them to the food.

I told her to leave it at that. There is no need to overload her with technical information, as it can get very confusing.

We had a day at sea, which gave me ample time to continue my work.

I noticed in the storeroom that the wine storage is at the ship's bow. The bar manager knew this and had been searching for a mid-ship location.

We approached the housekeeper and agreed to switch locations. It gave them a larger space and the wine found a quiet home.

Tonight is a grand show I want to watch; Nicole was asking if we could go together.

It's too obvious, remember I still work here! Come a little earlier or later. It will not look so obvious.

A classic Revue show with individual acts and dancers made for an action-filled evening. The passengers like it. It made up for the dismal first night's show.

Hollywood has talented entertainers who get the limelight for a time or a show and fall out of favor afterward. It supplies a pool of talents to tap for shows like the one tonight. These talents must bridge the time until the next call comes from the agent.

The Mamas and Papas had been last week's main act. Then the agent called, and off they went.

I wanted to see the bar action, but Nicole had other ideas. She is hooked on pleasures.

A warning signal for me was when a girl gets hooked and becomes aggressive, she will become possessive.

Give me advice. How will I find another man who will give me the same satisfaction I receive from you?

First, find a decent guy with character, stability, and compassion. You have to teach him. Train him in the art of making love. Do what I do to you; he will learn to follow your lead. Patience is going to be a challenge for you. He will realize the rewards are much more satisfying by taking the time.

******

Niguel showed up to see my work. In the butcher shop, I was in the middle of showing the butcher the proper specifications for the strip loin. This tail must not be part of the loin. Look at the angle cut at this side. It will lose you one steak. Then, the inside skin from the bones must be cut off, and also, this tough bottom part is not edible.

Your next delivery will include a lighter striploin and tenderloin. The eye is smaller, giving us a thick steak while cutting two ounces off the weight. We will save money that way. It will be delivered after I meet with the vendor.

Do you know meat specifications? I was looking at Niguel and the butcher.

"Not that good."

The quality grade is stamped with a blue round stamp about here. Sometimes, it is a clear mark; other times, it is a bit smeared. You cannot find one on this strip.

Any idea what this means?

It means this loin is ungraded, not the quality to deserve the grade choice or prime.

An old cow gets this no-roll, as they call it. This meat is used for sausage making and burgers because it is lean. Niguel, have you ever inspected the deliveries?

"No, never; I am too busy in the office handling the rating!"

I understand; you sort out the bad ratings before turning them in to be graded.

Did my predecessor order you to do this? "Yes, he commanded me to do it."

You can blame him now that he is gone. All the crew members are relieved by his departure!

"How can you insinuate this?"

I do know all about it. I spoke with the victims. He is a sick man who needs professional help or jail.

If we catch another person doing this, I will chop off his balls with this cleaver on this wooden block and feed the rotten balls to the rats.

Niguel turned pale and left.

The butcher was holding me by the arm; you have hit the nail on the head. He will be sacred and leave the boys alone.

It was the last I saw of him for the rest of the cruise! Ari told me he went to his cabin to hide.

When I repeated the scene, Ari laughed; good for you, don't take any shit from anybody.

That afternoon, Captain Anderson asked me to come to the bridge.

Come here anytime; we welcome friendly visitors. He showed me the electronic navigation system, the safety and watertight door chart, and the fire drills, and then he offered me an Aquavit. It is the Swedish equivalent of your Schnapps.

He gave a history of his family's maritime tradition and the routes he has taken ships through storms.

Like the Flying Dutchman in Wagner's opera, every Captain has storm stories.

"I know that one."

We talked about operas and classical music. I told him my first opera was like the first love; one never forgets.

Carmen was on the program at the Zurich Opera. The fiery Gypsy women with pitch-black hair and music to drive the Spanish rhythm. It stayed with me forever.

I purchased a tuxedo and the lowest-priced ticket in the nosebleed aisle. It is still my all-time favorite opera. Hearing the overture on the radio still gives me Goosebumps.

His favorite composer, of course, is Mendelson, the Midsummer night's Dream.

I love all classical music and listen to it exclusively; it is just so difficult to find a female friend who will love the same and go to performances.

"Have you made plans yet on how and what to improve?"

I must start with the basics. The first steps are buying good quality and checking the goods. We have room for improvement in handling the food, plate presentation, and temperature.

My list is growing; I told him what had happened earlier with the Chief Steward.

It's good to get rid of him.

We will bring Mike from the Columbia over to this ship.

"We look forward to having you onboard often. The work is endless, and you have big plans."

The bakers start by midnight, three Greek men with big arm muscles and a strong voice. It must be the language that forms the vocal cords!

The loaves or rolls are a given because they can produce crusty rolls.

To satisfy the need for it, I saved the leftover soft rolls and took them with me in a plastic bag.

Then, I checked the supply of Canadian hard wheat flour.

I asked the storekeeper to transfer the flower to the refrigerator or freezer. He looked at me with a question. It will prevent it from going live; you know, the weevils! Warm climates have more insects to find a home for eggs and a built-in buffet once they hatch.

These fine soft rolls are just not appreciated, and we want to have bread that will be consumed. Crusty rolls are always depleted. I see it in the officer's mess, and we serve them in the dining room on the night.

"We like these better too!"

Can we forget these soft ones and go with the crusty rolls or loaves?

"We love it, and it will be less work for us. One large batch of dough, and we are done early."

Tonight OK. Yes, by all means. The flour is in the freezer, and there is no extra meat.

Good. We will pull a day ahead to warm it in the bake shop.

I know Calimera. It was easy; I needed to learn a little Greek besides Malacca. I must ask the bar manager.

Magandang Umaga in tagalong means good morning; this is a starting point!

From 1 a.m. on, my night's sleep was like a whole week's rest. In the morning, I felt like a newborn.

******

Acapulco awakened emotions that still stirred in my guts from when we had to say goodbye to these beautiful employees.

I wished to meet and find out what had turned out for them in the aftermath of the hotel's closing

I was torn between visiting and not visiting, but I had to see the man selling blankets and Gonzal doing his sales magic at the beach.

The taxi ride was only five minutes, and I asked him to wait while I looked around.

The Building had the Radisson Brand on the top, where the proud name of my former company had once been.

The inside was fully renovated. If only they had done this when we still had the hotel. I met one housekeeper taking care of the public area. When she saw me, she remembered me from when my wallet had fallen out of my pocket.

She searched everywhere for me until finally she found and returned the wallet to me. I gave her a twenty-dollar bill, which she refused at first but took for her Children's sake.

She told me that the older people had retired, and the younger ones had once found work at the Hyatt and the big Princess hotel. It was to their advantage since the training they had received was well-known in hotel circles. They are all happy.

Back to the ship and a nap to get a head start for the busy night.

******

Captain's dinner again. The Hostess has since learned of my liaison with Nicole and invited her to the table.

At dinner, Captain Anderson hinted that there might be a merger. He received rumors from his homeland.

Merger? With whom will it be an actual merger when both sides come out ahead, or will it turn into a takeover? A big fish swallows the little offered as bait.

My thoughts went to Nina at home and how she is holding up since we still haven't bought this computer. Her son is looking forward to playing the expert and teaching us the workings of the software. The opportunity cannot be missed.

A merger will bring dramatic changes. All sorts of possibilities crossed my mind.

******

Next week's market visits in San Pedro came into focus. No doubt it will get testy.

Do I have enough proof of collusion with this lobster deal? The lobster deal is not clean. The surcharge on the price may prove such an opportunity.

Yes, we can consider stocking up for Alaska. If they want to force the sale, we will buy it at market price plus storage. Delivery will be taken as needed.

I can always put pressure on them by buying Canadian products. It will be Main Lobster and superior to this stuff.

It will cut them out of business for five months.

I should see a humble vendor.

These thoughts crossed my mind in preparation for my vendor visit. I have two days to prepare, but something could go wrong and put me in a bind.

Our inventory looks high. I judge this by the amounts still not consumed. We must make efforts to reduce it. Too much money is tied up in here.

I dealt directly with the storekeeper, who had proven to be a responsible man. Please work with Greta to get this under control.

******

At the Captain's reception, I saw the receiving line. It rubbed me the wrong way. Can we do better, and what can that be?

It occupied my thinking, but I could not find a solution. Too many things are wrong, such as the dress code under the Mexican sun, high humidity, and handshaking. The Hostess must get the name and pass it on as an introduction. I can read from the Captain's expression that he despises it.

I had seen this in documentary films when royals staged a reception. Are we trying to copy them and stiffen up the atmosphere?

183

Questions upon more questions until I heard the word "Party."

Yes, now I have it.

We must be staging the reception as a party. Loosen up the people and let them have fun.

The Margaritas are a beginning, and I noticed the Captain is enjoying one. He signaled his approval to Ari.

He left from his introduction to the officers and gave a little speech. The final words compliment Ari and the quality of the Margarita. Passengers applauded him while Ari turned red in the face.

I had just assembled all the components. My next step will be to format it in script format and present it to the Captain and Eva. Then, the rum punch will become the starting cocktail. It will take the wind out of Champagne consumption.

I explained the concept to Ari in a rough format. "Aren't you afraid to take this risk?" I can calculate the return.

It will become a money maker. Remind me to tell the wine story; it will amaze you.

"Are you going to have time later, with a smirk?"

I will make time with her by my side. I know she will be glued to me. She does like a story and would not want to miss out.

As expected, Nicole was seated next to me. The Hostess placed the wine order from the dead inventory. I was hoping that the wine was still OK, and it was.

She impressed the Captain, who promptly remarked to see positive changes all over.

He mentioned the crusty rolls and the Margaritas, and what would be next?

I started the Gala night and would receive a facelift if he approved the concept.

You must tell me I have time tomorrow afternoon.

Here I go again, putting my foot into my mouth." I want to hear it, also said Eva;" now the game is on.

The time has come to let him in on my plans.

I have adjustments in mind with the food and desserts. But the one I am planning next is not really in my territory.

When serving the Captain's reception, I see how displeased you have to shake hands with every passenger. It is a boring chore and does not allow you time to mingle with the passengers.

Here is my solution!

We will move the passengers into the room and serve them a complimentary beverage.

From the stage, we have the cruise director announce the arrival of the master and his senior officers; drum roll or a march, and the Master enters the room followed by his trusted men.

He takes the microphone. You do a short introduction with humor and then roll right into a funny story about something that happened on one of your sailings.

Keep it short and to the point with the punch line: "Got RUM"?

The bar will bring you a rum punch; every passenger receives a free drink.

It gives you time to mingle. I see that you are good at it. Have fun with the people.

If you agree, I will work it with the cruise staff.

I can help you with the speech by accentuating certain words and pausing for the suspension to deliver the punch line.

If we get this off to a good start, I will work on changing more old traditions on the food side.

The desserts will be reworked to deliver a grand finish to the meal. We have a letdown while parading the tired old baked Alaska, which nobody consumes.

There will not be a need for a pastry Chef. Most components can be produced on board.

I planned it this afternoon, and we will create a trio effect: three components with different textures, flavors, and colors to create a more exciting taste sensation.

******

The show had feathers and hats, like in Las Vegas. Skimpy costumes and skin-colored dance wear projected the illusion of naked dancers.

It will stimulate blood flow, I remarked to the two women escorting me to the lounge.

It is not my preference. The presentation was overdone; too much makeup, too many costumes, and all these feathers gave me the feeling of dust. The music is on a tape; it's missing a human touch.

Eva remarked that you would not recognize them without the makeup. "The only thing real is the body they have to keep, and for that, they go to the Gym."

To the wine story, but where do I begin?

I was on my first hotel visit with this company. I asked the F&B director how he was selling wine.

He told me very proudly that we had a house wine!

Ari was now all ears.

I told him my theory of the cost relationship, which I had told every manager in the past. It never fails to confuse them at first. Once they process it and think outside the norm, they get it. There is no risk in selling any wine by the glass.

The story continues with me attending a cognac tasting from Remy Martin.

The effects of sales of these middle-tier premium wines by the glass had started to move inventory. They had already prepared to ship it back to Europe when suddenly, the product was depleting the inventory of certain regional storage locations, and they woke up to the call to replenish the stock. The product was now reallocated, and now comes the question.

What and who is responsible for it? The company people started a trace of the wines to the biggest deliveries. Multiple hotels from one brand have turned the corner and are now the leading sales outlets.

Visiting numerous hotels revealed the idea and was now traced to me. It is how an unmarked box turned out a Louis the 13th cognac as a take-home gift.

I still have this bottle, but little is left in it. End of story!

"Will you let me taste it when I visit?"

I shall save you a drink from it.

The hotel has stories for me; it was the most challenging opening, and since the property owner had me do special projects, yes, there is another story for another day, please.

After we docked back in San Pedro in the morning, I ran into Niguel, the Chief Steward.

He said he had been looking for me and wanted to say goodbye.

He had seen the wrong he had done, and now, he is making it a turning point. He thanked me for being brutal but honest with him. It gave him food for thought, and he sought professional help.

The bar manager Ari had seen the farewell and said he would make it for as long as he stayed away from the other guy. For that man, I have no hope.

******

I called for a hotel room and rental car from the office and then sat with Greta.

If I run into a wall with the purveyors, will you know who to call as a backup? "I have already prepared for that. I have a hunch which one will be tough, but you'll find out."

I have a good idea from looking at the products from last week's delivery.

187

"You have the names and contact persons and addresses with directions. Here is all this information. They are all in the same industrial park. Once you make it there, you will have an easy time locating them."

I have one more request: Find out the phone number for Fantasia Confectioners in San Francisco. I want to talk to a high-level person tomorrow, and please book my return flight for the day after.

Alex will be in later. In the meantime, I will approve the proposal for your position.

******

A new hotel building that had not yet found its soul provided me with a room. OK, the rooms are nice and still smell from new materials, but the check-in was cold.

Do they think the cookies at the desk made a caring impression?

They did not follow through with a warm welcome or explanation of services.

The breakfast was not mentioned; there is a bar service until eleven at night, and I had learned the pool and gym hours from the in-room book.

A forty-minute drive took me to the industrial park on the South side of LA.

The first one on the list was the Vegetable vendor. I expected an attack since we complained about last week's delivery.

Greetings. Can I have a tour, please?

The owner offered breakfast. Thank you, I had it at the hotel early this morning.

The dock workers were busy loading delivery trucks with the same aged stuff we had been receiving.

Which one goes to the ship?

"This one!" Can you find fresher lettuce and celery? The spinach is dead. I see rotten oranges in the boxes; is this the best quality you have on hand?

"We are getting it from the guy that brings in railroad cars of fruits and vegetables from the Valley.

The cruise line wants the lowest price; something has to give. For this reason, we must buy seconds."

What is your price, for example, for this case of Iceberg lettuce?

He quoted the price, and I looked up a bid sheet from various vendors.

His quote was two dollars higher.

When he saw me check the price, he looked a bit nervous.

I understand that you also sell us fish.

Please do it this way. He proudly showed it and pointed to the workers cutting the filets from the bones.

"We buy the fish from the fisherman and process them here. These men are professional at their craft."

He was proud of his crew and the work quality.

When was this fish caught? Do you know which fishing methods the fishers are using?

"The fish is caught in nets. You must understand that this method is productive but also brings unwanted fish."

Do you mean those protected or on a quota and even sea turtles?

"We select the species we sell. I do not know the details; the fisherman will not tell us this. What he does with the rest is not my concern.

Why is there such a strong odor if you get the fish that fresh?

"Why all these questions? We are cleaning up when all the work is completed. Meanwhile, you can see the waste on the floor and dirty bins.

"I want to talk to you about the lobster you canceled on me. This deal had been agreed with your predecessor."

We better get to your office to talk about this issue.

"Your cancellation of these lobster tails has bound us and disrupted our cash flow."

I can imagine it well, but I saved the cruise line from taking out a loan to pay for it.

Why was this order placed?

"The other man had told us he wanted to load up the ship for the Alaska cruise."

This is weeks away; was there any discussion about a price increase on the horizon?

"Yes, this too."

But I can buy the same lobster in Miami for half the price and add shipping; I find it strange that it should come to this price!

Are there any other cost factors built in? He now acted nervously and was lost for a good answer.

"No, just the margin for us."

You are sticking it to the ship's company with an inflated price. Why not get it while you can with an increase of three dollars over the going price?

The getting has just ended. We have enough products on board to last until Vancouver and the first voyage to Alaska. Then, I will buy locally for the season up there.

"Won't you take any at all? You are committed; you must honor the agreement."

Do you mean that you have a contract?

"Your company's commitment to buying the entire inventory."

Can you show me a written commitment?

"No, we did this on the honor system."

Does the inflated price fall into the same honor system?

Let me tell you something from my heart. I would take this lobster next winter if the price were based on a current market quotation. I will pay for storage and honor the commitment.

But this is just not the case; there is no basis for honor amongst thieves!

I am done with you and cancel all this stuff; it's below our quality standard.

Your business relationship is now canceled! Have a good day!

I left without turning back. The next vendors were dry goods and grocery purveyors.

Greetings to you; nice to meet you!

May I use the phone to call the office? The secretary dialed and handed me the receiver.

Hi Greta, go ahead with new suppliers on produce and seafood.

"Thank you, as predicted, I took a little chance and placed the orders elsewhere already. Here is the information if you want to meet the new company."

She is a Jewel, and I am lucky to have such an efficient employee.

The secretary agreed. She has everything in good order, is precise, and has excellent follow-up.

She will assume a long overdue and more significant role.

I came to see your plant, to get an impression. My background covers a broad spectrum of food and beverage.

From the operation, I know that my predecessor was a penny pincher. I also understand that products may save a penny but lose a dollar in yield. Can you recommend brands that give us better yield?

I glanced at his list and placed it in my briefcase. There is so much to sort; It will make good travel reading. We will increase the Canadian hard wheat flour and reduce the cake flour. I trust that you keep it in the cooler.

"Yes, we have recommended that the ship do the same."

"The Moon Dancers' storage areas are not in a cool place. Canned goods look overstocked on both ships. You are running the risk of getting the cans blown up."

You are so right; it amazes me that a vendor is interested in protecting his ware after the sale.

"It's in our interest to have you as a satisfied customer. Any problem created on account of neglect will come back to us."

Inventory will be reduced, so do not be alert when the orders are a little smaller in the next few weeks. Is there a way to date mark the dry goods cases?

"Glad to stamp it; we do it for the Hyatt and other hotels."

The flower is now in the freezer; the cooler was too full.

"What about Canada?"

I do not have an answer yet. I will advise.

"We can ship it in bond and avoid duty; keep that in mind."

Hmm, good to know. A purveyor up there obtains from us often; you can cherry-pick the goods for him and provide a steady flow of supplies.

Do you know the confectioner Fantasia?

"Very well, we carry the products, but not the complete line, just what the hotels order."

Can I get this list? We are thinking of using certain baked goods to combine desserts.

"If you need a product we don't show on this list, give us a couple of weeks' advance notice. We will source it and get you the price."

Thank you, this was a highly informative visit; see you next time in port.

Did this former guy ever hint at inflating the prices for the company?

"Glad you are asking; for the last six months, he was darn right straightforward to ask for a kickback, citing his upcoming retirement."

"We told him to take his business elsewhere. We would also go to the company to report his pressure tactic. He backed down and begged never to show this request to anyone; he was sorry for it. We do not work under such conditions."

At the meat purveyor, I saw these butchers working in a chilled room in heavy coats and protective gloves.

The manager gave me a heavy freezer coat and a hard hat to look around.

From my days as a butcher, I realized the strict rules of the US Agriculture Department.

The chilled room was one of the harshest rules which had been imposed. These men looked cold and worked in warm clothing, but their faces gave their discomfort away.

"Are you hungry?"

It was two o'clock, and yes, when I smelled cooking, it awakened my appetite.

"My wife is test-cooking Argentine steaks. We can talk about it and whatever you wish to discuss."

The place looks orderly.

How was your relationship with the former man?

"A testy one, but I must explain. It is not our standard to do what he had commanded us to do.

He had me over the barrel.

I was a young plant manager. Do you want me to continue?"

Not a problem; I know it all.

"I was young and naïve, and this man came and told me the amount of meat he would be using on these two ships. It made a big impression on me.

He produced odd suggestions for concessions on unique cuts and trim.

The amount was overstated, but I did not know better. In any case, we had been smaller, and I saw the chance to grow the business.

Then he told us that he would order choice and US good, and the trim had to be the strips with such a tail, and the ends can be uneven, as he preferred it that way. He has items on the menu suitable for such odd lots.

When all was set and done, he started to inflate the price by 20% and pay him a broker's commission.

These are the terms, take it or leave it."

"I took the bluff seriously. The hook that came along with weekly payments had never come out."

He is gone; you must stop these payments at once.

Any checks not yet cleared, put a stop payment on them.

"Good, we were getting ready to do last month's check. I know that this is illegal. I wish I could take it all back."

How much of the inflated price had been kept back? About 5%.

Here is what we will do. The trim will be 1x2 on the loins. All other standard USDA specs will be used. Only choice grade and yield grade 3 will be used.

I want you to pick the smallest loins and send them on board.

I know it means sorting.

"No problem; we have an oversupply and find it difficult to be accepted by the hotels and steak houses."

We help each other this way, which yields better and serves our needs. I am not asking for any reparation from you. I want good service and a consistent product.

The pork is the standard USDA! What else? You carry lamb for special occasions. Like whole carcasses? "I can get it with one week's notice."

I want to make the ship's engineers happy for their holidays; it keeps the kitchen equipment in good repair!

"Thank you, that sounds fair and square. Let's try these steaks.

My wife is just cooking; getting food into the system is good.

If we get a good deal, I will talk to you about using it. We find it so much more flavorful, grass-fed, and less fat waste, yet tender."

The steak was terrific; yes, we would like to hear your proposal.

"Since my conscience has been bothering me and I was getting sick to my stomach, I will throw in strip loins at no charge. Tell that to Gracie."

We can go ahead with this order and switch to the right stuff.

We have not had quality time to set it all up. Can I call Gracie now; let me talk to her about the changes.

Thank you for lunch. I am a straight shooter, as you may have learned. I grew up in this business in Germany and have compassion for it.

You have cleaned up what needed to be done. From this day forward, I am happy for an honest business deal.

When I returned to the office, I gave Gracie a full briefing on my visits. From this day forward, we have a straight business arrangement with all vendors. The guy we canceled will be off the vendor list.

"I was thinking of a vendor list. We should set up an approved vendor list and have Alex support it. It will give me a way out and shield me from the constant solicitors."

I know this is an annoying timewaster.

"Anyone that wants to get on this list must apply, and if we need his service, we approve him as a group and with an inspection."

******

The wine list will follow, but first, we must drain the current inventory. Keep an eye on this and let me know when we run low.

The wines are now being sold as wine by the glass.

Gracie, my able right hand, we covered every issue. I will meet with Alex for a debriefing. I have seen his signature on my request. He wants to present your promotion to you in person. Look surprised.

195

"I get feedback from the vendors you visited. They are pleased and speak of a new breeze in the company. The meat vendor mentioned a Scirocco."

Alex did as I predicted. He called the office staff together and handed Gracie a bouquet.

Congratulations to our Purchasing Manager. Here is your first paycheck.

I heard Angela popping the cork of a bottle. We celebrated the promotion.

Gracie was in tears of joy!

"Oh, this is so much more; I love it and will do an excellent job for you."

Angela wanted to get an update on the changes.

We sat in the fresh California air, ordered appetizers, and listed every change I had implemented in part or fully.

From the Captain's party proposal, I went to the meat purveyor and ended with this crooked lobster deal. She was in Ahh.

"No wonder you are tired!"

Yes, that too, but I had a little help on that. I said this with a grin on my face.

The terrace of this restaurant had become our favorite place to chat or talk business.

"Don't you need Miami's approval?"

I do, but to this date, I have already made so many changes to the Turquoise Seas. Nobody has said anything to discourage me.

I have a nut to crack in purchasing. This visit with the fish guy was a dress rehearsal. I know that hands from the past are meddling with vendors. Quality and price do not match up. It will be my next battle.

But, as they say in Paris, take one after the other. She punched me in the ribs.

I will return to California once I have that battle behind me and under my control. It will be a time to cool my heels. Should you run into any challenging situation, I will give you my home phone number so you can contact me.

I arranged for the hotel shuttle to take me to the airport.

There is no service on the Red Eye. I must remember to take food from an airport food stand with me.

CHAPTER 10

Arriving early in Fort Lauderdale has the benefit of making it home on the short stretch. It's only twelve miles on Interstate 595. Thank you, Gracie, for thinking of me. She had changed the arrival airport from Miami to the nearest airport. Gracie has her heart in the right place. I learn to appreciate her more with the care she applies to her work.

Nina had been waiting for me with breakfast. Her son was also up and ready to eat and then off to school.

We will buy this computer tomorrow, are you free, Derick?

"Yes, I look forward to it, Dad. Can I use it too? "

You will have to teach me. Of course, you can use the computer. All I ask you is that you do not load up every game.

I will need it for my job.

I went to sleep and finally woke up late afternoon. My shirt was drenched with sweat. I wondered if I even slept and rested. No, I was dreaming, tossing, turning, and dizzy from the crazy dreams.

A shower will do me good.

Hunger and thirst set in as I searched for food. But there was almost nothing in the house. I had to settle for eggs and bread. I might as well have another breakfast. My time clock is turned upside down.

Nina came home early from work. Derick will be home soon, and then we will go to the store to buy this computer and printer.

Did you hear him calling me Dad this morning?

"He is fond of you; he cannot show his affection. He has never had a father figure, yet he has wanted one for a long time; his birth father is a bump. I would not let him near him as a baby, which is why I am here in Florida. But do not ask me for details; letting a sleeping dog lie is better."

I will see if I can get him to open up, man to man, boys talk, cars, girls, sports, that stuff.

"Can you give him a bit of sex education? The use of protection and how to treat a girl. He wants to know, but I have a handicap with it; he will not take me seriously."

OK, that must come organically in the contents of a conversation unless he asks for it!

Shopping for the computer turned him on; he was a different person and knew this so well.

It is his calling for the future.

"He wants to go to technical college at the junior college.

With his grades in High School, he has the first two years tuition free. After, he must come up to pay for tuition or search for a scholarship. I am saving up for this to aid him with his technical college education."

Derick selected a machine with a higher price tag. It will be worth the money since it has faster memory.

The technical data confused me; I had no choice but to take his word.

My trust in him made a big impression. He was different towards me. During the programming, he explained every step in layman's language. You will not get this explanation from a salesperson. They rattle all information and rush you into a sale.

I had that experience once with a fast-talking guy. I walked away from him.

Nina wrote the California reports on our new computer. I did not plan to share the full information with the Miami office. Somehow in my guts, I felt the need to hold back on the lobster situation.

I will share a condensed version to appease the boss.

At the office, I could feel a certain tension. Ignoring it did not make it go away.

Kerry was scribbling notes down and came to see me.

"I have a concern. Jim is accusing us of abandoning the bidding procedure. He is talking to whoever is lending him his ear."

I wish to know where he obtains such information.

I will give you a clue to follow up. I had a situation in California with a fish vendor selling lobster tails. He came on to me as if he owned me. But his fruit and produce were also of the lowest quality and at a higher price than the competition.

The situation here looks and smells the same. We will find out the connection he has with Jim. The lobster is another story, but first, this produce.

We have a supplier who dumps poor quality on us. One driver pushes the others to go first on the delivery. Who is that? A visit will clarify this situation. You will come with me; I need you as a witness.

Tomorrow is a good day; the ship is in the day after. I must look over my notes; the head is still buzzing from the last two.

Did we get a case of alcohol from Bacardi or Barbados?

"Yes, I have it. It's another issue; guy Jim is claiming that the bar cost will be running out of control. He tells our boss that we are buying expensive products, and it will never make the company any money."

Tell him to see me if he has any complaints. You do not report to him any longer.

Be blunt and have courage; he is a coward, and all bullies are cowards.

This stuff is called Falernum and is made by the Appleton Rum Company. Bacardi has signed for the distribution rights. We are going to make it famous with rum punch.

We will serve it along with champagne at the gala reception.

The fresh fish is still going strong. The fish purveyor has his saltwater ice maker ready and delivers the fish packed in snow.

"I had to fight the storekeeper from tearing it apart."

"The Captain is in seventh heaven. He advertises the fresh fish and the drinks at his reception."

We must inform him about the rum punch. He may already know about it. Plan to bring him a bottle and ask him, "Got Rum?"

It will be a surprise since he knows Barbados and the rum brand.

Think of an approach with this Purveyor tomorrow. How would you start the conversation?

"I would confront them and accuse them of meddling in my business."

No, Karry, you need to set a trap and lure them to the bait; explain!

We will go to the plant and check for rodent droppings and cleanliness.

Do not show any reactions; just keep listening. When you get a chance, start asking questions.

"I better let you do the first visit."

I will ask to see if the order has been staged and is ready for delivery. If it is prepared, then we will tear the boxes open. We do the talking in the office of the Purveyor. I will not make any remarks if I see discrepancies.

He will ask for our impression. We cite the inconsistency in quality, and if we found the warehouse dirty and in disarray, it would give us more to discredit him. At last, we talk about to price.

Help me understand why you are charging more for the bulk items. Are there circumstances where we are causing you a higher cost? Those kinds of questions do not come as accusations. Remember that!

This question will be difficult for him to answer. Somehow, he must justify the price.

The trap is set!

It's late already, and I must get home to rest. I came up a little short in California. Jet lag and red eye will do a number on you! We are now ready to face these guys tomorrow.

A visit to a supplier can be testy. The behavior of a guilty person is unpredictable.

This Jim has reasons to protect his past dealings. He is going on the offensive and is accusing me taking a kickback.

The offense may be his best defense, but what is there to defend when my hands are clean?

******

Good morning: we will not take much of your time, but since I am new, I thought it proper to meet the source of our food products. May we have a look around?

"We are staging the pallets for the trucks here. We are loading for Hotels today; they prefer the mid-week delivery. It's best for us, too, since the weekends keep us busy with the cruise ships."

Have you staged the ship's order by now?

"My worker is getting started over there. The order is much smaller than expected, can you tell me why?" Let's have a look. We will talk about that in the office.

How do you handle the rodent problem?

"It's a constant battle, and we must use heavy poison to keep it manageable."

Do you use a Broker out West and get it shipped by a truck? No, we are too small!"

Can you make a co-op arrangement with other smaller dealers? We get it from a large volume buyer. We are too small for brokers.

"There is fierce competition; we fight for every customer. Let us go inside to talk about the situation."

I looked at Karri. Tell me why you are always so much higher in the items we buy. Is there a particular reason?

Our buying strategy is simple. The one with the best products for the best price gets the order.

In the past, the order was split into four different companies.

We find it inefficient to complete the loading in time, and it does not make good business sense for the others who dropped off only a couple of pallets.

You were awarded the largest order, yet your price was higher than the others. Can you explain this to me?

Are we the cause of not paying the bills on time? Or are other factors outside your control that cause extra costs? Karri saw his body language.

"We run our business our way, OK? Fair enough?"

It's not my business how you run the show, but if I have to pay more, it is my business.

"OK, I see that you must know something. Let me tell it straight: We are making payments to a specific bank account for a so-called broker's fee."

What does this amount to?

You don't want to tell me!

How did this all get started, and since when is this in effect?

"Three plus years."

To whom does the money go?

"This guy before you. He came and put the squeeze on us. We had then been smaller and thought it was OK and it would go away as we grew in size.

We called him, and he told us that the new man had reported to him and that he would fix it.

Nothing happened until this week."

From your gut feeling, is he acting alone?

"No, the account has two names on it. Latin banks are doing that."

Would you have a canceled check on hand and make us a copy?

"Reluctantly, but level with me now; are you reporting to him?"

No, I report to the VP directly.

Jim is in the marine department. He does dry dock.

This young man is Karri; he is learning the robes. He reports to me.

I appreciate your honesty. We will put you on the approved vendor list. Just be in line with the price and remember any inferior product will be rejected at the dock. Make the best of it, or this arrangement will be short-lived.

Karri was surprised. We will alternate the orders weekly; this way, we get them from two vendors and keep our efficiency.

I did not cut him out for simple reasons. He will tell Jim about this visit. I want to prove that we dealt above board and knew about the payment. I am not sure he will go that far as to tell Jim this information.

In any case, he must explain the stop payment.

This action will tell Jim a message. Watch "they do know," and he will back off.

It was certainly interesting, and now we have proof to use if he gets nasty, and he will.

The next is for you, Karri. "What if they deny it or play hardball?" We walk away because of a hostile business environment.

Never accuse; let them talk and ask questions. The accuser must bring the proof.

We have Jim's back against the wall; his choice is to back off or face the judge.

Backing off is better for him and us. We can exercise control at will. Remember, we need kitchen equipment, which falls into dry dock projects.

We must think ahead like a chess player.

CHAPTER 11

It did not take long, and Jim came storming into my office. "You are now threatening the suppliers that have served us over the years. What has gotten into you?"

Too many inferior products had been dumped on the cooks; they are pissed and never piss off a cook. Sharp knives, you know, laughing and making it a joke.

"I do not think this is a joke!" We can exert pressure on you, kids; we have connections, too.

We understand the influence you have.

Let me assure you that we are not easily intimidated and have insurance!

"Oh yes, and what is this?"

I showed him a copy of the canceled check. The original is in a safe deposit box. We have the conversation on tape as we do this one right now.

We know the bank and have seen the signature card. Do I need to tell you more?

Then I handed him the equipment list.

Can you do us some good with this list?

His head glowed like a lighthouse beacon. He would have found the way home in pitch darkness.

******

The office was noticeably quiet, secretaries doing what they do best, gossiping, and drinking coffee." Do you have reports?"

Not at the moment.

The woman from purchasing stuck her head in the door and asked about the visit to the purveyors.

We narrowed it down to two and look for a weekly rotation of the entire order to keep two companies happy for a safety backup.

The others were told that we revised the approved vendor list, and they did not impress.

We cited the obvious reasons, their conduct towards us, the dirty facility, rodents, and the pricing policy.

"This approved vendor list is a great idea. Can we do it for all suppliers?" Yes, please make a list for review by the boss.

Can you transcribe this tape? It holds sensitive information. Do not share it with anyone. It will self-destruct after you are finished transcribing.

"I like this man; he always has a lighthearted comment!" You will see the other side when you hear the tapes.

******

Your birthday is coming up, Derick. At last, you will be eighteen, and we will make it a fun party at the pool. I will reserve the BBQ area, and then we will grill.

"I will connect speakers from my friend, bringing a boom box.

I plan on tasty food, drinks, and a punch for selected invitees. I bring a bottle of Falernum, my secret weapon.

I make you an honorary German citizen for your birthday, making you of legal drinking age.

Invite your friends and girls. We must have attractive girls.

"I know one who has her eye on me. Would you allow me to use my room?"

Mom and I have already spoken on this subject.

She asked me to talk to you to teach you the right way. You would not want to disappoint her.

Use protection, and with this, Derick and I went into every detail to make a woman happy.

We will give you privacy and we go to a movie. That should be enough time.

******

My son Martin called to say that he went to visit his mother in Santa Fee.

"She is a social worker for alcoholics and found a man to spend time with.

Her guilt feelings are bothering her; how stupid of me to let myself be abused."

Tell her the past is called history. You cannot reconstruct history, can never re-live it, or go back and redo it. Today is the day you live, and make it count.

Tomorrow will be a new day after a good night's sleep.

She is doing something good and found peace in her work.

Life is not so complicated when looking at it this way.

"That is great; my girlfriend needs to take this to heart. She has this need for never-ending debates over nothing. She keeps asking the what-if, questions."

"The Air Force is transferring her to Alaska, and she is pushing me to go with her."

Tell her that Alaska has long nights to find someone for these endless talks, and in summer, the day is 24 hours, and too much to do to sit and talk. You cannot be around wasting time on her behalf. You have a job and a career.

There will be others; you are a good-looking man and have a great head on the shoulder.

How is the money holding up?

"The boss is helping with the extensive renovation projects. As a tradeoff, I do his side work. I am doing good and getting more rent now.

I am training my roommates to be handy and productive for the massive amount of food they consume.

The EPA will scrape the contaminated soil around the house.

I will get rich-composted material and plan to start a garden."

Stay in touch, and you know if you need help, I am here.

******

The Port call to a ship is always a busy day. The Captain must be seen first and ask permission for a visit.

"I have a question: How did you get the Falernum so quickly?"

I have a daughter in Barbados. She made the arrangement.

"Spread around your seeds there? Not exactly, but a story no less! I will tell the story when we have more time.

I have to be on the ship for a four-day voyage. That will be the time for stories.

"It's a deal, I will remind you! The rum punch is as good as I have ever remembered."

"The next time I tell my rum story, I will tell a lie and fool them about Black Beard.

Make sure you have a good supply on board; they are buying it like hotcakes.

But all kidding aside, you knew that I love this punch."

"Barbados has a special place in my heart; what better way to promote this product than by an old salt Captain?"

"Appleton should make a commercial of it, and then I can retire in style."

I will talk to my daughter! Here she is again in the play; suspense is building!

Chief Francoise was in a good mood. The loading is easier with the lower inventory. The boys are happy for time off to do their shopping.

For the dessert, I found a company in California which produces outstanding dessert components. They will ship, but it would be convenient if a local food purveyor would carry the products on hand.

Karri, make sure you double the Falernum order. The cruise director must record the Captain's story on tape. He will tell pirates stories next gala.

He is sucking the rum punch down like water, like in his apprentice time with Black Beard!

"Really for sure?"

I had you almost believe this, funny!

Next week I will make the four-day trip.

The visit was over, and the ship's horn was signaling all visitors to get off the ship.

Fair winds and calm seas, Captain Black Beard!

******

Do we need to get any food for the party? "Buns, salads, and chips! have burgers and hot dogs;" and? OK, I need more things! What? Stuff to eat, real food! Pork ribs, the one with half a chop on it, smoked Kielbasa, Potatoes to make my salad, Tomatoes, Pickles, real mustard, onions to smother them, hot sauce, fresh fruit, I am going all out.

Derick gets to be eighteen only once. Besides, he has to make a good impression on the female guest. Burgers and dogs are what everybody serves. Your son is worth the attention of better food.

The proud Mom was glowing; then let's go. We have the fast-burning charcoal type and extra for the marshmallows, long bamboo skewers, ply napkins, quality disposable cups, a couple of mosquito torches, and Balloons, and now we have it ready.

I will come home from work early enough to set up the Barbeque.

"Dad, I will have my friends helping us; they want to learn from you. It will be excellent; the food will be great. It's always the focal point."

We will make a punch for everybody and a punch with a kick for selected guests. Lemonade and Iced tea to offer a variety; yes, this will be fine.

Are you happy with the way this party is developing?

We will get a picnic cooler and ice cubes from the convenience store. They carry the type that is frozen like a tube, which will melt more slowly.

The trash bags from the hardware stores, the ones we buy for lawn waste, are made from brown paper, which makes a statement about being eco-friendly. Kids learn by seeing; it is their world now and more so in the future.

The plastic utensils will be separated, and the bags will be marked with a black marker.

Food waste must be isolated for disposal. I will take this bag to the dumpster on the way to the movie.

Party time!

Everybody had shown up to help with the setup, and the guests arrived.

While Derick was playing the gracious host to the arriving friends, female, and male, with handshakes and cautious little cheek kisses from the girls, he started the music.

Help yourself with beverages and chips.

I had the fire almost ready to start cooking. At first, the kids needed to talk and stayed in groups of girls and boys. Infrequent glances fell on the food table, and the girls had to size up the boys from the corner of their eyes.

The boys talked about sports until the latest news had been exhausted.

Hot dogs and burgers are ready, while the Kielbasa and the pork ribs need more time.

Nina tried to entice the guest to start eating. The boys took a burger, and the girls held back. When one of the girls took a hot dog and made a comment, uhhs, this is different! They were still nibbling on chips and sipping the lemonade. It awakened the curiosity, and others took a Frankfurter sausage. Wow, what kind are these? I had never had one this good. Inquiries to Nina are referred to me.

I explained it to them; you do not need to load up this sausage with mustard and ketchup. It's OK if you want it in a bun, but I eat them as they are.

The girls came in tiny summer dresses and feared getting their clothing soiled. Then they realized that the food would not soil the dress, and all the girls started to eat.

Keep room; there is more to be had; look at these pork ribs.

I made them without BBQ sauce. You can use your fingers and wipe them on paper napkins after eating.

The boys noticed the pork and Kielbasa and went for it like hungry wolves.

"Wow, this is real food. Your Dad is a super cook!" The chit-chat had stopped while everybody was eating.

Nina and I had a rum punch and joined them on the picnic table.

The questions are now coming at me. How did you make these ribs, and what kind of spices is on the meat? Why did you not use a BBQ sauce as everybody else does? What kind of punch are you drinking? Yours looks different."

I gave them answers to everything they threw at me. I wasn't sure that everything I had said was completely understood. I noticed blank faces.

I saw the kids and the manners they practiced. Girls came with a nice hairdo and kept the makeup to a minimum.

I did not care for the others; too much makeup and arrogant behavior made them seem cheap and pretentious.

I noticed that the boys had the same reactions.

Derick cranked up the music and the beat to entice dancing.

The girls danced as pairs while the boys stood there watching the moves.

Derick and his best friend had the courage to break into two girls dancing. Nina took one to the dance floor and handed him to a girl. He strategically moved to the girl of his choice.

She had him in view all evening.

When finally everybody was dancing and the party was in full swing, Nina and I watched while we sipped our rum punch. It gave us a chance to eat.

The music tempo guided the dance activity. It took me back to my teen years, when Mom had her three sons sign up for dance classes.

Those days, we learned etiquette by asking a girl to dance. If the girl was with her parents, the father or mother must give permission first. The girl would act very shy and lose her inhibitions once the parents were out of sight. On the opposite side of a busy dance floor was her aim and be shielded from her parent's view.

It took me a while to understand her urgency, but the language was much clearer when her body pressed against mine.

Derick introduced his girl to us: meet Kasey and ask for a rum punch. We had made a promise and gave him a small cup. The girl quickly shared his drink, and a quick refill was asked.

The dance floor showed partner changes; occasionally, one or two boys found themself without a girl. They came back for more food and drinks.

Derick and his girl kept on dancing. Her body language spoke volumes of affection to our son. He was proud to show off his catch and kept looking at me for approval.

Yes, a little nod made him move forward with his plan.

Jealousy flared up between two boys when one was dancing too closely with his girlfriend. She was one of those painted faces, yet the girl preferred the other boy.

Nina managed to prevent an ugly fight. Kids will be kids!

It had damaged the mood, and the girls headed back into little groups.

Derick stood up for what looked like a speech.

Thank you for coming to mark my coming of age to manhood. I am eighteen years and an honorary citizen of Germany. I celebrate my birthday, but I want to recognize the most incredible Mom and my newfound Father.

It's my first birthday party, and I want to show Kacey my birthday presents. Please excuse us for a little while. He took Kasey by the hand and walked to the house.

The party continued. The boys took another helping of pork ribs, sausages, and burgers; the hot dogs were gone by then.

More questions came from the girls.

I gave them a pre-printed recipe to take to Mom and instructions on the cooking procedures.

The comments on the food came from girls who must be interested in cooking. "Are you a Chef? And where did you learn to cook like this?"

I named places, and it amazed them.

Are you into cooking?

"No, I help my Mom and dad grill outdoors. Our food is not as good as it was tonight. I want a birthday party like this when I get eighteen."

I handed out papers with the recipe since I had raw pork ribs untouched. I used them to show how to apply the spice mix. It is a simple procedure. Make sure you measure the spices correctly.

Let the meat sit inside the cooler and cook it on low heat. Do not rush it.

Can we help with the cleanup? Please, that is nice of you. I guess the other girls don't want to break the fingernails!

The boys laughed; yes, good riddance. Who needs friends like these?

We made it back from the movies by nine o'clock and found the two lovers watching television.

A technical program captured Derick while Kasey tried to follow him on his technical terms.

They looked happy, and the girl thanked us for the private accommodations. She clung to Derick and asked him to take her home.

Is there anything left to clean up? Cups may still be around; we do a sweep with flashlights and pick them up. The rest we leave to the Yardman. I gave him a nice tip already.

Kacey wanted to recipe for the ribs; they were terrific. I gave her my last paper with the spice rub and told her how to prepare it.

You have lovely parents; I wish my Dad were more involved in my life. I miss having an adult to talk to, but now I no longer need it, as she looked Derik deep in the eyes and smiled.

He drove her home and returned 45 minutes later from a drive that took ten minutes.

"Yep, he has the bug now. Nina smiled, it worked, and we will be looking forward to a happy and responsible young man."

Nina saw her son making such a turnaround. It had been her most significant concern as a single Mom. She could never bring him to bond with a boyfriend in the past. He grew up with school friends and stayed to himself.

Chores get done without a reminder, Derick is a changed boy, or do we call him a man?

When he comes home from school, he offers to help his Mom and takes an interest in cooking.

When he graduates, I will be in California. Mom must stand in for me once again.

We will take him out to a nice restaurant to celebrate the event. There will not be another party!

"Derick pulled me aside and thanked me for the instruction. It happened as you described it. She was fighting it at first and not knowing better. I took control and worked her slowly to the point where she was begging. I could almost not believe that she was begging me. But I stuck to my plan and took her to where she wanted to be.

She may be a keeper; I feel good about Kacey".

******

The Miami ship is sailing on Monday for a four-day cruise. The cruise is nearly sold out, and I received the last stateroom.

Passengers gathered on the upper deck and waved goodbye.

Live music playing Caribbean songs puts the vacationers in the mood to party.

Dinner was in full preparation, and everybody worked feverishly, completing the work. The cooks thanked me for the new knives. Finally, we have a proper tool to cut; it makes work that much easier. Handshakes and thank you came from everyone in the kitchen.

The aromas from the spices and herbs made me hungry.

Let us work on the desserts.

Let me do a sample plate. I have these Florentine cookies to use, and the rest we prepared on board. It will be terrific once we have these fancy cakes from the confectioner house, but I think it will be an improvement for now.

All of it looks great; I look forward to dinner; thank you for doing a fine job.

The flexibility is opening up a new market for us. It works even at lunch and on deck by the pool. When I entered the dining room, the wine stewards came up to me and said that the wine sales were making gangbuster sales.

The inventory is shrinking; please look into replacements soon. We will need a new wine list.

When the manager saw me, he came over and said, you will be happy with your table mates. They look like fun people and are all of the different nationalities.

The manager, Manolo, introduced each person by name and country.

One couple is from Canada, and another couple is from Mexico. Then came three people from Columbia who looked like Mom with the teenage children: brother and sister.

Mom was seated next to me and spoke excellent English and German.

Her husband is an oil executive and deals with refineries in Houston. He dropped the family off to go on the cruise and shop in Miami while he tended to his business.

I noticed the plates were decorated with two vegetables, and the meat part was reduced. It makes more sense to see the food consumed than feed it to the fish. I had seen the deserts and will now witness the reaction around the table.

An empty plate makes for the best compliment to a Chef.

I was reflecting on the food and the improvement in beverage sales.

It is mind-boggling how much the wine sales contributed to the total revenue. Jim would be green with envy if he were here right now.

Where have I been just now? I was daydreaming, looking back on my first trip and the changes we had made until now. It gives me great satisfaction.

"Tell us how a ship like this works came as a question from the Columbian woman. We mean the back of the house to produce all these services."

It works like a hotel or restaurant kitchen.

The food is loaded in the home port for the voyage. For safety reasons, we do not buy in foreign ports.

There is a Chief Steward or Food director, a Chef, cooks, and kitchen helpers to keep the workspace clean.

The storekeeper organizes the loading, which is carried out within four hours.

The daily menus rotate per cruise; like tonight, we have a fresh fish program.

We pack the fish filets in shaved ice to keep them fresh. This only works for the first night. After that, we must resort to a frozen product. Lobster shrimp do well from the frozen stage, but the fish suffer from being frozen. Precious juices are lost through the thawing stage. We want to avoid this, but I need different ice for it.

If I could get the fish delivered packed in sea ice, it would stay fresh to the last day. For that, the supplier must have this machine, and it would be great if the ship also had one of these ice makers. Sea water freezes at twenty-eight degrees Fahrenheit, and it turns into snow.

I know a fisherman in Pompano who pioneered it. It made him more competitive and profitable.

He can keep his fishing boats at sea until he has a full load.

"That is a great story! Tell us one more; we still have wine left."

Tomorrow you will be introduced to a new drink. The drink is not new; only the recipe is unique.

When the Captain has his gala party, he will introduce this drink in a way only he can do it.

The Columbian woman Sylvia took my arm and squeezed it. You cannot keep us in suspense. Is your daughter Jasmin of legal drinking age? Yes, we can drink at the age of eighteen in my country. OK, we are at sea, and this ship is registered in Panama. It will work in your favor, Jasmin.

We gathered in the bar and ordered more wine. Yes, story time tonight.

I started with the Castle and the Pirate crashing his ship on the reef.

Then the way he had built a Castle from the wood of the ships, he had lured to the reef to face the same crash.

He lured more and more ships to crash and took the provisions and treasure to finance his Castle.

After his death, the building was converted into a hotel and added more rooms in smaller adjacent buildings.

I became involved with expanding the hotel rooms and adding a restaurant.

It is a long story, which has already been told. But my audience was glued to every word, and time ran away. I took shortcuts, carried on with some details, and stopped at the point when we had the grand opening.

The pivotal point was now coming to the surface when Priscilla asked me to be her surrogate father. She had never been privileged to have the security of a father during her formative years.

I did see tears and napkins being used to wipe the faces.

We managed to drink four bottles of wine. Thank you, and all have a good night.

Sylvia held me back and wanted to make a date. Do you realize it is past two o'clock? I must be on the job early and have breakfast.

"All work and no play is not suitable for your health". We will talk tomorrow. It will be Gala night and no storytelling. Good night and sweet dreams.

The day was spent drawing up a wine list. The best sellers stay, and I will meet with a wine merchant for the rest.

While scouring the storeroom, I stumbled on a wheel of cheese. It was mildew-covered and not well preserved. I washed off the mold and found it wrapped in foil, with a hard crust below.

Francoise is a French man; he must know this cheese. How long has the cheese been on board?

Nobody had any recollection. Do we think it may be from an earlier ship owner?

Is it French cheese or from elsewhere?

I think it may be Italian. Let me see if the Captain has a clue. Should we cut it open?

Like a kid at Christmas, the crew assembled around this cheese to wait for the result by cutting it open.

From the texture, I can tell that it is not parmesan. I want to say Kasseri or Pecorino.

I am at a loss. Let's think this through. If the earlier owner left behind the cheese, then it must have been on this ship for another 12 years.

Somehow, the flavor reminds me of a cheese I buy at a store, but this cheese is not that well-aged.

The cheese is undoubtedly sharp and flavorful, yet it does not crumble. Walnuts, peppers, and olives blend in with a strong salty taste.

I will take a piece to the Captain and bring him wine. I know that he loves excellent and salty cheese.

Come along, Francoise; we must solve this mystery.

We dug up this cheese from the dungeon. Help us solve this mystery, Captain

"It was an Italian company before us. Going back further, you have to research the archives."

The wine adds substance to the flavor; I am getting close.

"Would you agree if I named it Asiago?"

We will keep it safeguarded as your private supply. Is that OK, Captain?

"You are the best I know."

I took a short nap on the pool deck and tanked Vitamin D to convert all the quality calcium from this precious cheese.

A hand on my chest woke me; it was Sylvia with a beer in her hand.

How nice of you, and you have your precious daughter Jasmine with you.

I love your name Jasmin, a flower that blooms at night and releases seductive aromas.

I believe when a girl is named with a selected name, she will grow up to give the name honor. Is that the case with you, Jasmine?

"In Columbia, we prefer to compare a child's looks to a flower.

The beauty of the flower is the beauty of the child.

Beaty comes with representation and responsibilities to live in harmony with nature and be an excellent example for the children.

My life has a purpose and must fulfill a mission.

"I am a night owl and do my best work at night. Schoolwork, reading, music, and whatever a teenager has an interest in, I do at night.

Daytime is difficult for me. I take short naps to keep up with the sleep, and after school, I lie down for deep sleep. It works out well for me."

******

The Captain's party is ready, the rum punch is prepared in bulk, and we are testing the first batch. It's a Chief Steward's privilege.

Hors- d' oeuvres are passed from small trays, and the passengers are making their way into the show lounge.

I noticed Jasmine with her brother in tow, and Sylvia made it to the door. Are we late?

No, we no longer have the receiving line; just watch for the Captain's arrival.

Music and a drum roll announced the arrival of the Master of the Turquoise Seas. He introduced his senior officers and went straight into a seafarer's story.

The Captain, in his dress uniform and the full beard, referred that he had been named Black beard.

In my earlier times as Captain, I was charged by the crown of England to haul back the wealth from the colonies.

The schooner was loaded to the brim, but he had not received the full complement of provisions. Namely, an essential element was overlooked by the provision sailor.

His smile returned when he noticed that his route would take him past Barbados. Despite the well-known pirates being on the lookout for a treasure ship, we outsailed them and are now heading for the harbor, we dropped anchor and went on shore with a dingy.

How can we be of service to you, Lord Master? We need gunpowder and foremost: Got rum? Yes, Sir, good, no mutiny.”

Rum punch from Barbados is now handed to him, and everybody in the lounge is offered a complimentary rum punch.

We were serving the same rum punch and added a new item to the rum punch.

Falernum is the liqueur made from sugar cane and our secret weapon.

From this moment on, this drink will be sold at the bar.

What a speech, Captain. You had them eating out of your hands. Congratulations.

People ordered more to consume during dinner, and sales are booming.

Sylvia and Jasmine showed that they would like to meet after dinner.

“We have met, and we feel secure with you. I have a special request which involves my daughter. Can we speak freely with you?”

Yes, of course, if I can help, let me hear your proposal.

“When a young woman transitions from girl to woman, she must get the service of a responsible man. Jasmin is still a virgin, and she wants you to help her with this transition.

Will you do this for her and me? It will make us both happy.”

He is the right man to transition you into a woman. Relax and follow his lead; he will not hurt you, my darling; I know you had wanted to do this. You will see the waiting is worth the time.”

Sylvia kissed her daughter and closed the door behind her.

I felt like a boy receiving a Christmas present. I had rehearsed it at times in my mind in the past.

I started to unwrap this precious gift.

A tall girl with soft blond hair stood in front of me. I sensed the anticipation and felt goosebumps on her skin.

She put her hand over a dark spot just above the bikini line. It's a beauty mark; it makes your body much more enjoyable. You do not need to hide it.

A photographer does not only photograph a skyline alone; It takes a boring photo. He wants to show other elements, such as a tree branch, waves, clouds, and a golden sun. All these elements make for a superior picture. The same goes for your spot. It makes you unique and looked at it as a natural gift.

Suddenly, she showed it to me and told me how long she had been hiding it." From now on, I will be wearing my bikini and offering the spot with pride."

I will tell everyone the analysis of your statement.

Did you like the rum punch?

I had only half of a glass and gave the rest to my brother. I am eighteen, but my brother is younger and only with Mother's permission was he allowed to taste the rum punch.

During this chat, I removed the few outer garments, revealing sexy lingerie and a bra with a back hook. She was not shy to show her underwear and started to unbuckle my belt.

Her naked skin and luscious body came unwrapped and profoundly affected me.

I continued with the bra, took her panty off, and started my process of caressing her skin. The fingers search for every sensitive area and stimulate the nerve ending. Soft kisses followed while she gave in to every move I made. Her breath started to increase, and little sounds came from her mouth.

My tongue is working its way to more sensitive areas. Her breast shows signs of arousal, with the nipples forming stiff peaks.

Down the chest cavity to the belly button and further for a visit to Venus. Her blond hair was soft and thin, showing the contours of the labia.

A short brush-up on this area told me to give it more time. She must be fully warmed up and show lubrication.

A massage of the legs and feet made her feel great. Then a back massage followed down to the buttocks and further down the thigh muscles. Then once more, the feet and toes.

When I had my hands reach the inner tough muscles, sounds of satisfaction appeared. Her legs came apart, inviting me to the center of attraction.

I knew she was getting impatient by now, but is she really at the point where I want her to be?

I probed the outer vaginal lips for moisture and found her more than ready. Her hips met my approach to get the fingers inside her.

Wait, my love, it is coming, and with a little more patience, it will be that much better.

She was lying on her back again while I probed the outer area, the inside, and the most sensitive spot.

She almost had an orgasm, but I quickly cooled her, a little longer, a bit more time

The activity lasted longer when I allowed her a modest orgasm.

I prepared myself in the meantime to make the grand entrance and turn this girl into a woman.

More kisses and now with all the intensity to get her to this point of no return. The first cry of pleasure gave me access to enter her and do the good deed.

I stayed inside while Jasmin was catching her breath. Congratulations, you are a woman now.

I did not feel any pain; how can this be?

You had too much to deal with having an orgasm; you did not recognize the slight pain. I will show you the proof; see here, the break had caused slight bleeding, but nature closed it quickly again. You are ready to receive the gift of nature and man.

Jasmin could not find words but recognized the intensity of her orgasm. It was the best of both; "You are a magician."

No, you had the patience, waited for the right moment, and received the reward in a big way.

I started little movements again, and she responded vigorously to reach another highlight.

I was at that point and took my reward while inside with protection.

I showed her the sperm. How does it taste? I do not know, but if you want to try a taste of it. You have to find this out yourself.

She could not bring herself to stick her finger in the sperm. It looks gross!

She asked to stay the night and tightly wrapped herself around my body.

In the morning she went to her mom's room and told her about the wonderful experience.

Sylvia saw me later and gave me a thumbs up.

I was wondering what comes next.

Mom spoke of us; she and Jasmin would be so happy. Does she have plans?

The day was filled with games and fun times on the private island. The illusion of living on an island like this is every child's dream in the way Robinson Crusoe made this dream a reality but only in a movie.

The cruise staff kept busy organizing groups for games while little children played in the surf and Mamas sipped on drinks while working hard on the tan.

Jasmine found me by the charcoal grill. She had a coconut filled with an alcoholic drink and drank it through a straw.

"I came to thank you again, and she kissed me. I will keep you in my heart forever."

The cooks and the Chef did see this gesture.

Then I noticed her bikini and how proudly she struts her body to the water.

Cooks must comment; it's in the blood to tease the boss.

The ribs are ready to come off the grill. As I expected, I was given a piece to taste. I smelled the spices while they cooked over the hot charcoal. The tasty, flavorful, and masterfully blended dry rub filled the air with aroma.

When Sylvia came over for a refill of rum punch. I warned her about drinking with a straw.

Be careful with this; it will catch up with you! It's the straw that will make you drunk faster. You are inhaling alcohol with air, which will make you sick. I would not want to have you spoil your time on this cruise with a hangover.

I told the bar manager to use crushed ice because it melts faster and dilutes the drink in warm air.

Lunch on the island was running past the regular mid-day eating time. The Chef adjusted the dinner to a lighter menu. Here is a man who thinks and acts in advance. Good foresight.

The sun had its effect on the people. Despite the amount of sunblock, red faces were everywhere, and most retired to their staterooms.

Sylvia and the children spend time together on deck to let the night air blow through the hair. No mood for stories?" Yes, of course, if you are up to it."

I looked back at my life and decided to give her tales from my time in India.

Did you taste the pork ribs today on the island?

"Yes, I did, and I found myself returning for more. Soo good, I was overeating."

With this comment, I began my stories about the time I worked at this Intercontinental Hotel and all the events that turned into funny episodes: the chicken butchers, cooking turtle souk, sending scouts out into the countryside to search for morel mushrooms, the milk coming raw in bulk from water buffalos, and lastly, the way we broke the social system in favor of promoting a cleaner to a cook.

Now I have to stop. It is getting late.

Sylvia said, yes, stop this story; a new one will be in the making soon.

Sylvia came to my room and thanked me for the treatment her daughter had received last night.

"She is a bit sore, but inside her heart, she is so happy I can see the glow on her face.

It was the best she has gotten and set her on the right path for life."

"I will now deliver how a woman must treat a man for keeps; it will be my gratitude for Jasmin.

Relax; Sylvia will handle all of it."

She started to undress when a knock on the door showed Jasmin.

"You always told me how important it is to treat a man properly."

With that, she joined the action.

Two gorgeous women are working on me to drive me to the peaks and valleys of making love.

Mom showed Jasmine the spots a man is sensitive; he needs to warm up the same as we do, and the areas are the same.

With this, I became the victim or the beneficiary of two women applying their passion to me. I had to surrender and endure, even when I reached the point of losing my mind.

What is it with Latin women that drive a man to such heights?

Jasmine spent the night with me again; I would not miss this for the world; it is as lovely after as it is during loving. She fell asleep and had a peaceful night.

At the gangway in Miami, we said our goodbyes, hugs, kisses, and joyful tears. "Be well and look after yourself. We go back to our life now and you to yours."

CHAPTER 12

"It's Priscilla from Barbados; I put her through to your line."

"You must have been at sea; I had called before. Happy belated Father's day; I love you, Dad. We miss you; when will you visit again?" I love you very much, and thanks for your attention; it still counts. I am revamping the program on the ships. I wanted to visit, but the work has me in the grips.

With every turn, I find outdated procedures that must be changed. I have had success, and the passengers love the new programs.

The rum punch takes center stage at the Captain's reception. We are making gangbuster sales.

When I get a breather, I promise you to visit. Kiss Kyra for me and a hug for Alex.

******

The Captain was amazed by looking at the equipment list for the kitchen; you pulled on the right strings.

Yes, it took motivation to get it; I explained how we gave the red devil an incentive, such as he gets to keep the job.

"I see you finally cut the umbilical cord. I had been telling his boss that something stinks in this kitchen, but nothing was ever done. Watch your back; actions bring reactions you have to expect it."

Thank you, Captain; the grapevine usually knows more than the shoreside.

"I will give you the signal, knowing you can read between the lines. Watch for changes away from the routine and always look him in the eyes."

******

At home was a dismal atmosphere. Nina can get down on herself, especially when she is alone.

It was different this time. Since Derick left for school with a healthy scholarship and was doing well, she missed him yet enjoyed her newfound freedom.

She was reluctant to come out to tell me what had been bugging her.

Is it the no-good Father of her boy, or is it the job? But the GM adored her; what could it be? I cannot force it out of her; she must unload in time and then I can console her.

Suddenly, she broke out crying and tried to talk, yet nothing came out to make any sense; all I could understand was her Mom, her Mom.

What about your Mom? Did she call; is there a tragedy again with your Steph brother and sister?

Yes, they are bastards and will not help but leave her to her misery.

"Finally, she collected her voice and told me that her mother had been diagnosed with advanced Dementia. She must be supervised from now on or be admitted to the nursing home.

I know she will cut her arteries and commit suicide if they admit her to a care home. I have to go home.

She adopted me to have a reliable daughter, and I know these two siblings are no good. They have too much of the Father's genes.

"I need you, my darling, you are the only one I love, and now I am in dire need of getting the excellent care I know you will give me." These were her pleas to Nina. She pleaded while crying. It tears my heart out; I must go!"

"I have to go tomorrow; I already called the boss to prepare my stuff, and I will drive to Minneapolis tomorrow afternoon. I know how much this will affect you but look at me; I am a basket case; just when all had fallen into place. It is my Karma I have to pay; I do not know for what."

The saying goes that the children pay the Father's debt.

"Forgive me, I have only one good relative in my life, her. She adopted me when my mother died at childbirth. The Father had something to do with her death. He took off and has never been seen again. He left me to the orphanage, and my Mom found me there."

"I will never know the details, but it was declared legal. She wants me to be her guardian and take power of attorney. After her death, I must settle the estate. These legal documents must be notarized at the location. She is revising her will and cutting the sibling out of the inheritance."

"It's the reason for her urgency. It must be signed while she is termed legally sane and is doing this of her own free will. Derick knows it and is upset."

He feels as if he has lost his Dad and his home and feels homeless."

You tell him I will be there for him, and he can move in again at any time. He will need a base with strength.

We made loved one more time, but it was not the same; her mind was in Minneapolis and the uncertain future. At least she will inherit her estate, which she thinks is large.

Be on the watch for these two criminals; they are capable of anything.

The dark history of a beautiful woman will remain a mystery.

She took the only cloth she could fit in her suitcases and drove westbound to the unknown future. "Will It be a one-way trip and an uncertain return?

" If I can come back, it will be in God's hands. Don't wait for me."

She will be missed, an empty bed again, alone, and left to my work. I was getting depressed over this and lost track of time.

******

"Who is ordering this?" The head of the marine department threatened to take away the equipment. The buyer wants an explanation. "Jim, the manager."

The scene was relayed to me in preparation to lose the kitchen renovation during the next dry dock.

Tell Jim if he rescinds the promise, we have recourse and mention Insurance.

Then came a note to see my boss!

"It would be best if you worked with the people in this office; we cannot tolerate open warfare."

Who is on the warpath? "Your predecessor makes allegations that the bidding has stopped, and he alleges kickbacks from the suppliers."

Show me proof; his form of bidding goes by a different standard. My bidding is for the best product and price, nice and neat.

I can only tell you that two of his former favorites have bad manners. We had been threatened, and Karri can attest to it. I have it on tape. I can make a copy of the transcript.

Do you want to back Jim blindfolded?

Look at the numbers and the passenger's rating; it speaks for our efforts. He had the opportunity to deliver these results while he had control of the department.

He will be well served to forgo his smear campaign. We have recourse if it gets ugly. He received a lifeline once, but that is the limit. I hope that I have made my point.

"I think so; let us forget this conversation ever happened."

******

I needed to get fresh air. Karri came out and wanted to know what the discussion with the boss had been.

He is in on it, and I let him know with so many words without saying that you and I know it. I hope this is the end of the redheads allegations.

I summarized the conversation and placed a copy in my file at home.

I will send the president a blind copy from now on. He must know what goes on behind his back. I have lost all trust in my immediate superior.

Alex at the West coast will be in the loop of every piece of communication from this day on. CYA.

******

We had called in wine merchants to give us the list.

Instead of the entire wine inventory of the various wines, they came with a selected list.

"Here is what we have for your ship. We have been doing business with the company since Jim took over, and they wish to continue this mutually beneficial relationship."

Jim saw the man in my office as he walked by and made an obvious detour.

They must have notified him of the appointment. It's a dead giveaway to me showing his dirty hands once more!

Is this all your company carries? "No, but these are the ones we can make a good deal for you."

Do you mean for the company? Come back with the complete list, prices, availability, vintage, and alcohol content by Volume. Then my assistant and I will sort thru it.

Jim is no longer involved. He is fixing the ship in dry-dock when it comes due. It is my show now.

Are you qualified to select the right wines?

I think so, check with this man, and I wrote the name on a note.

"Do you know him?" Oh Yes, I do. He knows something about me few people know. It is a good reference.

Karri looked at me and shook his head.

The following merchant came with the same scenario and received the same answer from me.

Then a young man in his 30th came in and asked permission to show us what he had to offer.

"We do not have an extensive selection because we are only two years in business, but we are growing and taking brands away from the competition. Give us a chance; we will serve you well."

"Tell me what type, price range and are there particular wines that may be attractive to your passengers. We do have an inexpensive sparkling wine if you are in the market for it."

We wish to divest from this cheap headache stuff and are looking for a nice white, light, a bit fruity, and with a spritz if you have it.

"We have that and just signed up the winery for an exclusive. It puts us in the position to deliver the quantities you need. A word of caution, we would prefer to deliver weekly to prevent spoilage. A low alcohol content makes the wine unstable. If you can store it refrigerated, that would be best."

If the price is attractive, we will use it as a replacement for the champagne.

We want a copy of all the wines you carry. We do not need a large selection, and the wine list we can print on the ship.

Another question: do you have remnants; I am talking about cases left over, which are hard to move into an account. A few cases of this or that at the medium to upper quality level?

We can promote these wines' sales and pour them by the glass. The sale is by word of mouth and will not require a wine list. It will be helpful to move dead inventory, and we will receive help from an attractive price.

"We accumulate these dead inventories when vintages change, or the producer cuts us short on delivery."

Thank you for your time; we will let you know within a week.

Karri wanted to know where I was getting these ideas.

Solving problems falls in the hands of the manager!

The other merchants mailed the complete list.

We selected noteworthy wines for our list and asked them for a sample for the taster.

Reluctant at first, the merchant cited that a case would be broken and cause a loss.

Do not worry; if you stand behind the wine, we will take the broken case, and you can bill us for the twelve bottles.

"Don't you want a special deal? "

No, we are not interested in that kind of deal. The last deal was not helping the company. The man stood up to close the office door.

"The Tasmanian devil with his red hair came on strong and muscled his way to extort a kickback from us. We do not like this method, but it never returns to regular business once he has us on the hook."

I am glad you are coming clean on this but give me more details.

"I thought you would be a straight shooter, so I came prepared. This is the last check he will receive.

Let me see it, and I will give it to him personally. We deal open. Tell me how this got started.

He told me how Jim used the same tactic as the other company: first, he promised huge volume, then reality set in, and it never changed.

Thank you, we will keep you as a supplier and keep it above board.

Are you finished with your work today Karri? Yes, just killing time until five.

Let's have a drink. We work more hours than these office workers, including managers; we can leave early once to compensate for OT.

"I know a Tiki bar, open-air with good oysters; perfect. Really off the beaten track but well patronized; It's a local hang-out for regulars."

"Once you have been there, the bartender will know your name and what you drink. Meet Bubba; he has been the bartender for years and should own the place now."

A Margarita will do it today.

"You looked a bit down this morning, Is anything troubling you?

You know the bout with Phillip, I don't even want to say his name, I was optimistic he would come clean and allow me to respect him, but after the evasive answers, he about told me that he is in with Jim in the kickbacks and now feels the pinch.

He must cancel the next Sahara Rally or buy another car; he is car crazy. It's his hobby, and it's good for him, but financing an expensive hobby on the company's books is not cool.

"But how do you know for sure? He will sneakily come at us. Until now, he used Jim and had hoped that we would break under pressure. Look out for behavior changes, look him in the eyes and read his transformation from the routine.

Any slight change is a warning signal. It will be our best defense. He comes from the culture that plundered the riches from the Colonies. I am glad we had this talk; I feel better and am ready to go home.

******

On the way home, I found something to eat: Little Caesar's pizza. I got two, and I took one home for another day. After that, I went to the lounge that had been my landmark signature spot and hunting ground.

I wanted to see if it is still going strong as an entertainment bar.

The few cars only told me what to expect. I turned around and looked up the cocktail lounge at the Intercoastal hotel, which had been my place to guard for the owner's sake.

Empty barstools and the room was way too cold. I had seen this once before when we had to turn this place around and make it the most successful lounge in the company.

Isabel greeted me with a kiss and unloaded her frustrations with the manager. They purposely killed the business, citing to set up a normal business flow.

"What do they define as a regular business level? Didn't they know that an action lounge needs patrons to generate energy and interact with other customers and staff? It was the driving force behind the success.

The hotel has a new owner and has replaced the GM and F&B director.

The new managers could care less. Nine to five and off on weekends, we never see them, nor would we ever have a voice to make suggestions.

As a bartender, I can make a living and you know how. It's not my style that bothers me, but they killed my livelihood.

I am considering leaving, but I am still in my studies and not ready to look for another job.

I am getting off soon. Would you mind if we went somewhere together? I want to pick your brain on management skills, the subject of my studies, and I hope to make it into management."

We went to the oyster bar on the Intercostals, which has a reputation for good food. She was hungry for food and knowledge.

I can think of mistakes that are made daily, but the care is not there."

You have just learned something, the way not to do it. You know, in both ways. One person will show you the proper way; the other will prove you the wrong way.

You will notice after this chat when a business is functioning correctly; few people will ask the question of why it is doing well. It is taken for granted. An effective manager will want to know the reason for the success. What are they doing better than us? I want to know. That is how managers continue self-development. Situations like this are all around you. 'I could tell you right now this bartender's mistakes, and the manager does not see it. But I better do this after we have left. Give it a try and keep it to yourself.

Now that you have pointed it out, I see it. There are other lessons you will never learn in school or from a textbook. You are learning from both right and wrong; both are teaching tools.

"I see; this as a revelation; why can't they include this in the course?"

They are Theoretical and do not come from practical applications. I will tell you that you already have more management skills than your teacher will ever learn. Just look at all the problems you solve daily.

Management is all about solving problems. Every problem has a source and, therefore, a solution. Once you track it back to find what or who the source is, the answer is in front of your nose.

You have done this a hundred times, but you have never recognized it as a problem solver. The other factor in management is dealing with people. Here, you have the advantage over the male gender.

Your intuition is much better than that of men.

When hiring a person, always make them do a task at the interview. You will see if they have professional skills. You will also know the attitude of new hires, which will tell you if this person becomes a team player.

If the person is hungry to learn, take this person, they will be appropriately molded by you and abide by the standards.

I will tell you another method to pass information or orders to the employees. When you say an order, there is always a level of resentment. To make it work, you must follow up on this directive until it becomes routine. Seven times is the minimum for it to sink in for good.

If you take the time to ask the employee questions about an issue, make the employee think, and keep asking questions until the employee sees the answer, you know that this directive or solution to a problem will be followed. You have made it the idea of this employee.

"I do not hear any of this in the school!"

Schools supply a fancy diploma, and it is given way too much importance. It serves as a tool to get hired. The ones with the most extensive certificates need a big wall to hang up on. Without that desk and the wall, they cannot function. Look back at your employment history, and you will recognize them.

What school did you go to? Grade one to eight. Then apprenticeship and out into the world, and it became my teacher. Today, I regret not having a degree, only because it opens the doors and nothing more. I was fortunate to meet the people who took the time to see me in my job. They hired me into the position, which I had worked my way up from the basic knowledge.

Today I carry my experience forward and build on it daily.

Finish your school; you paid for it but do not wave your diploma past HR at an interview.

Now you have all the material for your final term paper.

I will use it and give them your name.

I still have the waterbed. You did well in it, worth another turn, and who knows encores!"

We started dating and got to the point of getting the intimacy to a higher level.

Healing the wounds from Nina was coming timely.

The time with Nina will forever be embedded in my heart.

CHAPTER 13

The Moon Dancer

I will be sailing with you this time again.

"The Captain comments on the crew; they are much more relaxed and happier with the change. Mike is a good man and treats the crew with respect. I like the changes you have made in food and the portion sizes. The rum punch is a hit. "

I told him the story the Captain on the Turquoise Seas tells the passengers.

You know, how women fall for a romantic tale; it must not be the truth. Bring it to the punch line, like a joke, and finish with "Got Rum?

"You do much better; you are a natural in this field. I heard you telling half-truth stories, and they eat it up." It's not that hard; we will work on it later.

Mike and the Chef were checking the deliveries.

I like it when the Chef gets involved, it is his food to work with, and it's better to verify the quality.

During this voyage, I want to change our lobster preparation. Please ask the storekeeper to pull six tails to thaw. Tomorrow I will put on my old Chef's jacket and apron and see if I still have the touch.

Also, the dessert stuff from the confectioner is coming on board; keep it frozen and upfront in the freezer. Again tomorrow and every night after that.

The berries go on sheet pans with packing paper on the bottom and the top. It will absorb the moisture. Are the leafy produce still reconditioned? "Yes, but not far enough in advance." Change that, please, and gives it twenty-four hours.

Are you receiving enough Falernum? "I ask Ari, but he is running short."

I increased the delivery amount on Falernum. We need to look at a second vendor in Los Angeles; they are afraid to get stuck with inventory in their warehouse since we are the only customer ordering this product.

Hold off with selling the rum punch until the Captain's party. Making it exclusive is the key to marketing this drink. Besides the Master is our best salesman.

He will tell a funny story, and at the end, the question "Got Rum?" triggers us to start serving the drink. The first one is free; we will charge a little extra from the second serving until the end of the cruise, and this way, we will recover the cost of the free drink. Get the passengers hooked, and then the sale comes easy.

"You are shooting from all barrels already this early."

My time is four hours ahead, remember. Coming west seems more manageable but going eastbound is a killer. Adding the red eye on top kills a full day after getting home. Nothing is gained by flying home in a hurry.

I will now talk to Ari; he is up. Always the first one up, do you ever sleep?

A warm hello to Greta and Angela in the office, and then I saw Alex.

Insurance! I took the liberty to give you copies of my correspondence from Miami, just for information and safekeeping.

"Are you on to something?" I have the devil in check and keep a short leash on him.

The other had weaseled out of a delicate discussion so far, but I expect he will come back at me!

"You are right. I will give you advice on his method. He comes from the back, a coward, with a dagger in hand. Just watch your back and focus your eyes on the slightest habit changes. He is a prisoner of his habits, like High tea."

"Thank you for letting me know and keeping me in the loop. I never get anything from his office." Blind copies will now be sent from my home in Fort Lauderdale!

Angela came to give me a hug and a kiss. Life is boring without you, sure? You do not want to move here? I hear the winds of change are in the air! This is not the time for it.

"We hear the same, but no details as of today."

I know these people from the concessionaires are crooks. They will take the leading management positions. That is terrible news. It's time to start documentation and keep a file at home.

"Tell me how you swung all this new equipment."

I have the Red Devil from Tasmania on the leash and his feet to the fire.

"Is this the same situation we see here?" Yes, and he is not working alone. He does the dirty work.

I need bait; yes, this is it, a bait; talking to myself.

"Who?" Too early to tell but think of a person with an expensive hobby. I don't want anyone to get hurt; keep this to yourself. OK?

Greta, high, I saved the best for last, hug and a kiss, you look great.

"I have so much fun at my job now. I am glad about how it all works now. Efficiency and no more looking over the shoulders. makes dealing with the Vendors much more pleasant. They bring me little presents as a thank you. Is this OK to accept?" Yes, keep it small and share it with the office staff. "I do, of course. "Any repercussions from the skunk?

"He tried to muscle, but I referred him to you."

Good, there have not been any calls to my office. "He may have found a taker with Princess or Carnival to unload the tails." I have an idea. Let's talk in private.

Should he come with an attractive offer, tell him the proposal goes to Miami for approval. I will then tell him about a special request.

My boss is into cars, particularly VW Beetles. " I hear that one is coming in from Mexico."

If the lobster guy can secure a car for him, we can make peace and keep the boss happy. If he takes the bait, then Alex will do the rest. Secret classified, top secret! OK.

"She smiled; what a trap."

I developed this idea while talking to Alex. I will have him take the bait, and then I will set a trap for his visit.

We know in advance when he travels here. "Remind me never to get on the wrong side with you!"

Have no fear; I do not harm the sweet and innocent like you, Gracey.

"The Falernum supplier has a little hick-up." Tell him to get it from the other Bacardi distributor in Long Beach. There is no shortage. He is just too timid to stock up.

We will increase our load for Canada. He must prepare for it now.

I saw the Fantasia Pastry goods coming with the delivery. We will begin using them starting tomorrow, and the lobster recipe will also receive a makeover this week.

The inventory on the ship will receive scrutiny. We carry too much on board as dead money.

Schedule wine merchants here for my return; I have an idea for a replacement for the Champagne. We changed it already in the East to a fruity wine with a little fizz and serve the wine with a berry garnish.

Karri will be sending a report here. I will call in from one of the ports of call.

"Before you go, Hostess Eva asked if you would be here this week and sail with the ship! What is going on with her?"

She is into wines; I gave her a lesson on it and let her taste wines. She feels that she is an expert and now wants to talk about wines.

"Do you want me to believe that story?" Yes, and I have more stories to tell!

"Don't get cute; I should get on the ship and see the action myself."

"I can do the Alaska cruise when I have more time. When are you going up there to select a vendor?"

I have a proposal here; do you want to see it? Hold on, I want to be covered with my supplies too!

My information gives us a one-stop shop by a company that also coordinated the delivery. They work closely together, saving time and delivery costs.

******

I should settle on board to get the room. Have a great week. The purser has a surprise on board; you will love it.

The stateroom was a suite looking aft with a beautiful view. It had a queen-size bed and fancy linens, which beat the twin bed in a standard room. Thank you, people; I value your attention and the welcome presentation.

I went to greet the cooks and Chef.

The kitchen is busy with the preparation for the welcome buffet on deck.

I gave the Chef my priorities for the week, naming the lobster recipe, desserts, bread, and plate presentations. If we can involve the photographers in taking pictures, we will have a permanent reference.

I need time with the storekeeper to reduce the inventory.

Awareness, dating the products, proper rotation and setting goals for each item will ensure that we have an inventory turnover at the bare minimum when the ship returns to its home port. The menu remains the same, and any change is planned in advance. There is no excuse but caution: work with the kitchen and check the status daily.

Can you get started on this list, please? I wish to call Gracey from Acapulco and give her advance notice.

******

Ari was expecting me and made his usual sarcastic remark. Any wine tastings this week?

I have a nice room; it would be a shame not to share it. "Eva is always available for you; she cannot stop talking about what a lovely man you are."

A little engine hick-up caused the ship to leave late. The engineers had been waiting all day for the part. They will repair it during the first port visit when the engine is shut down.

The Greeks have their Seaman's Patron Saint's holiday coming up. On December 6, Saint Nicolas Day is celebrated by seafarers of Grecian descent worldwide.

I must remember to send a whole carcass of a lamb on board. They will roast it on a spit over charcoal. It's normally never allowed to have a live fire on the ship, but with a long port of call, they can open the back gate and do it safely outside the ship. There is always a way, and I must credit these Engineers. They are excellent mechanics and problem solvers.

******

My dinner table of six was filled. A father traveling with two teenagers filled the vacant seats next to me. A boy and his sister sat next to me, while the Father sat at the end of the table. I am Chris, and my sister's name is Olivia. I learned from the boy that Mom stayed at home for fear of getting seasick.

It's nice to meet you. Can I have your name again? Olivia, thanks. You have a beautiful name, and it fits you perfectly. Someone made a careful choice.

"My aunt and godfather made a choice. Are you from Europe, Germany, or Belgium? "

Germany is correct. "How is Konrad? I know he is long dead; we had this post-war subject in our history class. We learned how this German Chancellor negotiated with the Americans and managed to change the Image of the German people. At that time, he agreed with the allies to start the rebuilding process and borrowed money from them. He appointed a genius as his Finance minister, who created a miracle, also called Wirtschaftswunder. Payback will come once Germany is back on its feet and has a thriving economy."

The table had listened to our dialog. A mature girl is taking an interest in the history of post-war life!

Olivia continued with a million questions and asked if I remembered anything from that time.

I told her about my childhood years when there was hardly enough food for the people and when we kids first met the armored vehicles. French soldiers handed out peanuts and chocolate, and the kids fought over cigarette packs. The silver foil became recyclable for pennies as pocket money.

It had to be saved and deposited into a bank account. Each boy had a booklet in which every penny was recorded.

The food shortage drove the women to the butcher shop with the milk can each Tuesday. My parents carried the business forward from my Grandfather and expanded it into its pre-war time.

My mother handed out the broth used to cook the sausages, which became a soup with bread as the daily meal.

We never had any toys but made our own. Imagination drove the inspiration by using materials we could gather in the town, junk piles and often an empty spool from mother's sewing supply. At times it even involved an empty beer bottle, filled it with Carbide and by adding water we caused an explosion.

The danger of such activities was kept secret from our parents.

The entire valley was our private playground. The kids were looking for a swimming hole, and for that, the river was banked up, and now the water created a calm pond.

Olivia had switched seats with her brother to sit next to me while dad listened with great interest to my conversation.

We were not always the good boys; Dad sometimes punished us with a stick. The best time came with the first fruit ripening, especially the cherries.

We used to pick a tree and climb it. While everyone was stuffing their face, one boy had to stand watch. When the farmer came, we took off with the mouth full of cherries. If he caught us, he would ask the stupid question; "Are you stealing my cherries?" With the entire mouth of ripe cherries, we could not answer and the juice running down the chin, it got us a spanking and a smile all the same. He knew this game from his own childhood.

******

The food was now in front of us; I could see the efforts to dress up the presentation ant it is making an impression on the passengers.

"You must be working for the ship, the cruise line?" Yes, we have three ships split between the East and West Coasts. I do work for this company.

I handle what you get on your plate and in your glass, food & Beverage.

"Where do you live?" Fort Lauderdale. "I work in a hotel as a restaurant hostess."

Do you know the hotel directly on the Beach? "Yes, that's the hotel I work at."

As the regional director, I opened this hotel. "I have heard your name there."

What a coincidence! Yes, it was my last and best opening. Creating a four-star hotel was fun and challenging work. The hotel is very efficient. We put our heart and soul into this project to set up the service and excellent food.

Is the Girl from Alabama still there? "She is the restaurant manager for the fish house."

I know her and take her from Alabama to the hotel as a task force personnel. "She is talking about you sometimes."

"We have things in common: she is a good manager. The employees wished you would still be their regional. The man that followed is such a primitive man. He uses foul language, no class, and no experience, but he is good at kissing up to the arrogant Indian. The General manager is still the same. We lost his secretary. Nina was super-efficient and put out such beautiful Menus for us. She will be missed."

I know, I miss her too; she was my girlfriend.

"It's a small world. Can we talk some more on deck? You have so much to tell, and I want to know everything. I am pursuing a hotel management career. FIU accepted me when I finished high school."

OK, Hon, I love the fresh ocean air and cool nights out west.

I have things to look at first and after I will meet you by the pool.

Olivia wanted to know everything we did to get the Beach Hotel opened. They received four stars from AAA. The GM was breathing lighter; it had been a testy time between the inspection and receiving the award.

The talking carried on with endless questions until I had to cut it off and get my rest. "Can we continue tomorrow? "Yes, as time allows, remember I work here!

I went to Ari and informed him that we were testing a wine to replace the cheap Champagne. I will look for a similar wine for his ship.

"What about the cost?"

Wouldn't you want to pour a product you can be proud of and turn it into a sale? I am tempted to go all the way. Why give it free as the worst product and earn a bad reputation?

I should hear from Karri when I call him from the next port.

"I call my honey from there too. Yes, she is a beauty; Rosa is a Spanish girl who lives in LA. She comes sailing at times to make Ari happy. "

"I got the idea from you looking in your eyes after last time. What am I doing wrong? I should be living it up instead of gambling?"

Olivia was at the pool looking out to sea; the moon at half is more beautiful than the full moon!

"Do you say that because the other half must still be discovered?"

Life is that way too. "Do you have a new girlfriend yet?"

Not anybody serious. I started seeing a girl last week whom I have known from the other hotel for years. She is attending the bar but wants to leave and go into management.

"Do you want to go someplace private; I have my cabin." How old are you, still in high school and with a fake id?

"I will celebrate my 18th birthday in 3 days. Can I get a birthday present from you please, pretty please!"

Only on your birthday and in your birthday suit and very discreet in my room!

"I like that; here is a kiss for sweet dreams. You are a wonderful man, a real man!"

I had a note on the door from Eva. Knock three times. I am next door! She had a taste of the forbidden fruit already. She came in a loose gown and carried a Chandon Blanc de Noir bottle.

"I had a tough time tracking you down, and when I saw you talking to the girl, I thought she was your daughter."

She is almost young enough to be a daughter, but no, she works at my favorite hotel on the Beach in Fort Lauderdale. I have a special affection for that hotel. I opened it, and it has now reached the four-star level.

You can guess that had stuff to talk about this hotel.

"I wanted to see you tonight. Tomorrow, I have a duty and the Captain has me hanging around the group he is hosting after dinner."

Eva sat across from me while she opened the Champagne bottle and poured two glasses. Her dress opened up and slid past her leg to reveal the view into the area, confirming that she came ready to play. The brief peek gave me the reactions I was looking for.

We can finish this bubbly after; let's make the best of this time. Is she that hungry for sex all the time?

The Champagne was still cold and fizzed.

"This time it was just a quick release. It has been a while. The next time we will do it nice and slow with peaks and emotions."

I have to attend a birthday party for my new friend Olivia on Thursday. She will be of age and is planning a big celebration. I need a good night's sleep tonight, so forgive the short visit, but it was worth it.

The Captain's Gala party is important on every ship. I was wondering if I planned to serve little snacks during the reception.

I missed meeting with the cruise director; this will be my priority. I know that the Captain has his story rehearsed; he should be OK.

First, a good, and healthy breakfast from the buffet! They are doing the best job of all ships.

Yogurt, nuts, dry fruits, fresh fruits, a Granola-style cereal, juice, and great coffee. The baked goods are oven-fresh, and the rolls are crusty— all the best life can offer with fresh ocean air and California sunshine.

Eva joined me and looked at my plate. "You are eating healthy." It's the best and most important meal of the day. Especially after a raw bar the night before! The comment earned me a jab in the ribs.

It marks the beginning of the day; look at the Sunrise; I find it much more beautiful than the sunset.

The rising sun brings the hope and anticipation of a new day and hopefully a great day; the sunset buries the good and the bad. If you get up early, you get the freshest air, the cleanest water, and uncomplicated surroundings because you are by yourself; what more can you wish?

The brain functions best when it is just up from rest, with fresh blood streaming through and bringing hope, the elixir of life.

"It sounds like poetry!" She crossed her legs frequently. "Do you have a busy day?"

Like all days, I do as much as I can, but Captain's Night is always a busy time. We want him to look good in front of the passengers. We cover a wide spectrum of services in Food and beverage.

Olivia has since joined the breakfast table and I introduced her to Eva.

"Will you be at my table for dinner?' No, Olivia, the Captain invited me to his table. He likes me there; I am like the jester at the King's banquet. "How do you do that? "

It starts with the same question you had. Where are you from?

"I will miss you and don't forget the birthday party."

By nine, the lobster test and I must get the Chef's jacket and apron, and now again rehearsing the ingredients I remembered from the San Blas lunch.

A hot pan with little oil and a quick fry. But how did he keep the vegetable texture?

I envisioned the sizeable electric pan that could make a difference. The test will show me the way.

After the lobster, our pastry man will work with me to create desserts for each day. I have good notes and pictures from food magazines and pastry books.

Now, the Garde Manger prepares snack bites, and the fry cook makes sweet potato chips and sprinkles spicy salt on them. Then, we tackle lunch on deck. Here, I have a tough nut to crack. Despite the excellent food choices and a daily rotation, the passengers do not recognize the changes.

There must be a way to create awareness. I had the Chef and Mike with me, and when I mentioned the issue, Mike patted me on the arm. "You have the idea already. Awareness of all the senses, including the nose. The nose will be the first level of understanding. We are thinking only about the looks and taste."

Yes, you are right; we must rotate flavors and food penetrating the air with its distinct aroma.

"Chef Bobby quickly tuned in to this conversation. OK, I will do Asian food tomorrow; I have been itching to show my skills from the Asian world. After that, we can go generic or do other ethnic food."

I think that will work. We sat together after lunch and mapped out the rest of the cruise.

The lobster test was an exciting task; too many cooks spoiled the broth, which is what almost happened. Many cooks added their ideas, claiming to experience from their own recipes.

One young Filipino cook said in a low voice, "You must remove the Lobster meat from the pan after the quick stir-frying. Then, add the other ingredients and seasonings to the pan and cook fast to remain crisp. After that, return the lobster meat and toss it; it will be perfect. Taste it, and you will find two layers of flavor. The lobster keeps its flavor and will not be overcooked, and the vegetable keeps its flavor and texture and brings forth the seasoning we added. My Mom taught me that at home."

We did a second test with adjustments to the spices, and voila, this was perfect. All the cooks celebrated the moment and named the dish after this cook: "Lobster a la Danilo!"

He was immensely proud when I promised to feature his name on next week's menu.

Desserts are making progress. His artistic talents are being displayed in the arrangement, bravo. He has it right, and it looks too good to eat. The Pastry Chef is a true Artist. He paints pictures as a hobby and does the ice carvings for the late-night gala buffet.

******

The reception has started. Passengers are in the show lounge awaiting the arrival of the Master of the Moon Dancer.

Drum roll and the officers are making an entrance in grand style. After a short introduction by the Captain of his senior officers, he rolls into his story.

We were Sailing the bulk freighter from South America north to Sweden with a whole load of Brazilian coffee beans. Surinam is an area known for piracy at the northern tip of Venezuela. We knew that and prepared for an attack. I had met with pirates before when I sailed the waters of East Africa.

This time, the pirates managed to get hooks over the railing since the ship was fully loaded and low in the water. With swords and Sabers in hand, they demand ransom money from the sailors.

"Pay, or we cut your throat." When I heard this commotion, I dressed up, put on my belt with the sword, and went on deck to confront these hoodlums. What do you want, money? We do not carry cash; we carry coffee. If you don't believe it, then have a look." We do not believe you and want to see the cargo; please tell your crew to open the hatchways and let us check it out.

He motioned the sailors to do that and let them into the bulk cargo space.

The sailors quickly closed the hatch and locked the access.

The belly of the ship is hot and humid, creating fermentation for the coffee beans. Little oxygen brought them near death. After two hours, I ordered to open one door to see if anyone was still alive.

Two heads came up gasping for air, then motioning to open more to get the others pulled up. Half dead, they were thrown into the sea, sink or swim. Make a choice but learn a lesson from it. I told the helmsman we needed to celebrate. Got Rum?

Ari was ready with the rum punch, and we introduced our famous drink at the end of the story.

Olivia felt left out when I spoke with the Captain, and then I introduced her to the Master of the ship. He kissed the young lady's hand and invited her to join him at his table.

It was the highlight for her, getting a hand kiss and a personal invitation to his table of VIPs. She must have grown an inch. She sat next to the Captain at the head of the table. I sat beside her, and she held and squeezed my hand under the tablecloth. It did not take long before she relaxed and joined the conversation.

Word had gotten out that the company would be merged with World Ocean Cruises shortly. The conversation centered around this merger since the table guests were travel executives. They had to know if the bookings were honored and if the commission was secure.

Olivia listened and whispered to me not to forget her birthday party. It will be much more fun. "Are these dinners always such a bore?

No, it depends on the people's diverse backgrounds, and the mood dictates the subjects.

Her mention of her birthday reminded me to get her a gift. But what is right for her at that age? I was at a loss.

Should I buy her perfume to mark the transition from girl to woman? It would be perfect if the gift shop carried the same perfume, but more for the mature customer. I know she has a burning desire to experience the love of a mature man.

I thought it might be best to postpone this encounter to home base. A meeting can be less conspicuous since both live in the Fort Lauderdale area. I do not need a scandal and a father to accuse me of rape. I will guide her to visit my house when she is assured that neither her Father nor her brother will ever find out.

To celebrate her birthday, I thought I'd plan a private party with Champagne on deck and make plans for the at-home reunion.

There are always other passengers on deck to observe, and a harmless kiss will demonstrate the affection and gratitude of spending time with her, marking her special day. Plans for an encore can then be made at home base in FTL.

While talking to Olivia about the dangers of tomorrow's plans and the consequences if her Father gets involved, she starts to cry.

"I had high hopes for this, mainly because of you." She had seen her Father's looks and knew trouble was on the horizon. Plans at home gave her fresh hope. She settled down with hugs and kisses and went to her room.

A knock from the next door, followed by a knock at my door. It confirmed a lively night ahead. Eva had a protein-rich dinner with wine on top of the rum punch, making her a little light-headed.

Something had gotten into Eva to be so aggressive. I thought she was going to rape me. She must be ovulating, or is it the food?

She approached the activity with a warming-up period, and when the moment arrived, she let go with all her force and emotions. She could not speak while she was gasping for air. It must have been the biggest one yet.

I gave her water and let her settle down. This time, she stayed for the night and changed into a new outfit in the morning.

I made my phone call to Karri from the agent's office.

He confirmed that the wine was a hit. This gives me the confidence to go ahead on the West Coast with the same program. I told him about the lobster's effects, but the cooking method had a trick. I have to show it to you and the Chef.

"The Chef gave me a letter from India. Another daughter? "

No, I broke the law there, but I will not be sent back to face justice. It's a good story for the Tiki Bar.

The letter came from Anil, and I bet it will start this way.

"I trust my humble words will find you in good health and great spirits."

They are polite while we get straight to the point—no beating around the bush. Which way is better? He confirms that his family is doing well and expresses his eternal gratitude for taking the risk of promoting him. The hard times presented by the other cooks were worth the sacrifices he endured. The benefactors are his children entering school and making a new life for themselves. Bless you, and your kind heart. May heaven protect you and your family. Respectfully. Anil

******

I found a lovely perfume, the same brand she uses now, but with a more mature, less pronounced smell. The saleslady described it as seductive. I hope she likes it.

Do I give it to her at the dinner table when the servers sing Happy Birthday? Can I hide it from her Father's eyes, or wait for a better opportunity?

Her Father seemed distant to her. There was no usual tight bond between a girl and her Father; He missed out on her most critical developing years.

A girl needs her Father in these difficult times. A man will show more sympathy, while a mother will nag and drive her out of the house. Is this a natural move? Look at nature! Nobody understands it.

Being there for her is enough to show compassion and genuine love even when the worst of tantrums are played out.

She will try to sit next to me again. I can slip it to her under the table and whisper to hide it.

The rest of the afternoon allowed me to write my two reports. The one with every detail goes to Alex, and the condensed version is on a need-to-know basis, and that one goes to Phillip, my boss.

I found time to meet with the Captain. He is a straight shooter and has expressed his position where he stands with the Brits.

"You take him; I know he wants to unseat Alex; that is very obvious, but Alex is the better man, and he is honest. This man comes at me as if he wants to put his hand into my back pocket and reach for the money. He has suggested changing to another company to bunker oil.

But I know the other captains are calling this man a thief. They know the Mexican mafia runs this outfit."

That fits my suspicion; I cannot get a straight yes or no; I always get an evasive answer without commitments.

Then he has this Tasmanian devil on the leash doing his dirty work.

"How do you deal with him? He had your job!"

We have hard proof from vendors, whom he has blackmailed up until now. They wanted to come clean and gave me a check he was about to mail. Then we received a check from Phillip from the wine merchant, and this deal was linked to the Champagne.

It's my reason to have this conversation with you; as the Master, you have the last word on the ship, and this is my backbone if he wants to muddy the waters.

"Good, count on me. I will get a quote from an independent professional in San Diego and a price quote from the Mexican oil company. I can almost predict to find a booby-trap in the deal. I will keep you and Alex in the loop."

Thank you for your time.

******

What will I do in Acapulco this time?

I have always wanted to see this magnificent Acapulco Princess, with bungalows, private pools, and fancy restaurants. I will ask Eva if she wants to join me.

The seating at dinner did not change. Olivia was filled with anticipation.

I requested a better-than-regular cake made with cream and berries filling. She sat next to me, and I could smell her freshly shampooed hair and flower-fragrant perfume.

It's her special day to come of age. She was in a chatty mood that kept everybody engaged. Her Father looked more relaxed since she talked to the entire table, introduced subjects an adult would bring up, and participated in back-and-forth dialogs.

Her Father had seen a change in her and took off the alarm. She must have manipulated him to pursue her original plan.

Then the cake came to the table, and a group of servers sang the song like it is done in Asia. Rattles and percussion devices accompanied the soundtrack over the speakers in the ceiling.

It had everybody engaged in giving this proud girl the attention she so desperately wanted.

Eighteen candles must have been blown out, so she asked for my help. I did it in disguise to manage it in one sweep.

Her Father noticed my closeness to his daughter and wanted to learn more from the man his daughter had latched on to.

"Where had you worked in your career before the cruise line?"

I will backtrack my resume. For starters, I opened the hotel where your daughter works.

I was the Regional Director and had the owner's assignment to put the seafood restaurant together. That was just a tiny part of opening a hotel. The company did an extensive job of training, testing, and even a dress rehearsal.

A task force from other hotels is applied to aid in this training phase.

Olivia nodded, " My boss came from Alabama as a task force and landed a manager's position after the grand opening. It is indeed a jumping board recognized for future promotions. I want to do this once, too, and I hope she nominates me for the next opening nearby."

Before this, I opened up Miami, Tampa, Raleigh, and Hilton Head, integrated Tampa airport, and closed Acapulco.

"What happened there?"

The owner was a prominent radio company, and the hotel needed a significant renovation.

Warnings were ignored until we finally removed the name and locked the doors. It was the most emotional experience in my career. Employees had worked at that hotel for 20 years and longer and loved to work for this Gringo Company. They received fair treatment, training, and good pay.

The company withheld money from the owners and gave everybody healthy severance pay. It was gratifying to see them cared for and provided funding, holding employees over until the next job.

His tears could fill a river in itself. It had the same effect on me now as when I was there.

I had to wipe my teary eyes at that time.

When I stopped there on my last visit, the hotel had reopened under the Radisson Brand. I found one person cleaning the lobby, and she recognized me.

She told me that everybody had found an excellent job.

These employees had a reputation for being the best trained and honest. To secure these employees, other hotels have been bidding for increased pay.

It will be an emotional day. I must remember to bring extra tissues. The Princess hired most of them, and I am going there this time by taxi.

It was so quiet around the table; I thought they had lost their voices. Olivia's Father broke the silence and said," This is huge." He came over to shake my hand, and all the others followed as Olivia expressed her pride in me. It took me a moment to regain my composure and wipe my face. I know my eyes get a washing tomorrow.

As we all left the table, I saw Olivia's Father pull her aside and whisper something answered by her nodding her head.

She returned to me as I noticed the gift still in my pocket.

I gave it to her, and she started to tell me with full excitement that her Father liked me and gave her the green light to spend time with me.

Spending time and having a birthday party are two different things.

"He said yes, you are an adult; you must decide. He sees you as kind, especially when you wipe the tears. He wants to invite you to our home for dinner."

When I saw Eva from a distance, she motioned, tonight? I signaled to hold off. The alternative may be on again. She received the green light from Dad, and I am sure she will take the opportunity.

******

I embraced and kissed her on the lips, soft and long, then a breath and again, but more intense.

Olivia wrapped her arms around my neck and held me tight. The slow undressing started at once. I reminded her to let me do it at my pace, relax, and let it happen to her. She relaxed and breathed while I took off her blouse, skirt, shoes, and socks.

I undressed myself to my underwear and then touched her skin all over her back.

She laid down on her stomach when I loosened the bra hook and gave her back a feather massage. My hands are brushing over her legs and moving down to her feet. Hard-working feet are abused all day long and deserve the fullest attention. When the foot had relaxed from the anticipation of getting tickled, I had the toes in my control with a soft bend, and pulling on each toe, I heard a soft moan showing pleasure.

After that, the Achilles tendon was stretched, and the entire foot and calf area was cream massaged. Her thigh muscles came next, and with them, the body was fully relaxed.

Olivia turned on her back, giving me access to the tender, young and still budding breast. Her little pink nipples are demanding attention. The girl is guiding me to her sensitive areas while being impatient. She had an incredible body, a dream, a treasure, and my fingers made circles around her breasts. I noticed how the nipple hardened, and she reached for them to give a soft pinch.

Give me the time; it will be worth the wait. Gradually, I reached the pubic area and followed up with the lips and, at last, the tongue.

It was too much for her to hold back any longer. With a loud moan and a shaking, she had reached her first orgasm. OK, it will continue after a pause. There is more and also more intense.

Her eyes showed a glare, which I took as tears. No, they are not tears; they are joyful expressions.

My body had reacted, and I took off my underpants to let him free. Olivia got a glimpse of it and reached to touch him. Wrapping her fingers around, she said, will it fit? Am I a little girl?

She will be well-lubricated, and I will go slow.

My tongue approached the inner thighs as she opened up, allowing me access to her fleshy parts. The sight of this area exited my body, but I knew I must go slow. Olivia may still be a virgin.

A sin to touch, but necessary to make a woman out of her!

The tongue opened the lips, revealing the pink inside, the sweet smell, and the wetness, showing her readiness. Her hips met me with urgency; yes, I know, but not yet, my love.

She took a deep breath and returned to give her body to my caressing. Then the tongue finally reached her trigger point, and she could no longer hold it back.

She moaned with pleasure and moved her hips, telling me to back off. It's intense, be gentle!

It's just the beginning! "What? I thought this was the big one, indeed the biggest for me. Doing it alone is never that big." I know it has to build; the slower, the bigger it gets. Oh really?

I am ready with the protection already on.

"You do not need it; I have been on the pill for two weeks; I had to get my mother's permission; she frowned about it, but better than coming home with VD."

I continued to build the excitement, and she reached the pinnacle, but I backed off and got her down to cool before exploding. Carefully, I took her up again and realized she was super sensitive and quick to go.

I took her so slowly and gently to get closer. Yes, that is the way, and then she climaxed. At that point, I went inside to drive the excitement to the maximum.

Bucking up towards me and driving my penis ever deeper, she was going on for minutes before she had to breathe and slow down. All the while, her inner muscles pulsated and contracted to milk every drop of my tool. It was as intense for me as for her. We collapsed on top of each other and slowed our heart rates down.

"Stay inside; it feels so good. I wished you could have been my very first man. But in a way, you are my first. The boy tried, but he failed." He took the finger to break the Hyman and never made it inside. He soiled his underwear.

Interesting, but my first time was no better. Poor girl. She was not satisfied and got angry with me. It took me time to understand.

"How did you learn all this?" Practice, practice!

I will not tell anybody about this practice; it will be my secret. Never kiss and tell!

You must tell your little brother once he comes of age, teach him what I am doing verbally, and then, if you ever have children, teach them, too.

******

Olivia and Eva joined me on my visit to the Princess Hotel. The ride took 40 minutes and fought the busy main street.

It is worth the trip; this hotel is truly world-class, projecting luxury from the minute one enters the driveway and portal, with sharp-looking door attendants, bell staff, the front desk, and the gigantic open-air lobby.

The ocean was visible from this point of entry. Wings of buildings with ornate architecture resembling a royal palace housed the guest rooms. It is surprisingly affordable. Anyone can feel rich.

We took a stroll on the grounds and passed various pool areas and bars to swim up to get a refreshment. A separate area had supervision for children.

The appointments for the guests are detailed and plentiful. They have thought of everything!

We had a drink at the bar, and the bartender recognized me; "Palenque bar! Do you remember the Hora Feliz?"

Yes, of course, you served us when we had the hotel. How has it been since the closure?

"I am happy to report that 80% of the employees found a job here. Employees were promoted to junior management positions in restaurants, bars, and housekeeping. The training was not practiced at this hotel. Our employees knew how to train and received added assignments with a boost in pay.

The hotel runs buses to pick up at a central location in the town center.

I no longer work for the hotel company. I run the F&B operation on ships now. I love the new challenge and ability to interact with the public, which I did not have!"

Meet my new friends, Eva and Olivia. "You always had good taste!"

Which place would you recommend for lunch? "Go to the one with excellent fresh seafood.

You may find Ignacio there, the deputy director in F&B." Thank you for your gracious hospitality.

Ignacio told me started as the deputy F&B manager and has a promotion in the wings. The department is growing too large for one person. I learned good management techniques from you. You must know this: how you ran and always presented questions made me realize the ease of getting employees to buy into a suggestion.

On the way back, Eva commented how impressed I was with all my contacts. Most importantly, I left behind a positive mark. Olivia echoed this with the efforts I made at her hotel.

"Do you have any duty on your agenda tonight?"

No, Eva, it's just dinner and holding the inquisitive women at bay.

It went down as predicted. Olivia had a private conversation with her dad, likely to explain why she was not sleeping in her room.

He was OK with it; you must know that your Mom and I had sex on her 18th birthday, and history repeats itself.

If she sees what I see in you, she will be jealous and accuse you of having sex with a stranger. Tell her that history repeated from 20 years ago. It will shut her down.

I have a wish, but you decide, no pressure.

I would like to know his technique; if you give that to me by verbal instruction, I can give her this glow on her face, too.

"Good Dad, at home, when we are alone. I will show you on my body the areas that turn a woman on. A kiss on the forehead and a hug, and she went on in search of me.

I was on my rounds for the people program. I learned this from a man who practices this like a religion.

Olivia watched me in action and stopped me. "That kind of activity has not been practiced since you left the company. The veterans are always commenting on it; we miss getting a pad on the back from the suits."

His time will be short-lived. I told Olivia about my experience when the chairman made a beeline to shake my hand. After I had been out for three years, he still remembered my name. That is the epitome of the people program.

"Why did you never come back?" I tried, but this Doberman loaded my employee file with dirt and lies.

It's beyond my understanding how people find satisfaction in hurting others or, for that sake, the company that gave them work.

I have a list of these types of situations that I cannot name. I refer to the ones that I keep on a short leash.

******

Back in the home port, Angela greeted me and wanted to know the latest changes.

"I know you by now to make changes on every trip."

I told her about the Lobster change, the desert improvement, and the Captain's story, which made her chuckle. But in reality, I changed the reception to the grand entrance by the Master for his party. I hope I did not step on your tail since this overlaps with your territory.

"I am OK with it, and the Captain has the right to approve such changes. Phillip will have a cow! "

Let him have a herd of cows; the Captain has the last word on the ship. He is the Master, and he loves it. Finally, this awful handshaking is gone, and he gets time to mingle with people.

I will handle him in time; just let it mature. Are you up to something now?

We must keep life interesting! But if you have the stomach, you can take part in this! I need information on his expensive hobby. Can you find out if he has any cars?

Is he buying a VW and may have put it on hold? "I know the dealer that supplies these rally cars. Last I heard, he tried to cancel the order."

Can you get me the dealer's name and contact information?

"OK, yes, but this is sensitive and dangerous. No secret shared stays a secret." So far, it is you and me."

With the information in my pocket and confirmation of the rally and car cancellation, I had enough information to know that the timing was ripe. I told Alex that a trap would be set, and he would get the date for the final kill.

I told Greta that this lobster vendor is hurting and will go bankrupt unless we take the inventory off his hands. I will call him to get good terms. Canada has not been committed, and it remains an open question. We have the space to store it, and he may invoice in installments.

I called the vendor and said that my boss was forcing me to make a deal to take the inventory to Alaska. Can we talk? We can meet at the restaurant. The one with the deck should be undisturbed.

He agreed at once and is ready to talk this afternoon.

I ordered an iced tea, but there was no food as we started to talk.

He feels wrong for hurting you in such a big way and wants to see if a deal can be struck. The price cannot exceed the market price, but it works in your favor since the market has gone up.

The sticking point is the company's cash flow; if he could bill it on a weekly consumption basis, it would show a straight business deal, camouflage the earlier shady deal, and preserve the company's cash flow.

He is asking you for a favor. Seeing the VW on hold is putting him in a bind. Can we count on you to have the car delivered to the port and give the papers to the office manager, Alex?

He knows that you have a connection to this car. The car will not be used as a streetcar, so it does not need license plates and CHP clearance. The title will be sufficient. Place it in a sealed envelope.

Will you call me at my private number? We keep the girl out of the discussions, OK?

"Well, yes, better than cash, and I can trade. It does make it easier; OK, we have a deal."

The timing depends on your call. I will have the girl order both ships, which will be used weekly on the Columbia and the rest on the Moon Dancer the following day.

Alex closed the door; it was set up, and this is how it goes down.

The bait is the car; the trap is the title in your hand. The dealer will call Phillip to inform him to pick up the car in LA; he is releasing the vehicle in good faith, as well as all the prior deals.

Payment for the car comes from the lobster deal. This guy is so desperate to unload.

He will be told that the Moon Dancer will take the entire load to Alaska.

All these promises are fake. I will place the order, and when he delivers, the storekeeper will reject the entire load based on freezer-burned products. The supply we have on board now is already burned.

Next week is the target day. OK! Phillip is scheduled to fly here to take the title and car.

The title will be in a sealed envelope and delivered to you, Alex. You will then go in for the kill and call the fraud.

He will seek a way out, but you can deal with him and keep him on a leash only with a confession. Papers become evidence if he dances out of line.

Tomorrow, Columbia will be in for a short port visit. After, I will fly home by noon and make it home at a decent time.

I thought of the mouse trap to look for downfalls. Playing the devil's advocate, it looked solid. It had the elements of desire, desperation, greed, reward, and a cover to disguise, and the timing fits. Yes, it has to work.

Alex and Angela came and said, did you swallow the canary? Your look is so dark and severe; what have you been thinking?

I told them the idea was going through my mind with the midnight buffet and, in a rough frame, the belief in principle. Alex was encouraged by another albatross nobody wanted to attack, and a big waste.

It bothers me the most. Nobody can be hungry when they just had dinner two hours ago.

Do you have any rough ideas? Not yet, just conceptional thinking!

The first night was a large spread since we were catching the late check-in passenger who missed dinner. Then, the Grand Gala follows the extensive menu and overeating on the crustacean.

By now, we are in Mexican waters and tying up in the first port. There is more to think of by designing contrasting food that helps digestion. A Viennese dessert table could serve as an attraction towards the end and make good points for the rating.

I am leaning toward setting up a deli, much like the New York ethnic place, with hot and juicy pastrami, pickles, mustard, Cole slaw and brownies. It will give the kitchen a break, and the leftovers become hash with poached eggs. There has always been the popularity of the past, and I am sure the Chef wants to show his Asian spicy morsels—nothing elaborate except the Gala with the culinary art on display.

"You have it down, pat. Just work out the details."

Yes, I am getting there. The Gala buffet still bothers me. Will the repeaters complain? Then there is Phillip; he will skin me alive. I want to divert the attention from eating and limit the eatable food to bite-size snacks.

"Give it time; there is no rush, then implement it in Alaska; Phillip is usually on the second voyage. Does your brain ever shut down?"

I do have my moments, Angela. On the last cruise, I thought my light would burn out.

When you invent a new mousetrap and build it, you must test it mentally!

"Are you talking about the Truly Nolan Car? Yes, dear, we are on the same page. "I hope this beast has gas in the tank." I do, too; peeing in the tank would be the wrong energy.

Nobody would understand the sense of this conversation except Angela and me.

The breakfast cook at the hotel greeted me and offered me eggs.

I want an omelet, but if you allow me, I can teach you how to prepare it like a professional. I am a Chef!

"That is kind of you; nobody has shown me anything; I had to learn it alone. I worked as a houseman in housekeeping."

I took the skillet and added a pad of butter. I added a ladle filled with beaten eggs and seasoning when the butter was hot enough.

It has to cook a little, and when you see it solid on the bottom of the pan, you start moving the eggs around until you can see them almost cooked. Now comes the filling. I use cheese and lift on the handle. With the rubber scraper, the eggs are folded from the handle forward. You see how they follow the pitch of the pan. The omelet is ready to be tilted onto the plate when it's a half-moon.

It's all straightforward. Do not let it cook too much; you need the softness to fold, and it will continue to cook and form one unit.

He watched with great intensity and said, "This is beautiful."

You have to make one, please. It's for practice, and you get to eat it.

Danny did as I had shown it to him, becoming the best omelet cook in town. I just made his day!

Tugboats pushed while the linesmen worked the thick lines to the cleats. A winch on board the ship pulled the lines back tight to secure the ship to the pier. Two spring lines finished the job.

I remembered the procedure from the time I owned a sailboat. If you try to do this alone, you will need four hands. Gooday mate! Good morning, you an Aussie?

I come from the land down under, where women glow, and men plunder, do you know the thunder!

"That is correct and glowing they do if the job was done right." The Long Shoreman smiled and gave me a thumbs up. He told his fellow workers that I was from Aussie land, and he had been there and tasted the forbidden fruit.

The new Chief Steward met me at the dock. Magandang Umaga Danilo. Good to meet you. Did your first voyage go well?

"Yes, Chief, I noticed changes; I like it."

There will be more to come soon. For now, you get a break in the action. The only item I wish to change is the Lobster. We tested a recipe on the Moon Dancer.

We stir-fried the Lobster with vegetables and spices and named the recipe after the cook that had supplied it for the test. "Lobster a la Danilo"

Is he your son? "Yes, Chief, he is into cooking and took the recipe from my wife."

I looked at the meat and noticed the strip loins were smaller.

Let me walk you through the changes and explain the purpose.

It took me twenty minutes to give an overview, and I promised to sail with the Columbia and then go into every detail.

"Anything else for me?"

Yes, a special delivery of Lobster. Next week, there will be a small delivery from the old lobster inventory. Keep it aside; I must see the condition and decide how we can use them. Do you know the man?

"I do not like him; he is always rude and bossy."

He will not be bossy anymore. Accept them even when they show freezer burn. I will explain when I come back because it must serve a purpose.

CHAPTER 14

Back in Miami, I met with Karri to update him about every change. So many changes are implemented without first seeking approval.

I am not concerned since we can back it up with results. I Look at the numbers and the customer comments. "We had never reached such heights with Jim. He has been quiet since we found his shady deals."

It serves us. We have a solid base to defend it. In California, I informed Alex about everything, and we have the backing of the Captains. They are grateful for the changes we started with the party.

I was unsure if I should feed Karri the upcoming trip details.

It must remain a surprise. Otherwise, the risk of a leak is too big. I will be in Vancouver, which makes him vulnerable if he knows too much.

"Tell me what's bothering you; these changes are not the only issues. Is there something I can help you figure out a solution for?"

You read me very well; yes, there is, and it isn't easy. It is also dangerous. If I give you information, and if word gets out, these two will squeeze you for information. I don't want to expose you up front, but you know that I will be in Vancouver to set up the Alaska provisions.

I have a code name that I can tell you. "Truly Nolen."

I am working on a better mousetrap. Sorry Karri, I must leave it at that.

Your next project will be the lunch buffets. The Chef on the Moon Dancer and Mike had this idea. Bring in new flavors and fill the air with food and spice aroma.

We recognize food with our eyes and forget the most powerful way to communicate a change in buffet food, namely our sense of smell.

Here is what I penciled in my brain. The first night has a Caribbean theme with jerk pork, roast chicken fish with sofrito, plantains the Cuban way, and there is more to add. Challenge the Chef to use up midnight buffet food and develop other items.

The Gala buffet can be smaller and concentrate on the artistic side.

Passengers want to see this and take pictures. It also makes the cooks proud.

Snack bites will be sufficient for those who are tempted to eat. Who can be hungry after a big dinner? It was only 2 hours ago. We tie in with the decorated pieces, which aligns with the buffet idea.

My mind is searching for some more. It's midnight and, hopefully, a clear night. The stars are out, and all we need is music.

Yes! I have it. We can stage a Party and call it a "Starlight Dance Party." I will share the idea with Lynda in Entertainment and the purser.

Other lunch themes can be Italian or Mexican; even a New York Deli will be a comfort food concept.

Each theme brings a different aroma. We are testing this on the Moon Dancer. My head is spinning.

"Can I come to sail with you once in California?"

It would be good for you to see a different clientele. The passengers are fun and loose, topless girls on the pool deck asking for a nudist section on the highest deck.

I'm not sure that will be a go. The bridge officers would be sidetracked and get the ship to Hawaii. I'm kidding. But you may get lucky!

The evening at home was quiet until the phone call came from Olivia.

"Can I come by your house to talk? I am still jet-lagged. I only want to share the latest mood at La Casa.

Mom was asking what had happened to me. She has been pushing my father for answers. Her precious little girl got hurt or bewitched; she looked different.

She turned eighteen, an adult, and a year older. We all do this every year; what is so different? She was with me, remember? It was her father's explanation.

She would not let go until my father told her I had lost my virginity. Don't you remember our first time; it was your 18th birthday?

This man is a stranger, and is he older? What does age have to do with it? He brings experience; in her case, she learned how to do it right. Do you mean orgasmic? Yes, she told me that she had multiple orgasms.

Mom sucked in the air, held it for five minutes, and only let go when she had to.

Drama queen. You and I never reached that point, and we still have not managed it with all the practice.

But this will change now! What do you mean?

She explained and showed me what he had done to get her to the arousal stage that produced these high points. Is she that open to you? We had an open discussion.

The man told us stories from his life. He showed us a big heart. It moved the people to tears, and he was wiping his face just the same.

Yes, Mom, I said; he told me more stories, all different and all authentic experiences.

We want to invite him to dinner, but he is a world-renowned Chef. Olivia will arrange a reservation and get permission from Amanda to dine with us. You will like him. But do not give him an attitude; he will teach you a lesson.

I saw him become a man, and he thanked him for realizing his flaws. He has a unique skill with people, but you would not know it by just saying hello."

We kissed, hugged, and said soon, very soon, this week when we are all recovered? Yes, darling, yes!

******

Derik called and filled me in on his Mom.

"I could not talk to her; she had locked out the whole world, but I got the neighbor's number from the phone company.

She is taking care of her mother, and all seems OK. Nina stopped any actions the siblings had planned. Papers had been ready for signature, and pressure was placed on her Mom. It was just in time.

Now I understand, and she still refuses any help. Yes, but she has done everything herself all her life, which is not unusual. The mistrust towards others stems from these older siblings; their mother calls them criminals." OK, how is school?

"Doing great; I am at the head of the class and piling up the credits. I will graduate early and start work to make money. If she needs it, I can repay her for everything she has done for me."

Great of you, son; you have a good heart. Stay connected, and I will take you on a cruise when you graduate.

"Wow, that's so cool, dad!"

******

The lobster guy called and confirmed the car. All the ducks are in a row, Alex.

It's time to get ready for Vancouver. Greta had made an appointment with a grocery purveyor, and he has connections to good meat and fish.

Greta mailed the product list ahead of time to save time.

I looked at a flight connection. There are no direct flights from either Miami or FTL to Vancouver.

I will change planes in either LA or Denver.

Other options are Chicago, Montreal, or Toronto. Denver won out because it has the shortest layover to connect to Alaska Air.

I was met at the hotel by Sanjay the Merchant, a former sea Captain with Indian heritage.

During the drive to his office, I gave him a bit of my background and explained our aim.

I need you to be my ears and eyes since the distance does not allow frequent visits.

Trust is the operative word; you will get it from my side, and I, in turn, will count on yours.

"I would not do anything to screw up this business. In winter, there are only the hotels for all to compete. We have the edge because we understand ships. My company can also service the materials for the marine department."

I told him about my time in New Delhi as a Sous Chef! "It must have been difficult for you."

It was at first until we learned to understand the people and class system.

He told me how he escaped the caste system by going on a ship at age fourteen. He worked every job and showed a strong interest in learning every job and skill. In time, he earned promotions and worked his way up in the ranks. He needed the education to earn his stripes.

The story continues how he studied the navigation books, picked the officers' brains, and eventually earned a wage. He got to maritime school with company sponsorship and finally received his Captain's license.

Bravo, that is a great story.

"It freed me from the Indian system, and only through this could I marry a doctor." Sanjay, congratulations!

The food list is self-explanatory, and Canada's specs are the same.

We will have a small backup supply of warm-water lobster, but I prefer the cold-water East Coast Lobster. We like the Lobster cooked and split. We can turn it into a Lobster thermometer.

Greta will be your contact person. She is an intelligent girl and easy on the eyes, too.

Then I come up to check and will sail the voyage to see the onboard action.

"Who is checking the deliveries?" A storekeeper is a capable man and trustworthy!

"Do you like fish? I love fish. When you come up the next time, we will have a halibut for you to take with you." Thank you for your time and business.

Then Sanjay told me how they work together to maximize the truck space. Tell the storekeeper not to worry if he does not see multiple trucks.

"Would you like Indian food? My wife is a terrific cook."

Yes, we'll go to my home and relax. Then I want to hear this story about India.

His wife, Soya, practices medicine. Yes, he would not be allowed to marry a doctor in India. He would cook in someone's house and manage the other employees.

I told them I promoted the pot washer to the cook's job.

With my help and protection, he has held on for all these years while I took a chance for humanity! If only they knew the word humanity, it would be another country.

India's population has the highest IQ. If you give them the opportunity to learn, they will make 200% of it.

Soya made Chapattis, Basmati rice, chicken, and lamb in different sauces, yellow lentils, and fresh yogurt with lime juice.

I noticed the aroma of the spices. Cardamom, Cloves, Nutmeg, Curry leaves, Turmeric, and Garam Masala and more are carefully blended to harmonize flavors.

It took Soya one hour only to prepare a table full of food. Déjà vu for me to my time in India.

Dutch beer by the brand name Orangebum followed, followed by a reminder that this would be for the crew bar. He wanted me to approve it first.

It was an easy trip. I expected it to be more complex to put a deal together.

The ship will be here in two weeks. I will sail on the first Alaska cruise. Thank you for the beautiful food and hospitality!

Sanjay dropped me off at the hotel.

A man in a Chef's uniform filled the lobby, singing opera arias. His tenor voice carried through the lobby and stopped all activities. People are staring at him from every level inside the lobby.

After two arias, he disappeared into the restaurant and continued there. From the desk staff, I learned that this is a promotion to lure guests into the restaurant. They must be fighting the same hotel restaurant stigma.

The view over the harbor showed the piers, where the Moon Dancer will berth in two weeks. It will be a busy place for six months.

US immigration processing took place on the Canadian side. The airport was quiet while a woman Immigration officer looked over my passport and green card.

She commented on the dark tan I showed on the green card.

When she switched to German, we had a little chat. In the conversation, I told her about my situation in Miami. While going through Immigration, the officer questioned why I had never applied for citizenship. I was shocked at first. I searched for an answer, and he let me go on with a lame excuse.

The officer in Vancouver was shocked.

This woman told me that he had no right to question it. He violated policy. Tell him, should it ever happen again, "It's none of your f""'g concern and do use these words. It will mark him as having violated the rules.

When I called the home office from the Denver airport, Karri told me to call Alex in California. He has the plan's result and says it has worked.

At once, I called his direct line. Alex was so pleased and told me everything went like clockwork, and you should have seen his face! He is on a joke collar and a short leash. I made a deal with him to stand down and be a good boy; insurance policies had been taken out to assure his compliance.

Thank you, my friend; this is one for the memories.

I was wondering how he would treat me. He must have added up the cost and included me in the equation.

Do I set the record straight and pull my proof, or do I let Alex pull on the joker? What if he did? It will be good to stay in the shades.

******

The pool allowed me to swim laps after I had sat in the place coming back home. I fell asleep on the lounge chair.

A woman poked me and pointed to the sunburn. I can give you Aloe, fresh from my plant. It will take the burnout and prevent the skin from peeling.

I had never heard that, but I was willing to try it. Come to my house at number six. I will apply the Aloe. You will need two or three applications.

As promised, she cut a thick leave, trimmed the outer thorny skin back, and applied it directly on the skin. The skin sucked up the slimy substance, then a second application, and we must wait ten minutes.

She offered me a beer, and we talked. I thanked her for the service.

She responded with the promise of another application tomorrow but will take a trade-in instead of payment. "Are you available after work? I travel every week. It's a better time for me. I have a job, but today I took a day off to rest."

Carmen told me that she sells appliance insurance to homebuyers. Breakdowns and hidden faults are never shown to the buyer at the closing. We offer protection to pay for repairs and, in severe cases, replacement. She dealt with brokers, who directly contacted the home buyer and earned a commission.

'We give excellent service'. I can see it from the Aloe treatment.

We exchanged business cards, and I went home.

The Aloe worked wonders. My skin cooled and felt normal, with only a bit of tightness. I was pleased.

Saturday was a quiet day in the office. The On-duty staff visited the ship and made themselves essential.

Karri was there to inspect provisions. Phillip snooped around, but he stayed clear of meeting me.

His travel schedule confirmed that he was in California and would be on this ship for the weekend.

It will give me time and peace to catch up on loose ends and the reports. I can fax it and do not need to hide it from the secretary. Copies go to Alex, and instructions go to Greta.

Review the repositioning cruise up the California coast and double-check every detail.

Karri was eager to find out the urgent matter with Alex. Tiki bar talk, OK!

No good stories today; the bartender is a confidant and sworn to secrecy. Rum punch, please.

"I finally received Falernum. This purveyor is an asshole and puts me on allocation. The ship buys the bulk of his deliveries."

Get Karri a drink first, then I start, and you want to be sitting!

Alex and I had been busy building a new mousetrap. We suspected our boss of having sticky hands and expecting retaliation for cutting off his funding.

Now I found out the details of this lobster order. The wine deal and produce purveyor had cut into his cash flow. I cut the delivery to weekly consumption, but they had a freezer full of tails on the delivery.

There was a dollar hike in the price, and it looked like a sweetheart deal to fund the purchase of a VW. He needed one for the next Rally.

I told him how I had structured the setup as a trap. It's a mouse trap big enough for a Truly Nolen VW. Get it now? I gave them every detail of how I lured him in and the lobster vendor's deal with the Mexican mafia. The money was borrowed, and the tough boys demanded action. He was scheduled to visit and sail the Moon Dancer, and we managed to get word to him that the car was waiting in port and the papers were with Alex.

He took the bait hook, line, and sinker and walked into the office to pick up the envelope from Alex. At that point, he was in the trap, and Alex put the noose on his neck. It serves as a choke collar, like a dog's training tool.

Only a few people knew a part of this transaction, but nobody knew the entire plan. I Studied this and realized that I could not do it alone. I must have people in the game doing innocent, regular duties.

It became the trigger to make this trip successful.

When the ship received delivery of the entire amount, inspected the quality, and then rejected the entire lot on account that the lobster had suffered freezer burns, it was a shock at first to the vendor.

However, he turned the deal around and returned it to his supplier.

They passed the pipeline back to the Mafia, which owned the production plant.

It left them stuck without paying for an inferior product while everybody washed their hands because of the poor quality. Suffer the loss or peddle these tails to other consumers.

With this action, the Lobster guy was off the hook. The Mafia, which had by now blackmailed Phillip, lost their leverage, and Phillip got off the hook. The car was returned to the dealer, and everybody came out of this deal unscathed.

"I understand why he is all of a sudden so friendly."

******

A visitor from the past came calling. "Do you still have the waterbed?"

She left the bartending job and is now working at a new hotel as a bar manager. The lessons she has learned have been beneficial for her. She made a big impression at the interview and scored the top job in the bar.

The F&B director's job will be next. He has no clue how to handle people, and his days are numbered!

OK, let's make waves. "Here is my way of showing my gratitude. Let me treat you!"

She worked out the rhythm, and the waves took it to the top, which relieved stress.

******

Phillip motioned me to see him. He closed the door and shook my hand.

"I have to hand it to you; this plan was done in a grand style.

I created the dire situation to start with, and now you have set me free from these Mafia guys.

The blackmail and pressure became unbearable for me. I am in the clear with the lobster man. He received help from the rejection based on freezer burns and could return the lot to his supplier. He is off the hook for payment. Only the mafia is facing the loss.

You and Alex acted in good faith. Can we keep it quiet and between us, boys?"

"I do love the changes. We had been blind to hang on to the old stuffy ways. A fresh set of eyes now has set a new direction. It's well-received, and the numbers speak for themselves. Congratulations, carry on and keep me in the loop."

I tell Alex in Vancouver; he will be pleased too.

******

There is no ship in port, no reports to write; all is calm and happy until the red devil dreams up something dumb. What will we do today? We go to lunch with Alberto; he keeps asking.

Alberto immediately pointed to Anguilla's in garlic and olive oil, a traditional Spanish dish with aromas of Saffron and garlic.

Eat bread and even more wine. We had a fun time with this lively man, and for a change, I was the one listening to stories. Alberto had a terrible experience with Jim.

He thought he had met the devil when he saw his red hair and evil eyes.

279

Jim lured him into a deal with the promise of overstated consumption, and he wanted to impress his father.

The story is the same as we had heard from the others, and it ended up costing him the business. He was forced into chapter eleven and reorganized under his wife's name.

We knew the outcome when he started telling us the strategy. Only this time, we did not have to clean up after him. He never took the bait to pay the surcharge to an offshore bank.

"I threw him out the door and never accepted another order until I heard he was assigned elsewhere. You do not look surprised."

No, it's not a surprise because we caught him red-handed. If he dances out of line, then we are squeezing his cojones. We could have blown it up big, but as you said, the repercussions of the unknowns with fingers in the cake were risky.

We settled for his confession and documented it for safekeeping. He is served by staying on his best behavior. We decided on another situation last Friday, which coincidentally involved Lobster.

We tell this one another time. Ciao Alberto.

******

Olivia made the reservation for six pm.

"Why so early, her mother demanded to know. Mom, the busiest time is at seven; I work there, remember? We do not want to get in at the busiest time. Food and service are best if we are there no later than six."

Amanda greeted us in her charming southern way.

She gave me a kiss on the lips and a long hug. "I missed you, darling; I still keep a special place, you know where! Other servers came over to say a nice word and a warm welcome. Mom had noticed it.

"He is extremely popular, she whispered to her husband."

When the Chef came out to shake my hand and offered me to cook something special, Mom was getting a little envious.

"Are you celebrating a special occasion?"

No, we met on the ship and made a date to meet once everybody was back on firm grounds.

We will order from the menu. A red hot iron will serve my dinner well. "I thought so. I see to it."

Mom looked at me with big eyes as if she wanted to say something. Olivia cut in at that time!

"Mom, this is his restaurant; his name should be on the door. He created it, cool it; he trained these people to make it what it is today."

She is a bitch right now, I heard Olivia whisper to me.

What are we drinking? Olivia ordered the wine and then appetizers to share. Is this OK with you?

"I heard you asking the Chef for the tuna. I will have the same. I let her and Dad order the main course, and my brother asked me for advice."

The bottle of wine arrived, and Olivia was asked to smell the cork and take the first taste. I noticed her expert handling of this ritual, and then I gave the server and the wine service the signal to proceed with the service of the wine.

Mom had this look on her face and finally spoke.

"How do you know all these procedures? You look like an expert!" Amanda gave me expert training.

Olivia is taking over the role of the table host—a toast to our friend, cheers.

The appetizers were excellent. The most popular item on the menu was a combination plate with stone crabs, a couple of shrimp, and lump crabmeat salad, beautifully presented.

The entrees that everybody had chosen came at a random pace. Pompano, grouper, snapper, and last came the blackened tuna to the table. The Chef made sure it was perfect.

Olivia's Mom was asking what it was. "It's a transformation; the cook turns a fish into a filet mignon."

"Come on, do not pull my leg." Olivia is correct; we take a thick piece of tuna, spice it with all hot peppers, and put it in a red-hot iron pan. The intense heat burns off the hotness of the spice mix and blackens the outside, and the flavor turns to a beef taste.

Do you want to try it? "Oh no, thank you."

"I had no idea how it was made; will you give me the recipe?"

Better yet, I will cook it at my house the next time you visit. Let me know beforehand; I must drive to Pompano Beach to get the fish.

I felt a squeeze on my thigh, which was extremely high up. This girl will go places; she gets her point across.

Olivia was asking me about the mousetrap.

The mouse trap had worked; we caught three in one catch, and all were happy except one, who did not know me. Nosy Mom had to hear the details of the mouse trap.

I minimized it, telling her it was a cat-and-mouse game. That confused her even more. It's not a suitable dinner conversation.

Olivia ordered dessert and made it to allow exchanges if so desired. I wanted the cold sabayon with raspberries but did not wish to share.

What a wonderful evening. Thank you for your generous hospitality.

Olivia handled the check, added the tip, and handed the credit card to the server. For the final signature, it went back to Dad.

Amanda came by and looked at the empty plates. There was no need for the question. Olivia received praise from her boss for the fine work she did. She will be moving up to assistant manager soon.

Amanda pulled me aside as we left and asked if I was in town next week.

I am traveling to Vancouver and then sailing to Alaska. She punched me; I want to go there too!

Tell your husband to take you there! I will work on him; it would be so much fun if you were on the ship on the same voyage.

I started the season when we had new programs. It takes a lot of effort to get everything working properly.

Follow-up sailings weeks later are a better option for a joint sailing. Goody, I will stay in contact to coordinate it; he can go anytime.

******

On the flight to Denver, I had an older couple chatting about this upcoming cruise. Changing airlines and heading to Vancouver, I had the pleasure of a young female student sitting next to me. We entered into a conversation about her studies.

"Oceanography, they have a great program at the University of BC.

How are you getting into town? "I will look for an inexpensive bus or hitchhhike."

Can I offer you a lift with my taxi?

"That's nice of you. You must know that students are always starved for money. I wonder if I ever make it to the level of everyday life and not worry about every penny or go begging my father."

At the airport, we took a taxi to the center of Vancouver and said goodbye. I gave her my card.

"Oh, Fort Lauderdale, my favorite city. I love to go there when I finish school. The Florida Keys Marine Sanctuary is always looking for professionals." Give me a call if I can help.

This cab is on me, and it is a company expense. I wish you success with your studies.

She hugged me; "you are a nice man; I like you!"

Sanjay greeted me in the traditional Indian way and then passed on the storekeeper's comment. We can see that you know ships; the orders are aligned like a ship's storeroom.

I will see the Master; come along. I will introduce you to Captain Anderson.

The sailor will issue a pass to you. It is valid for the season.

Captain Anderson, good day. I'm meeting a colleague of yours, a former Captain turned supplier of goods and services to ships. "Welcome. It's good to have someone that I can talk to on a professional level. Do you handle other materials besides provision?

"Yes, Master, we have excellent contacts and can get you information about anything for your electronics, the engine room, paint, supplies, or whatever the ship needs. We act as the in-between man with a small markup and deliver to you on time. I know the urgency of the ships is due to the schedule. Here is my card, and we are set up with billing; this cuts out the agent and his commission."

"I like the direct approach; as you know, too many times, we find ourselves at the agent's mercy. Please check with me weekly; we can talk about a little shop and old times."

My room was again the mini-suite I had once before. A large queen bed is always a welcome amenity for a restful night.

The average age has increased, so we need to alter the drink choice. Since Phillip has accepted all other changes, the gala will undergo a transformation.

"Don't set your hopes up too high! The bar manager Ari cautioned. He mentioned at times that the sales would drop dramatically. This generation of passengers does not consume drinks or wine."

I know that we will do better than last year. I have plans for hot drinks.

The concept of hot spiced wine, nonalcoholic cider with cinnamon and orange peel, and hot chocolate with a shot of Baileys Irish cream or Kahlua were alien beverages to Ari.

For the Chef, the scenery was new. This was his first Alaska, with unique cold climate scenery and wildlife as one of the high-level attractions.

A chorus of cooks sang, "Welcome back, Chief. We love to see you again." It was a heartfelt welcome.

Did you all have a chance to call home? "Yes, Chief, thank you for asking. All is fine, and everybody is happy."

I want to rework the midnight buffet, make it more efficient and less work for you. We want it to be still artistic and give the passengers a show with your culinary art and decorative pieces. Just less eating food and hopefully less waste. More details later. Nice to see you all again; happy and healthy.

"We don't like waste also. So much food and our efforts go to the ocean. We could feed our village the amount we give the fish, and then someone else catches the fat fish and makes big money.

We should get the fish free!" All are laughing at the analyses of this young man! Danilo, you are always thinking, your papa is on the other ship, you know; "Yes, I know the Columbia."

I talked to him because he wants you on his ship, but relatives in a supervisory job bring problems. I then told him about when I worked for my father and how he worked his sons twice as hard.

He understood and had no problem with working extra, but the suspicion never disappeared.

I have an idea in mind, but it's too early to tell if I can get other people to agree. You will be happy with it.

I had a short talk about it at Columbia.

Ari waved to take off for his shore leave; "We have too much to do. Besides, I do not have a place to stay. My sister and her lousy husband occupy my house in Athens. My girl here in LA is sharing her apartment with another starlet. Not enough bed space: otherwise, I would not mind a bit of crowding, you understand?"

The mugs are here; send your boys to get them, and we will do a test with every hot drink.

"I am still skeptical about selling hot drinks; I am unfamiliar with them. It's not a beverage for the bar!"

Give it time; when the register rings, it sounds the same, Chief.

Think about a starlight drink with sparkle. We will change the Gala buffet and bring a band to play dance music. The drinks must look like the sky.

"That sounds like a natural drink; I will get my boys to brainstorm the idea."

I will motivate the assistant cruise director to set up and run a show. Yes, showgirls but not in makeup and feathers, just all natural and dressed. We let them loose and have fun. The men will be looking them over, and I want the girls to grab the older men and drag them to the dance floor. Get them good and hot and turn them over to the wife.

It should be fun. If the wife plays her cards right, she will have a tiger in her bed. The comedian can do an adult midnight bash. I know they all have a program in their treasure chest.

The cruise director's replacement is a young man.

He is more inclined to work with us. It will give him an addition to his entertainment program, an interactive one far more enjoyable than sitting and watching a variety show.

When I sail, I always have a passenger table, and the interaction I experience with the passengers stays with me as the most enjoyable time. Making friends sometimes comes with benefits, no complaints!

"You are getting the best out of it!" Ari said this with a grin on his face.

I still meet people from the same town; just last week, I had dinner with the girl's family.

As operators, we need to see it from the consumers' point of view. I read this in the comments.

Can we do a late-night comedy show? He can go off-color for the adults.

"The comedian is a friend and will do it for tips only. Give him a barstool, not even a microphone. Throw in drinks and all the ice cream he can eat."

I must tell you the situation I discovered in LA.

It will be an entertaining cruise; I loved seeing these fuckers get caught with their hands in the cookie jar. It was like catching a monkey.

"How do you?" You mean catching a monkey? If you want to catch a monkey, you need only two items: Peanuts and a Coconut.

Cut the top of the coconut big enough for the hand of the money to slide inside. Now add peanuts inside.

The monkey reaches for the peanuts, grabs them, and makes a fist holding onto them. Now the opening is too narrow for his fist, and he will not let go, so this is how you catch a monkey.

Good, so simple a life lesson applied to the sting? In principle, I saw it more like a rat trap. I did get three rats in the trap.

"Boy, I have to hear this. I have to tell the Captain too; together? Yes, he is eager for the details. "He said to me earlier that something was going on."

Do you know that he was pressured to bunker oil in San Diego?

"Yes, I have his name. He also sells lobsters." It's the same crook I had in my trap.

Back in uniform like a Chef, the kitchen crew was surprised to see me in working clothes. We will make potato salad, and then I will show you how you handle these fresh sausages.

Potatoes are boiled with the skin on. We will peel them while they are still warm. If they are still too hot to handle, you have a hot potato, meaning you pass it on to the next man, and he does the same or gives it back until the potato has cooled.

"German joke, we know, so funny, Chief!"

Once peeled and cool, I need them sliced thin with the Mandolin. A paper towel will protect the hand while working the warm potato. We apply spices, mustard, oil, and Vinegar and add finely chopped onions and a little chicken bouillon. Then, after two hours, we will adjust the seasoning as needed.

You already know how to arrange all the other items nicely.

You will still do all the artistic work you do so well. You are masters at it.

Any returned food can be worked into the lunch buffet, and we have zero waste.

"Chief, zero waste, we like it."

My war against wasted food has just begun. Within the hour, the slogan was in every cook's mouth. I am off to a good start.

Travel fatigue and time change are forgotten. A hot shower and transitioning into casual clothes make me feel human again. Adrenaline running through my veins will keep me going until late at night.

In the dining room, I met with the manager. He had finished the seating assignments. We have open tables, but I filled every table to get a conversation going.

Single tables are not available on this trip.

At dinner, my table was a mixed bag: a Table of six with four single women and one other single man, all of whom were travel agents.

"We have been all over the world." This will be the theme of the conversation.

I ask for advice on tour travel and if it has a future. It focused on the domination by European Agencies like Neckermann, Cooks, Tui, and others. Americans are getting into it, but it is more about organizing the coordination, hotel choice, rental cars, and not much else.

Are you a travel agent? No, I work for the cruise line. Before you get carried away in guessing my position, let me explain.

One ship is in Miami, and two are on the West Coast. I handle the food, beverage, and service on all three ships. It includes purchasing, crew training, menu planning, and wine and alcoholic beverages. To help with these duties, I have one assistant in the office on each coast.

We have set menus, and we buy only what the menu dictates. Special requests outside this line of products are impossible. We do not believe in purchasing outside our trusted vendors at home base.

This should clarify questions in advance. We can, therefore, have a conversation that may involve everybody's interest.

The suggestion did not result in anything. The conversation would then return to questions about the ship, how I got this job and what I have done professionally.

Hopeless to get another subject going, I ask them questions about their life and work. I had hoped that two or three had an exciting field of work. No such luck tonight.

As a last resort, I told them I have German roots and grew up in a small village during the post war aera.

It gave me the opportunity to discuss the war's aftermath and how the occupation affected a child.

Kids are not afraid of soldiers; they treat us to chocolate and peanuts, which is new to us children. We ask them for the empty cigarette pack to harvest the silver foil. Recycling was the only way to obtain material. Kids find out quickly where to earn pennies. The fierce competition taught us that life is a battle; to win it, you must get up early in the morning.

By now, I had an audience listening. Wide-open eyes showed me the astonishment these people could not imagine.

Towards the end came one question. Have you suffered mental damage since you were deprived of a normal childhood? Why are you suggesting this? The time was tough; we had to invent toys and make do with the gifts of nature. The situation was, for us, considered normal. We did not know another way and had nothing to compare.

The dinner had concluded then, and I saw the bar manager, Ari.

How are the politics in Greece? "This no-good Papandreou makes too many mistakes."

Talk to a Greek about politics, and you will have a full day of debates to fight. Are you going to have your honey on a sailing soon?

"She wants to come on board, but her roommate friend wants to accompany her. She does not have the money."

Can I take her on my ticket, and she shares? "No sharing: all the goodies are mine."

Ari reminded me to meet with the Captain for the results in San Pedro.

Ari and Captain Anderson met me in the bar.

I know that this action has concluded. Phillip dropped a note about this during his visit. He had praised you. Tell me about the way you planned and executed this stunt.

My plan was complicated because it involved other people. Each one had a role to play, but none could know the complete action plan.

I had sleepless nights about it. The danger of losing my job over it was immense.

Then came the unknown factor south of the border. I could only judge the reaction from bits and pieces of information.

The only face-to-face contact was with the lobster dealer. When the car was set up for delivery, I used him to call Phillip. Payment for the vehicle came from the three-dollar surcharge on the pile of lobster.

The stunt went down during my first Alaska trip. My attendance was unnecessary since the deal was set up with the whole amount of lobster as a regular delivery to this ship. When the storekeeper rejected it because he found the lobster freezer burned, it was over for us.

Meanwhile, Phillip was in San Pedro, thinking he would pick up the car.

He had to see Alex for the title, who knew his part to play. He confronted him, and the game was over. Alex received a confession, and for this, he is on a tight leash.

All the materials, like the lobster and car, were reversed to the former owner, and Phillip was free from blackmail. The following week, he thanked me for it.

This last part could not be foreseen. It came as a bonus to Phillip. I did not know that Phillip was blackmailed.

Alex and I have the case fully documented and locked in a safe deposit box.

I received confirmation when I called Alex during a layover in Denver. I can assure you when I made it home, I had a good night's sleep.

Ari and the Captain took a deep breath.

"How do you handle all this pressure and not show it?" I have experience with situations like this, but this one was nerve-wracking.

"You need to write a book!"

******

For breakfast, the baker had mastered good crusty bread loaves. The fruit was peeled and ready to eat, and Bircher Muesli and more nice additions pleased me. The crew is proud and satisfied to see empty plates.

These kids have it figured out to 100% recycling.

Landing the frozen food waste container has occupied my mind more than I liked.

It is easy to love these cooks. They generate so much imagination and show care for each other. I cannot let them down. A solution must be there.

Does anyone have a relative in San Pedro? Yes, Chief!

Do any relatives live outside the city, far enough to have space for a pig?

"Yes, my aunt used to have one; just the cost of food made them stop it."

Place the food in heavy-duty plastic bags and freeze it. In San Pedro, we disguise it with plastic material which must be landed, and your uncle makes the pickup.

The port will allow a new recycler to remove this material. These kids can almost taste the pork roast already.

******

The pool deck is packed with people enjoying Canada's warm sun and landscape. On occasions, an Eagle was sighted, and fingers were pointed in its direction. The eagle then flew away in search of food. There must be young chicks in the nest!

Hot chocolate plain or with Bailey's Irish Cream was the day's hit. Ari smiled." You proved me wrong again, Chief."

After the critical passage, the Captain's party was ready for the ceremony.

White wine, fruit garnish, and Margarita are offered to guests entering the lounge.

Music and a drum roll announced the arrival of the Master of the Moon Dancer.

A short introduction of his senior officers and the Captain rolled into his story.

His story was well-received, and when it ended with "Got Rum," the waiters answered, Yes, Master.

Rum punch was served to every passenger and became the hit drink on the cruise.

At the Captain's dinner table, the atmosphere was dismal. Usually, the Captain or the Hostess would start a conversation. Otherwise, probing questions about professional and private life became the talking points.

This night did neither. It was the choice of the guests who showed no interest in anything Jenny tried to introduce.

The dinner was a flop, and the Master was annoyed.

He told Jenny that she could have used me to tell a story. He had done this at times and captivated the audience.

"How do you do this? Can you tell me one of your stories?" I don't do it like this, cold out of nowhere. We need to meet privately, and then I will show you.

"Let's get together and have a conversation."

It is chilly, but I love these evenings; we do not get this fresh air in Florida.

We met on deck and helped ourselves to hot chocolate. A bar waiter offered the enhancement, and both accepted. It was a nice touch and heartwarming, like at Christmas in Vermont!

The first time I ate chocolate was when I was three years old in Germany.

The border was closed even though Mom's cousin in Switzerland was producing chocolate. It would have been considered contraband.

French soldiers gave me chocolate and peanuts. We had enough to eat since my Father ran the butcher shop.

The occupying French soldiers confiscated cattle, and we had to slaughter it for them. Then, they took the best cuts and left the rest behind.

My dad would tell us stories about how people would line up to get a small piece of meat. He gave it for free but ensured everyone received a fair share.

People would come to the store to get a milk can full of sausage soup; nothing more than the water in with liverwurst and blood sausages had been cooked.

Casings always broke and spilled the meat and mostly fat into the water. Add bread to this broth and serve it as dinner for the family. We did not have toys; we made our own.

When my Mom was sewing and had an empty spindle, it became a simple toy.

The valley was our playground. We ran barefoot all summer long. It was saved on shoes and stockings.

I can see how a story is created when others stop talking and listen to one person. It is a smooth transition, and for that reason, the story is believable.

"You are so right; I never thought about it that way. If all of your stories transition this way, it makes them much more interesting because they come from a subject already proven interesting to the audience."

Bravo, smart girl Jenny. Now tell me, where do you live in Florida? Coconut Grove in Miami

Do you remember a restaurant called Peacock?

Yes, of course, I was a regular there. We used to go there to meet friends.

I must have missed you because I was a partner in the business and worked the service every other week. I write it off as poor timing.

I had the misfortune of getting cheated by my partner. He did a dirty trick, exploiting my novice corporate legal knowledge. It's water under the bridge, and I wrote it down to Karma.

"Do you believe in Karma?"

Inner peace is the real strength of Karma. People in India go by it and find inner peace. I have seen Karma work in mysterious ways and set the records straight.

I got my money back but nothing as back pay for missed salaries and the share of the profits from the restaurant.

I went back to the hotel business as a regional director. The job was in Pittsburg.

We went back inside and had wine in my room, which led to soft kisses and affection that followed and took us to the point when Jenny began to disrobe her body.

Your parents did a marvelous job by giving you a beautiful body.

"Thank you for the compliment. It's an excellent way to hand out praise to a girl. It's more effective as a direct compliment and never embarrassing.

She was gentle and tender, loved the caressing, and gave back just as much. When we reached the point of full arousal, we made love like old friends.

The follow-up took another turn. Jenny took over the role of an instructor.

Since you have spent time in India and know something about the teachings of the Kama Sutra, it is my turn to introduce you to it on a full scale. With this, Jenny took control of every moment of our time together.

The teachings go beyond the mechanics of sex. The level of achievement will reach high levels you cannot imagine.

You will find emotions that bond you with your partner with every encounter. It will last a lifetime as friends or as a family bond. Let me be your guide through this journey.

Jenny and I committed to her plan. She was right, I would not believe it at first, but with every love session, the results became real. We kissed and enjoyed each other's company.

Jenny joined me for breakfast on the upper deck buffet. The Chef had arrived to inspect the cook's work.

"Good morning sir! May I ask you for advice?" Yes, go ahead, and pull up a chair.

"I want to offer a different buffet. I understand how American passengers eat the same breakfast daily, primarily eggs. We have international people and those that prefer more healthy options. I see women with trained bodies that will seek a broader choice."

I agree with you, Bobby; I just started writing down my ideas. I see items missing from our food order list. Together we plan the changes.

We can start with the items we carry on board and go with the complete list next week. Jenny's eyes came to glow. Finally, my kind of food.

Everybody at the table suggested what turned out to be a long list. The idea was to rotate and use products that could be turned into innovative recipes.

Yogurt dishes, Bircher Muesli, Blini pancakes with a filling, Waffles, French toast, a souffle made with croissants and eggs, French Brioche, Asian breakfast items, Miso soup, Cereals, homemade Granola, Buffet meats turned into a Hash with poached eggs, little casseroles with baked eggs, and the list went on with new additions contributed by the cooks.

Lunch buffets are now planned to rotate different ethnic foods.

I wanted to include the sense of smell in addition to the sense of taste to conquer the negative comments finally.

The lunch setup was almost completed when I walked the stairs toward the buffet.

Unmistakably, it will be Asian food. The aromas announce the theme in the stairways.

It's the effect I was looking for. The cooks are happy with the results. It is your food; you can be proud of it. It looks appetizing, and the aromas make me hungry.

Mouthwatering dishes satisfied a hungry stomach.

Zero waste became a slogan. It made the cooks proud.

"Chief, we love you; we found a father-like person who looks out for us and gives us honor. You know how to give face; we are proud to work for you. We must find a better title than Chief. Like Papa? How do you like that?"

Excellent, you honor me when you consider me a substitute for your family.

We shook hands and gave a group hug; with this new name, the crew adapted it all over the ship.

It's amazing how this ship has turned around in such a short time. A happy crew is a healthy ship; I cannot wish for more.

The Captain made this statement when he heard them calling me Papa.

Ari, I'd like to discuss selling techniques with your bar crew. Please schedule a fifteen-minute meeting before dinner.

The assistant cruise director told me that her boss was taking a nap.

I judge you as a sharp person. I will not waste time waiting for the cruise director. Time is of the essence.

Let me explain. The Gala buffet is the only focal point on the night of the Captain's party.

I wish to do more with the event and see a missed opportunity to turn the night into a party with music and dancing. It will keep passengers on the upper deck and create a social atmosphere.

Can I recruit you for this idea?

"Yes, great idea. Keep them on deck, and with a band and jazzy tunes, our staff can stimulate the dancing. You know, the men need encouragement while the women dance alone. How do I get the director to sign on?"

He has two bosses on board: the purser and the Captain. I have already cleared this idea with both men. The shoreside person is Angela, and she will love it.

Will you run it, please? With your enthusiasm, it will be a success.

Jennifer, you are a champion; you have the right spirit.

We will stage it next week! The cruise director will be replaced at the end of this run.

I took Jenni, the hostess, to the crew mess room." Welcome, Ms. Jenny. You honor us, and we enjoy your company."

"The food is delicious here, and I had no idea! It's well-prepared, simple, and healthy. Look at all these veggies, beans, lentils, and fish. Can I come here on my own?" Yes, you can see how much they love it. The crew chief cook took delight in seeing us eating with such enjoyment. Thank you, and please come often.

We tested five wines as a teaching class for Jenni. Hosting a table and offering wine to the guests is an essential function of a good host, who must be comfortable choosing.

I took her through the entire protocol, the rituals that are so often overplayed, and then the way to slurp the wine to release its aroma.

You can learn enough information from the front and back labels to satisfy any inquiries.

If someone is determined to test your wine knowledge further, ask them to tell it to the table guests.

"I suspect you had something to do with the Captain's story."

I know; he was treating it like a speech. Would you tell your grandchildren a story in this way? I got him to think.

"The story is lovely; it needs a punch line."

"I will coach him when to pause, lower his voice, bring in reflections, more volume when authority comes into play, and low, extremely low when making a deal."

"I had been searching for a punch line. I stumbled over it from a pirate's movie, and here it is."

"Got Rum? And then the response from the crew, Yes, Sir!"

"You must make this a standard phrase on all your ships."

Why did you give up on dancing?

"I have not given up; I had my fill of how these directors treat us. They think we are a piece of meat they can boss and use as a pleasure doll."

"I would not give in to it, and then the agents receive a call that the spot is no longer available. It's the kind of treatment that is a widespread disease."

Tell me what efforts go into producing a show like tonight. I love the theme of rustic Alaskan dance and music. Costumes and dance steps from the Wild West must break from the regular dance routines.

"It is not easy, and we often have difficulties getting the girls in the right rhythm. After the first visit, watching the Indian dances in various ports will help them to tune in."

All good things come to a pause!

We had a fantastic night together. If these people knew, the envy would be intolerable. I am thankful to have met Jenny, who is changing my life. Great memories and the hope to meet again soon will carry us forward. Soon, Love!

We said our farewell, and Auf Wiedersehen with tears in our eyes. Go and brief the Captain; you have work in the office waiting. Go, It hurts!

******

Gracey and Angela received the latest changes on the food and the midnight party.

That's good. I am sailing this week; I'll look after it. Thank you. I knew you would like the idea.

Alex is pleased by the great Passenger comments.

The cost is dropping, and the bar sales are double from last year.

"Tell me now, what is this Papa thing? Is the crew calling you Papa?" Word travels fast on the grapevine!

They see in me a person who looks out for them, a protector, trainer, mentor, and friend like their Father does. A sense of security has settled in; they are happy to see me. I give them a face.

Next, I must sail for four days on Columbia.

Please give me a short report, Danilo.

"No issues outside these freezer-burned lobsters. I cannot use them. Can I give them to the crew? The boys will make something from it, like soup, and it will be consumed."

Yes, go ahead. The deed is done; it had served a significant role in catching this man.

After I had received my room, I sat with Danilo, Mark, and the chef to map out the plan.

I will implement the program we have on the Moon Dancer and adjust it to the three-day and four-day cruises. Greta made copies for this meeting with notations that involved her.

The ship had always been a solid performer, which gave me the confidence that we would carry out the list despite the short time with the crew.

Mark received his instruction about the rum punch and the timing of the cocktail party.

They had heard from the Moon Dancer already. It was not a surprise to them. There are no secrets on board. The kitchen crew greeted me with Hello, Papa.

I often wondered how they were communicating the information.

It must go by phone call to Manila first and fed back to the next crewmember calling home.

Let me say hello to the Captain, Calimera Master!

"Got rum." I will get you a bottle. Did you receive the memo or the telex?

I received the information from Alex. He is excited about these changes, which make him look good because the ship's performance is way up on the numbers and ratings.

"You have either guts or steel - you know what!

"I am ready with my story. Rehearsals in front of the mirror and personal coaching by the Hostess helped me. I am not a good public speaker; my Greek accent has a way to go before the Americans understand me."

Good, we are all set to replace the champagne with a light and fruity wine. The rum punch is served when you ask, "Got Rum?"

All other programs are being implemented, including the rotation of the late-night food buffets. The Gala buffet will feature the culinary arts with only snack bites and become a starlight party. You will deliver the stars, OK?

There have been other changes, like changing the lobster recipe. The lunch buffet follows an ethnic theme and alternates with spices and aromas. We want the passengers to notice the food with their noses before they reach the buffet.

The breakfast variety will be enhanced, and items will be rotated daily.

"What happened to this crook and his lobster? "

The merchant had to take it back, and the trap had closed. Luck had it that the lobster had suffered freezer burn, and he returned them to his supplier. That flowed back to the production plant, and the Mafia owners sustained the loss.

The action had a domino effect, letting the car dealer off the hook, and Phillip emerged from a blackmail scam.

I cannot take credit for that part. It worked, and everybody received their share.

"Join me for dinner tomorrow night; we can go hunting again. We make a good team!"

Mark mentioned the success they see in the open wine sales. We are running low.

Great, send your inventory to Greta. She is on it already.

This girl amazes me. Whatever I give her to tackle, she gets it done.

Sometimes, I have the feeling she has a secret crush on me!

I stuck my head into the kitchen." Hello Papa!" I will come tomorrow to show you the new items.

 I waved to them and threw hand kisses.

"We love to work with you; you are the best teacher; see you soon."

"My service crew is gang ho, too; you must have produced miracles on the other ship."

No miracle. I treat them with respect and give them faces. "Thank you; it makes our job more enjoyable.

 Mark, can I beg a Negroni from you?

 You must have heard that your mentor has a girlfriend.

"I know; she seeks a sugar daddy to pay the rent. Aspiring something, she has a gig occasionally and cannot pay her bills."

He knows this, but it keeps him away from the gambling tables. Yes, one vice against another; he gets payback when she makes it on board.

"She gets free rent, and he gets his plumbing fixed. Funny, but to each his own."

What do you do when you go home to Ireland?

"I work for my Father to give him a break from running the pub. One day, I will have it as my own.

How about your love life? We have Asians in town, and I am hot after one to get her in bed and to the priest with a ring. For now, there is enough loose stuff to pick up. As the pub owner's son, I carry cloud."

Yes, no kiss-and-tell. It brings back memories of when I had a restaurant in Miami. "I bet you have stories about that time."

Mark is ready with a starlight cocktail, the food is all set, and the cooks are happy that it is easier and less wasteful.

Give a theme and let them run with it. I am pleased to see an operation with such harmony.

Word is out that the captain will join the party and may even dance at midnight.

I had nothing to worry about, so I settled in a quiet area to read a book. Add classical music, and the time was perfect.

The mind should concentrate on the book's storyline, but the music sidetracked me.

Brainwaves are activated to spawn ideas. I put the book aside and looked over the ocean.

It always has a calming effect when looking over water and waves.

Passengers do not seem to find this element of a sea voyage. They are too busy looking in all the wrong places.

Music enhances brain function. Is that possible? It must be because I get the best ideas when I hear Beethoven's compositions.

The work of a Genius is passed on to the recipient, and brain waves awaken. Is this possible, and can this be proven?

The time I passed while I re-visited the accomplishments. It was a long trip with a busy schedule. I am ready to return home.

A decompression period, a pile of mail to sort, and bills to pay at home will set in.

Long trips like this one make me feel uprooted. A day or two will resolve this. I had the same feeling when I traveled for a hotel job and was bound to a hotel opening.

CHAPTER 15

Back at the home office, the buzz was about the merger.

When will we find out, and what will it do to us and our jobs?

Uncertainty had set in, a doomsday feel, and long faces were displayed by everybody I met.

We knew that negotiations were in full motion. Only Vice Presidents received information.

Our leader assured us that we would be integrated into the department's labor pool. The other news revealed that the former concessionaire would take the lead position. No further information is available since he cannot speak for future decisions. It will be sorted out once we are moved to the primary office complex.

Do I update my resume? I have not yet heard of any good reference to their professional conduct. In California, the buzz has been that these people are used to fudge data and screen passenger rating cards.

It tells me that dishonesty is the norm. It will be there and play a role in everything that comes my way.

Be careful and keep looking over your shoulder. Yes, That will be normal behavior.

Reagan said it so eloquently to the Russians. "Trust but verify."

I asked Karri how they handled the purchasing. They want everything locked up in a contract.

Let's not worry. We have no control over it, but keep your resume updated.

Fortunately, I have since learned to run a computer, which allows me to insert the accomplishments from the past two years.

My decision was to give only the numbers and leave the changes to the interview.

Over three million dollars in cost savings, a twenty-five percent increase in bar sales, and a thirty percent reduction in inventory freed up thirty percent of the money on the ships. That will be enough to spark a conversation.

I plugged Karri in with a statement to show that he could manage a ship.

I debated whether we should work on a menu revision. Uncertainty made me abandon the idea. Keep everything status quo. If the wizards want to change, then we act on it. We can use the time to collect ideas: lighter dinner items, replacing the high-cost items and looking into a festive holiday menu.

The news came to us with a list of names and the positions attached.

That's it; we will be downgraded. Our resume was requested and will be reviewed. There is no word on when we will be able to speak to any of these big wheels.

So what? We are assured of receiving a job for whatever salary and terms. The process did not reflect a professional organization. It looked to me as if they had been given a task above their ability or they were not accustomed to a corporate structure.

It gave me hope to show my style and corporate experience. Will it work, or will it intimidate them?

I must listen first and then decide.

I received a call to interview their corporate Chef, Hans, also called Hansi. The date and time are set. The invitation sounded more like an order, but a friendly voice conveyed the message.

I read it as a conflicting message. He lacks corporate etiquette, and she had been told but wanted to soften the message.

A short man with an abundant body tried to prop himself like a peacock during mating season.

He greeted me and sat down with two other people in the office. Hans never introduced these two men. They sat and listened like witnesses.

Was it an oversight or done on purpose?

He gave me quiz questions on cooking skills. I referred to the resume, telling him I had not been working the kitchens in an active chef's ability. I do know all this, but he may be wasting his time. I am not interviewing for an onboard Chef's job. I can get a position like this in a 4-star hotel. My strength is in management. Can you put me to work in this field?

"You can be my assistant."

OK, that will be fine. Working together, we will make a formidable team. I can bring valuable ideas to the job.

He changed the subject to the way he is running his department.

"You should go on board and see for yourself."

We left it at that and another command: get your stuff over here.

There was never any word about salary and details of the scope. It looked amateurish.

"I'll make sure you get a cubicle. I am still looking for a secretary, but the work gets spread around for now."

The Vice President of Food & Beverage Operations received my resume simultaneously.

I came over and settled into the corner cube with a window. I liked the privacy and set myself up with the papers I took from the old office.

My neighbor's cube was still open.

Hansi called me in to review the new menus. I see you theme the menus by ethnicity! What? By country taste, that sort of direction.

"Yes, we do well with this. Any items you do not understand?"

No, I know all this stuff, but my question is, how do you train the crew on this, and who are your cooks on board? I mean, what nationality and what cooking background?

We have them from the islands and Asians, and there are no Europeans except the chefs and most sous chefs.

Do you have a task force to train these people on the new procedures?

"Task force?"

I mean a team that implements it. Surely, you do not personally have the time for it.

"I have these two men that sat in on the interview; they are from Puerto Rico, the hotel I had worked in before I took this job."

Good, that helps. What about a product list with specs and a recipe file for buying? Then, on board a systematic production system?

"The product list, yes, fine. We have never done this, but you can do this, and what else? Recipe cards, no, we do not have time, and who reads them?"

I just thought of having it as a reference when you have the crew and chef on rotation.

"It would be nice, but not now; we have more urgent work.

Then what did you mention on board? A production organization!

Explain, please."

I explained the short format I wanted to implement in the Pittsburg hotels to streamline simple tasks. The process frees up skilled cooks from basic duties and supplies them with time to cook.

He understood the value of separating the work, but I lost him when I started with the paperwork.

I dropped the discussion and took up my work to produce a product list.

I was able to fill in the specifications from memory.

It gave me a project to work on as an easy task. Knowing he did not want to see me for more work, I milked the days' time out of it. The man was over his head. He is a good chef, but he is a failure at organizing.

Karri opted to go elsewhere. A small company with one ship running and two in the making offered him the purchasing position.

We promised him an operations manager job quickly and gave him a modest pay increase. We promise there will be more later.

Yes, I know all about these promises. But stay clean, I gave him a stern message. Temptations will be there; you have seen the good and bad and how it ends up.

I worked on it in a rough format and had it in handwriting.

At home, I transferred my computer into a printed form.

I kept a copy at the office and handed the form to Hans.

"That was fast; wow, let me read it. I'll get back to you.

You can read our policies and become acquainted with them. If you see areas we can improve, please make recommendations."

Hansi was at a loss. Shuff me off to my corner to read policies I had known before. They are the same in most companies, and why would I make recommendations? It could offend the person who wrote these papers.

He must have felt threatened.

He called on Obermayer to get me into a management position.

Obermayer called me in, took another look at my resume, and told me to continue as operations manager.

"Stay with your three ships as you have done. Our guys are unfamiliar with them, and you have it under control. Carry on as you have done before."

Purchasing will take over that task and assign a buyer to your ships. Give it time; we have to organize now.

You have an office, and we are interviewing secretaries for everybody.

You report to me. The salary stays the same."

OK, this man looked affirmed and had made decisions on the spot. I can work with a boss like him.

I am my own man again and continue to fine-tune these ships.

My children will be pleased to keep me as the boss. It felt good; it felt like being at home again.

My life took on a routine with nobody bothering me. In purchasing, I was introduced to Bianca.

The girl was newly hired, and I could see a fire in her eyes.

She is alert, has sharp answers, and her charming personality is full of energy.

The Cuban accent is still extraordinarily strong but not a problem for me. I like listening to melodic sounds.

When I introduced myself, she said German, not Austrian. I can tell the difference, and I much prefer the Germans.

I did not inquire why but gave her my background and management style.

"I love it; it gives me a way to show what I can do for the ship, and I will also coordinate with the West Coast woman. Her name?" Greta, we call her Gracey. Spanish? "

No accent: She may be the second generation and was born in the US.

We hit off on a good note. I will bring you the order forms and specs, and I am tucked into the corner over there for any questions.

"Good, I will visit soon."

Bianca had an infectious smile, telling me, I like you!

Next came the interview of a secretary applicant.

She came to my cubicle with a sad look.

"I promise I will do a super job for you."

It told me enough; she had been rejected by the others who play the big shot so much now.

"Hello, my name is Stefani. May I present my resume?"

Her eyes had this trusting reflection, a bit sad from the turn-off before, yet her body language spoke of hope and instant trust.

Body chemistry told me, yes, she would be great.

She showed me her work and said she knew shorthand and dictation and could read even the poorest handwriting.

I showed her mine.

"Oh, yes, this is nice, not a problem for me."

I told her of my primitive computer skills and how I had doctored around on my resume.

Let me see. It's good, but to show my skills, I will redo this for you. Then you decide.

I detected a tiny reflection in her language. Although her address on the resume indicates she is a local, a tiny pronunciation of certain words suggests an accent.

Her personality is caring and warm; She is a person who is easy to like and hug.

I had seen the pain at first, and now, she is herself and comfortable with me.

I gave her the OK to be hired and signed by Human Resources to the payroll.

After, we can talk about ourselves and the work ahead.

She was assigned to a workstation in front of Hansi's office, which meant that she would be doing his work.

"Not a problem; I can handle it."

Her setup took only 10 minutes, and she received supplies. Immediately, I saw her working on my resume.

I was taken aback—wow, all this in such a brief time. I am blessed to have you as my assistant.

"The pleasure is all mine. I know so much about you from your resume. You have experience in the hotel business overseas, in Asia, the Islands, and the USA.

I am impressed."

I am thrilled to have a great secretary again; it has been my lucky side and support in every position.

I started to tell her about my first office job and how Maya was my lifesaver. I can tell you more stories, but now I want to fax the ships' captains to announce my position.

They will be pleased to hear about my continuation with their ships.

Do you work with the captains from this job? I do and have done so in the past.

She looked at me with respect. "We must make it memorable, not just a memo, a proclamation."

OK? Yes, they like that stuff, but it tells them I will continue with their ship.

Instantly, she formulated the text and showed it to me for my signature, then asked a shy question: Will this do?

It looked at her and said, you know it will; it is perfect, and then she gave me a soft hug.

"I like you; we will be a good team."

I was touched by this affection and felt like I was on to something big.

"Stefani said her name when she introduced herself. I write my name with an f in the middle and I at the end. I know this is different.

My Father was a tennis fan and wanted me to have a connection to Steffi Graf. Please call me Steffi!

Dad and Mom are no longer with me. I am an orphan, and she quickly followed with; do not worry about me; I manage on my own. I have relatives in Barbados. My parent came to the USA, and I grew up in Florida. Someday, we'll make time, and I will tell you more about me."

I noticed this faint Island accent. I know this Island and its people, as you know from my resume. It also comes with a story. We need a rainy weekend for that.

With that, we ended the day.

This girl stayed on my mind. She must have suffered, yet she looks strong; even the rejection did not bring her to tears.

These rude men from the operations team are Austrians. The arrogance spoke volumes, telling me to stay clear of them. There is trouble in that group.

In the evening, I could not get her off my mind. There is something extraordinary with this woman. An orphan is raised in an orphanage or by a foster parent. Either way, it is a hardship, yet she does not show the pain. The little hug and kiss prove a softness, a caring, and a big heart. Lucky me, once again.

The next day, we arrived at work at the same time.

Hello Stefani.

She looked at me with big eyes and asked, "Can I hug you?

I know I have a good boss. The rejections made this a reality. I would have been assigned to these rude managers."

We started the day as a team. I included her in all projects as an assistant. She loved the work and contributed her suggestions to benefit my work. I needed to organize my office and look forward to unfinished business.

The changes will only relate to buying and my reporting line to Obermayer.

I saw no conflict. He gave me the green light to run in the same way I had been doing.

Had he known the autonomy I had taken with these old ships? I realized at once that the free hand might be convenient for him. It was inconvenient to carry the burden of a product to which he had no connection. Suddenly, I realized to be cautious.

The question will be, should I brief him on my upcoming plans or deliver results and defend them with success?

Steffi noted frowns on my face.

"Something bothering you?"

Yes and no. Maybe I am making too much of it.

"Care to tell me?"

I gave her a situation that would be a potential issue.

She understood it, applied her female intuition, and told me not to worry. Time will tell, and if he makes it an issue, then you change.

He will receive financial statements. Numbers always tell the story. Then, there are the passenger's comments, which are received for review. It seems to me that the past has a history on their side of cheating. Those days are in the past; a different department tabulates it.

A controller keeps the numbers honest. The structure of a large corporation may make these ops managers uncomfortable.

Steffi hears them chatting about the good old days when these elements were manipulated to the concession owner's detriment.

Hello Master, got rum? I handed him a bottle. "What is your mission besides passenger relations?" A smirk on his face told me he knew and also approved of it.

I want to find the source of this odor, "What odor?"

I know you do not recognize it by now, but every time I come here, I notice it, and it is a source of negative comments.

"I see this, too; please let me know when you need help."

I went to see Francoise and the storekeeper to hear what they had to say about it. We do know it is there, but where?

I will follow my nose.

"Thank you, Chief, for the excellent addition to the purchasing service. Bianca was here today and introduced herself. She is so beautiful and fun. We love her. I know she likes to work with us; she has more freedom and can apply changes. We listen to her ability, which she values deeply."

The dinner table was occupied with small talk.

A passenger from the next table asked me; are you German? Her English pronunciation told me that she is from England, Great Britain, or the UK, which is it. I cannot keep it apart.

"She introduced her mother to me. Can we meet after dinner? I will clarify the question for you. Call me Tanja."

My table partners are dull, and nobody is interested in substantive talks.

Tanja and I had a social talk by the pool, during which she explained how her country's people choose their identity.

She is a caterer in London. Her business description was confusing. I was unsure if she had a restaurant or a party catering business. I know that different terms are used for different food operations.

My interest in her business and clientele was low and bored me. I wanted to tell her been there, done it." let's talk about something we may have a mutual interest in.

She took the hint and asked me to meet after the cruise. Here is not a good place to be intimate.

Too many eyes and ears. My mom will also be on the watch list.

She sounded cold, typical English. A handshake closed the meeting.

Being raised by a nanny and never receiving love and bonding with the mother must be the reason for the cold personality. A nanny is closer to the child, and when she is released from her duty, the child's bond breaks with the person closest to her.

In the morning, I ate at the crew mess.

Nice to see you, Papa; the word had jumped ship to the east coast!

I must go on a fact-finding mission.

Show me the path to the lowest part of the ship. The storekeeper helped me to open the access panel.

The stench was immense. Let me have your flashlight, please.

I saw debris and packaging material covered with mildew.

Who would put stuff in here and let it sit? The former storekeeper got fired for being lazy.

The engineers lent a smoke mask and heavy-duty gloves. When the debris was removed, we treated the area with vinegar, baking soda and bleach once more.

Tanja, the English girl, had hunted me down to secure a seat next to me. The manager of the change had tipped her off.

We enjoyed a good conversation about the business, and Mom also participated.

When people have something in common or similar interests, it comes to polite and informative conversation.

Mom revealed that her daughter is in her mid-twenties and is self-employed. She is single and could be served by a responsible husband.

After dinner and the show, she stuck to me like glue and wanted to talk more on deck or on the promenade. This girl is on a mission. Watch out!

She hinged her arm into mine and leaned on me to slowly walk the teak planks forward. The balmy night breeze was pleasant, and the fresh air was always good after dinner.

"Then a whisper: I want to get to know you. I have a strong feeling about you; you are a sensible man, assured and confident. You have life and professional experience. We can meet after the cruise at my hotel.

I do not want to engage here on board, but after, we can go out on the town and have fun." She kissed me passionately, kept my hands under her control, and then bid me good night.

I stood there like I was being let on and then dumped. The next day, it was the same.

Affectionate and attracted to me, but only to a certain point.

I was at a loss for what to do with her, which left me cold for the duration of the three-day cruise.

I finished my day at the office. Steffi and Bianca filled me in on the rumors and office talks. The operations managers were talking about me. No details: they hear my name in the conversation.

Let them talk; they can ask me personally if they want to know anything.

I thanked Bianca for her care and visit to the ship. You made an impression with attention to detail.

"She smiled; anything for you; I like you and love working with your people; they are all so nice and polite. Quite different than the other ships."

I can never let them take you away from me. Bianca, what do we need to do? "Do not worry; I see to it from my end. A hand kiss and she is gone."

"Steffi said she is charming; I like her."

Steffi then told me that the other operations managers were being questioned about the performance of their ships. The cost of telephone, food, equipment, negative passenger comments, and everything else was compared to the old ships.

You have the newer ship, and you should do better than them. That was everyone's question.

Obermayer must have reviewed and compared the financial statements.

In the aftermath, they stuck their heads together to see if anybody knew how he did it.

What does he do or manipulate to get these ratings? It must be cheating like we used to do. What about the cost?

A cheaper and lower grade of meat? One of them claimed to know from years back that the most inexpensive equipment was bought.

They would check with purchasing and the people who tabulate the comment cards. Something must be found to give Franz an answer. "What are you going to do?"

Nothing. Let them check it. We earn our rating, and the cost is managed. We buy the best equipment only once, and all this has been done already. No future equipment will be needed for a long time.

She smiled! "I thought so; you do not like a cheat. I just listened and avoided giving answers.

I do not know; I am new!"

The next step is to make me look bad instead of working to fix the problem on their ships.

The real problem is that they do not see any problems; it is business as before.

If everyone runs on the old inferior system or management, all ships are the same, and problems cannot be measured or compared.

Now, they have a basis for comparison. Let them sweat it; the way to me is as far as me going to them.

"You could be ordered to teach them!"

Yes, it may come to that point, but they will learn a hard lesson. I will not make it a cakewalk. They must pass a vigorous training program, starting in the kitchen by peeling garlic.

She laughed; it would be fun to see it from our side. I learned it this way, giving me the foundation to make decisions. My bet is they will refuse.

Any word from the West Coast ships?

No, just the regular reports, and they look good. It's another point of contention over in their camp. Cheap produce and cheap wine were rational. How naïve can one be?

"I read through the old reports and found points you refer to as a real issue.

Care to fill me in?"

Not at this time. We have too many ears listening, and you would spend excessive time here. We are the focal point. Remember that.

We must discuss it in private. There are three incidents, and I must leave them for later. But you have my promise.

I begin to get to know you from all sides. Do not fear me; I have a good heart.

Yes, it shows through everywhere, even with these crooks.

Let us stop for the day. I will walk you out to the car. It is getting dark early now. How safe is your parking at home?

"Not great and not the best area, but so far, so good. I usually sit in the car and wait until I see others walking, then join them at the door."

That sounds suspect.

"You be careful and take this flashlight; it has a strobe function. See if you push again. Point this in the attacker's eyes, and he will be blinded. It also alarms anybody nearby.

Thank you, a hug, and a kiss on the cheek.

We parted to drive home and looked forward to working together as a team. Both sensed a future ahead. Where?